D1295895

*Hannah Arendt and Leo Strauss: German Emigrés and American Political Thought after World War II* is an examination of intellectual migration from Europe to the United States and the resulting influence of European scholars on both the American academy and their home countries after 1945. This collection presents essays by German and American political scientists on Hannah Arendt's and Strauss's émigré experience and their philosophical work in the United States. The authors discuss Arendt's and Strauss's intellectual contributions to American political science as well as the evolution of their respective oeuvres that grew out of the emigration experience. As demonstrated here, the flight from totalitarianism, the Jewish experience of National Socialism and the Holocaust, and the critical transference of German political philosophy to the United States furthered a distinctive interpretation of American political philosophy.

This volume, which concludes with a roundtable discussion, also suggests common themes in the work of the two philosophers. Though in different ways and not uncritically, both of these philosophers viewed the contemporary American system as the antithesis to European totalitarianism. Finally, their émigré experience not only influenced their American work but also had a fundamental impact on the formation of the discipline of political science in Germany after the war.

PUBLICATIONS OF THE GERMAN HISTORICAL INSTITUTE
WASHINGTON, D.C.

Edited by Hartmut Lehmann
with the assistance of Daniel S. Mattern

# Hannah Arendt and Leo Strauss

## THE GERMAN HISTORICAL INSTITUTE, WASHINGTON D.C.

The German Historical Institute is a center for advanced study and research whose purpose is to provide a permanent basis for scholarly cooperation between historians from the Federal Republic of Germany and the United States. The Institute conducts, promotes, and supports research into both American and German political, social, economic, and cultural history, into transatlantic migration, especially in the nineteenth and twentieth centuries, and into the history of international relations, with special emphasis on the roles played by the United States and Germany.

*Other books in the series*

# Hannah Arendt and Leo Strauss

GERMAN ÉMIGRÉS AND AMERICAN
POLITICAL THOUGHT AFTER
WORLD WAR II

*Edited by*

PETER GRAF KIELMANSEGG

HORST MEWES

ELISABETH GLASER-SCHMIDT

GERMAN HISTORICAL INSTITUTE
*Washington, D.C.*
*and*

 CAMBRIDGE
UNIVERSITY PRESS

Published by the Press Syndicate of the University of Cambridge
The Pitt Building, Trumpington Street, Cambridge CB2 1RP
40 West 20th Street, New York, NY 10011-4211, USA
10 Stamford Road, Oakleigh, Melbourne 3166, Australia

First published 1995

Printed in the United States of America

*Library of Congress Cataloging-in-Publication Data*
Hannah Arendt and Leo Strauss: German émigrés and American
political thought after World War II / [edited by] Peter Graf
Kielmansegg, Horst Mewes, Elisabeth Glaser-Schmidt
     p.    cm. – (Publications of the German Historical Institute)
    Includes bibliographical references and index.
    ISBN 0-521-47082-X
    1. Political science – United States – History.   2. Arendt, Hannah –
Contributions in political science.   3. Strauss, Leo –  Contributions
in political science.   I. Kielmansegg, Peter, Graf.   II. Mewes,
Horst.   III. Glaser-Schmidt, Elisabeth.   IV. Series.
JA84.U5H35   1995
320'.092'2–dc20                                     94-13640
                                                         CIP

A catalog record for this book is available from the British Library.

ISBN 0-521-47082-X hardback

ACKNOWLEDGMENT: Chapter 7 was previously published as Alfons Söllner, "Leo Strauss." In *Politische Philosophie des 20. Jahrhunderts,* ed. Karl G. Ballestrem and Henning Ottmann. Munich: Oldenbourg, 1990. Reprinted here with permission from R. Oldenbourg Verlag, Munich, Germany.

# Contents

# Contents

# Preface

The essays gathered in this volume were originally read and extensively discussed at a three-day German–American conference held at the University of Colorado, Boulder, in early September 1991. The purpose of the conference had been to look at Hannah Arendt and Leo Strauss as German émigrés to the United States, and to assess the impact of this fact upon their political philosophies. This entailed, first, the examination of their respective German (or Central European) intellectual and educational backgrounds, as well as their political dispositions and experiences. It meant, second, relating their formative German backgrounds to the further evolution of their political philosophical views and experiences in the United States. And it meant, finally, attempting a judgment as to the definitive traces left by these various experiences upon the mature versions of Arendt's and Strauss's political philosophies.

Consequently, the main purpose of this volume is not a detailed analysis of all the recent literature on Arendt and Strauss published mainly in American journals. The conference participants were fairly evenly divided between political theorists and intellectual historians. Some approached Arendt and Strauss primarily from a point of view rooted in the history of modern German political philosophy. Others chose to assess the significance of their intellectual development from the perspectives of their fully developed philosophies, or in some instances to gauge the contribution of these philosophies to modern Western democratic theory. As a result, this collection of essays represents a great variety of often conflicting views, and to that extent reflects the original purpose of the conference.

Our gratitude goes both to the participants of the conference as well as to its sponsors. Participating were (in alphabetical order): Simone Chambers (Colorado), Helmut Dubiel (Frankfurt), Timothy Fuller (Colorado College), Jürgen Gebhardt (Erlangen), Elisabeth Glaser-Schmidt (German Historical Institute), Thomas Hollweck (Colorado), Bonnie Honig (Harvard), George Kateb (Princeton), Peter Graf Kielmansegg (Mannheim), Hartmut Lehmann (German Historical Institute), Harvey C. Mansfield, Jr. (Harvard), Athanosios and Gail Moulakis (Colorado), Robert B. Pippin (San Diego), Alfons Söllner (Berlin), and Ernst Vollrath (Cologne). The main sponsors were the German Historical Institute, Washington, D.C.; the Max Kade Foundation; the Goethe Institute of San Francisco; and the University of Colorado, Boulder.

Horst Mewes

Boulder, Colorado
May 1994

# Contributors

*Helmut Dubiel* is a professor of sociology at the Universität Giessen and co-director of the Institut für Sozialforschung, Frankfurt. With Günther Frankenberg and Ulrich Rödel, he has most recently published *Die demokratische Frage* (1990). He is currently working on a book about political philosophy after the fall of communism.

*Timothy Fuller* is a professor of political science and the dean of Colorado College. He has published extensively on Hobbes, Michael Oakeshott, and on contemporary issues in political philosophy. Recent publications include *The Voice of Liberal Learning: Michael Oakeshott on Education* (1989), "The Idea of Christianity in Hobbes's Leviathan" (*Jewish Political Studies Review*, 1993), and *Michael Oakeshott on Religion, Politics, and the Moral Life* (1993).

*Jürgen Gebhardt* is a professor of political science and the director of the Eric Voegelin Library at the Universität Erlangen-Nürnberg. He has published extensively on political theory, history of political ideas, and comparative politics. His most recent book is *Americanism – Revolutionary Order and Societal Self-interpretation in the American Republic* (1993). He is currently working on *The Interrelationship of Politics and Religion in Modern Society* (forthcoming).

*Elisabeth Glaser-Schmidt* is a research fellow at the German Historical Institute, Washington, D.C. Her most recent publications include *Amerikanische Währungsreformen in Ostasien und im karibischen Raum, 1900–1918* (1988), and *German and American Concepts to Restore a Liberal World Trading System after World War I* (forthcoming). She is currently working on a history of German–American business and political relations within the framework of the world trading system in the interwar period.

*George Kateb* is a professor of politics at Princeton University. His work is in the field of political theory. His most recent books are *The Inner Ocean: Individualism and Democratic Culture* (1992) and *Hannah Arendt: Politics, Conscience, Evil* (1984). His current work is on the moral and political philosophy of Ralph Waldo Emerson.

*Peter Graf Kielmansegg* is a professor of political science at Universität Mannheim (1985 to the present); he has also taught at the Universität Köln (1971–85) and Georgetown University (1976–77). Between 1977 and 1981 he was vice president of the German Political Science Association. His most recent books include *Lange Schatten* (1989) and *Das Experiment der Freiheit* (1988).

*Horst Mewes* is a professor of political science at the University of Colorado, Boulder, and, since 1979, also visiting professor at Universität Tübingen. He studied political philosophy at the University of Chicago with both Leo Strauss and Hannah Arendt. With Jürgen Gebhardt, he was awarded a major grant in 1993 from the German government to study recent German and American writings on democratic theory. In addition to *Einführung in das politische System der USA* (2nd ed., 1991), he has published articles in *Social Research, Political Science Review, Telos, German Critique,* and *Zeitgeschichte.*

*Robert B. Pippin* is a professor of social thought and philosophy in the Committee on Social Thought at the University of Chicago. He has published extensively on the modern European philosophical tradition. His books include *Kant's Theory of Form* (1981), *Hegel's Idealism: The Satisfactions of Self-Consciousness* (1989), and *Modernism as a Philosophical Problem: On the Dissatisfaction of European High Culture* (1991). He is currently working on a book about Hegel's ethical thought.

*Alfons Söllner* is a lecturer in political science at the Freie Universität Berlin and research assistant at the Zentrum für Antisemitismusforschung, Technische Universität Berlin. He has published extensively on twentieth-century political thought and the emigration of German scholars after 1933. He has recently published *Peter Weiss und die Deutschen* (1988) and, with Herbert A. Strauss, has co-edited *Die Emigration der Wissenschaften nach 1933* (1991). He is currently working on asylum policy and xenophobia in Germany.

*Ernst Vollrath* is a professor of philosophy at the Universität Köln. For many years he was the Theodor Heuss Professor at the New School for Social Research. He has published widely in philosophy and political theory. His most important books are *Die Rekonstruktion der politischen Urteilskraft* (1977) and *Grundlegung einer philosophischen Theorie des Politischen* (1987). He has also published articles in German and English on Max Weber, Carl Schmitt, Martin Heidegger, Hannah Arendt, and the "critical theorists."

# Introduction

PETER GRAF KIELMANSEGG

German emigration after 1933 and the development of political theory in the United States – does this comprise a single topic? Indeed, it does. A number of prominent names come immediately to mind, names of German Jews who, banished by National Socialism, found refuge in the United States, where they became engaged in the development of philosophy and the theory of politics, making significant, indeed definitive contributions. The list includes not only Hannah Arendt and Leo Strauss, of course, but also Herbert Marcuse and Hans Morgenthau – to name only the four most influential of these refugee intellectuals.

These scholars have more in common than merely their German-Jewish origin, the fate of being expelled from Germany, their new home in America, and the significance that they achieved as political theorists and philosophers in the United States. All of them had already completed their academic education in Germany (Hannah Arendt, the youngest of the group, was twenty-six years old in 1932; Leo Strauss was seven years older) and thus brought with them the imprint of the educational traditions of their native country and continent. But all of them, starting at different levels, attained their characteristic intellectual profile only after emigration. Their contributions to the history of political thought in the twentieth century were all published in the United States. Only for Leo Strauss does this statement have to be modified somewhat since he wrote his book on Hobbes, Strauss's first fundamental work in political philosophy, in the years just before he left Europe. It is true of all four, moreover, that once they had been expelled, they all turned resolutely and permanently to the country of their refuge. None of them sought and found a way back after 1945. And yet they remained the intellectual citizens of two worlds, belonging

This introduction was translated from German by Alice E. Kennington of College Park, Maryland, and the editors.

1

fully and indubitably to neither; they were no longer Germans, yet they had not become simply and exclusively Americans.

It seems quite clear that lives taking such a course will prompt questions of systematic interest. Does their thinking, in the questions they pose and in the answers they find, owe something to the fact that the émigrés belonged to two worlds? How, on the one hand, is their philosophy shaped by the world of their origin and, on the other, by their encounter with a new world that they first entered at the age of thirty or forty? Not all of the essays concerning Arendt and Strauss collected here use these questions as their explicit point of departure, but all contribute in some way to answering them. Thus, the individual contributions are linked not merely by the two names but also by an interpretive outlook that connects the work of the two Jewish German-Americans and their paths through two worlds.

With respect to Hannah Arendt, this outlook shows up most clearly in Ernst Vollrath's reflections on Arendt's concept of the political. Her search for the ideal definition of politics was given impetus by her confrontation with the most extreme form of perverted politics under the guise of National Socialist totalitarianism in her native country. The answer to the question of what comprises the authentically political, whereby the scales of human possibilities are once again brought into balance, she found in the country of her refuge. Arendt interpreted the founding of the American republic at the end of the eighteenth century, at almost the same time as, though quite different from, the epochal events of the French Revolution, as the model of political action in the modern period. She did not consider any other event of modern political history to come even close in importance to the founding of the United States of America.

Hannah Arendt's emphatically "American" answer to the question of what constitutes politics, what it can be in the best instance, that is, at the furthest remove from the pure nonpolitics of totalitarian tyranny, engenders new questions. Some are historical questions, which, though they might well be of secondary importance for the theory of politics, are anything but insignificant. Others are systematic questions. With respect to history, we must ask how Arendt's image of the founding of the American republic, elevated to the status of a myth, corresponds to the historical realities presented to us by the discipline of history. To what extent was Arendt at all interested in the results of historical research? How well did she know the writings of the Founding Fathers?

One of the accepted traditions of the American republic is the elevation of the story of its own founding to a myth. But Arendt's emphasis is not simply borrowed from this tradition. On the contrary, it reflects the liberating discovery of someone who had escaped the murderous, totalitarian perversion of all politics into violence and who had entered the republic of the United States as an outsider. Vollrath shows that Arendt's relation to current American politics was not at all uncritical. But her interpretation of the founding of the American republic as the high moment of modern politics affected her judgment of the institutions and the political culture of the United States in a manner that can only be described as nothing less than idealizing. Hence, not only her perception of American history, but also her thoughts on contemporary America need to be discussed.

The systematic questions presented here seem to me more important than the historical ones: Hannah Arendt's notion of authentic politics, in which a person finds his or her destiny as a political being, is firmly attached to the story of a founding act. The founding of a political entity or the drafting of a constitution, if one wants to express it in a more modern and technical way, represents for her the most political of all human activities; it is pure politics. But here one does not learn much about whatever else might constitute politics. All three essays devoted to Arendt expound in different ways this particularity of her concept of the political, which really must be called a weakness. George Kateb presents the most trenchant treatment of this aspect. He sees in Arendt's idealizing concept of authentic, pure politics the danger of politics becoming untied from its moorings in morality. Certainly, Arendt's concept of politics is inimical to everyday reality; it completely ignores what is everyday or routine. Arendt seemed not much interested in political action in the institutionalized context of a given constitutional order. Characteristically, as Helmut Dubiel points out, it was in civil disobedience that she discerned at least traces of the authenticity of the founding act. Civil disobedience is not an everyday act in an everyday situation.

Such a concept of politics, elevated to a norm and situated in a far-removed historical moment, seems almost necessarily joined to a perspective of decline. One cannot linger on the high plateau of pure politics. The actual practice of politics in a republic cannot remain, even under the most favorable circumstances, what it was at the beginning. In Hannah Arendt's view, the political decline most characteristic of modern societies occurs when politics becomes the instrument to realize "the social." Yet this formulation fails to reveal the exact purposes that Arendt does not want to see served by politics. But one comes away with the impression that she condemns practically the entire substance of modern politics. Modern politics almost always aims at satisfying the material needs of society, either directly or indirectly. Precisely the democratic process itself brings this about.

Hence, Dubiel is quite correct in stating that a concept of politics devoid of
specific purpose, which abandons the social sphere to societal self-regulation,
seems incompatible with the essential nature of democratic politics.

Ernst Vollrath connects this point with the way in which Arendt's thinking was shaped by her background. It is characteristic of the traditional German understanding of politics that the political is equated with the state, but
also that there exists a dichotomy between the state and society. For Arendt,
although the political has been released from being identified with the state,
the dichotomy between the state and society lives on in the dualism of the
political and the social. In any case, it seems hard to avoid the impression of
a certain emptiness in Arendt's concept of politics, which is the reverse of
her emphasis. And one is tempted to extend Vollrath's thesis somewhat and
to see something very Germanic in this idea of the authentically political,
strangely emphatic and, at the same time, devoid of content.

In all of this we have already touched on the theme of "Arendt and
Democracy" which, with differing emphases, forms the focus of the essays
by George Kateb and Helmut Dubiel. Despite some reservations, Dubiel
does indeed find the outline of a theory of democracy primarily in Arendt's
book, *On Revolution*. In her understanding of the act of founding a republic, he discerns a precise statement of the revolutionary reinterpretation of
legitimacy fundamental to modernity. And in her communicative interpretation of power, which is, in a certain sense, the centerpiece of her political philosophy, he finds the only conception of the phenomenon of power
that seems consistent with democracy.

Kateb assesses Arendt's relation to democracy much more critically.
Speaking of Arendt and Strauss, he says, "Both radiate disapproval of modern democracy." What seems obvious, in any case, is Arendt's nonrelation-
ship to modern, representative democracy. It means nothing to her because
authentic politics does not occur in this system. Kateb recognizes an aristocratic ideal behind this lack of understanding for the representative form of
democracy: A citizen is one for whom public life, participation in civil society, concern for the common weal, is the real purpose of life. And if there
are only a few such citizens, then there are only a few. Democracy, in contrast, is founded on the conviction that one should never leave politics entirely to the few, even if these are citizens in the sense of Arendt's ideal. The
few must be held accountable to the many who want to lead their lives in
the limited sphere of private existence, and that representation serves exactly the function of accountability. There is little of this to be found in
Arendt's writings. Her unconditional rejection of totalitarianism, as Kateb

notes, did not induce her to make a realistic assessment of the conditions that might offer the alternative of freedom in modern societies.

Leo Strauss has had a much greater influence on political philosophy in the United States than Hannah Arendt, who is read more and given more attention in Germany than Strauss. He still exerts this influence because, as is well known, a school formed around him – certainly a very remarkable state of affairs for an émigré. The theme that occupied his life, his "philosophical project," as Gebhardt calls it – whether one describes this in Söllner's words as "the rehabilitation of tradition against modernity," or using Gebhardt's formulation, as "restituting the dignity of the fundamental question about right and wrong" – does not seem at first glance to have much to do with his life's journey through two worlds, and the influence of these worlds upon him. His attack on modernity is not aimed at its specifically American variant. Rather, his condemnation applies to modernity as a whole as the destroyer of all authoritative traditions of value. It applies to the defection from the thinking of classical natural law, for this is how he interprets the entire history of modern political philosophy from Machiavelli and Hobbes onward. He is thus concerned with a process of error and decline (here again, the catchword "decline") that impinges on Western civilization as a whole. And in order to evaluate this properly, he deemed it necessary to return to the sources of this civilization, to classical Greek philosophy, which for Strauss means, above all, a return to Plato.

But still, it is not at all digressive to ask how Strauss's political philosophy might have developed, what effect it might have had, if history had permitted Strauss to remain in Germany or in Europe. It is certainly true that no break in the development of his thought exists that could be attributed in any way to his emigration. Alfons Söllner's essay, which examines the earlier and middle works of the philosopher, demonstrates this continuity in particular. His book on Hobbes, in which Strauss's political philosophy had already attained clear contours, was after all written in the period prior to his emigration. But that does not mean that no importance should be attached to his encounter with the new world to which he immigrated. More than any other society within the sphere of European culture, the United States has grown out of and is rooted in the Enlightenment. In terms of its basic idea, the United States is, as Ralf Dahrendorf expressed it, "applied Enlightenment." Thus, Strauss encountered modernity in its purest and most consistent form. It can be assumed that this constituted a special challenge for him. Conversely, when he questioned the essence of modernity while living and working within a society, like the American one, that derived its identity entirely from modernity, this questioning probably exerted a particular fascination.

The catchword "fascination" also involves Strauss as a person. In some respects he appears a very German figure, "a charismatic representative of Teutonic learnedness," as Söllner describes him, a representative of the nineteenth-century German tradition of higher education, the tradition of a highly elevated aristocracy of scholars of imperious manner. This may have contributed to the influence he exerted in the very different world of the United States.

Gebhardt's essay also emphasizes how Strauss's background shaped him. Admittedly, Strauss was a denizen of the German university world only as a student, not as a "mandarin," as Gebhardt formulates it with reference to Fritz Ringer's term. His first scholarly works originated outside the university, namely, within a Jewish research institute. But the style in which he later taught, the way he asserted his claim to authority, most certainly had something in common with that academic world from which he came. Moreover, Strauss was by nature a person in whom the European world, beyond the specifically German university tradition, seemed to be present in an overwhelming way. His almost cultic veneration of the "great books" in which he sought and found the tradition of wisdom and the wisdom of tradition might appear to alienate us in some respects as a kind of scholasticism. But it testifies as well to a deep-rootedness in the culture of premodern Europe that, like Jewish culture, was uniquely passed down through the written word. In a particular way, Strauss was a product of the coincidence of Jewish and European origins. His engagement with "the Jewish problem" during his early years in Germany – a topic Gebhardt's essay addresses—was certainly a significant step on the way to the European sources of thought in which he anchored his philosophical project. In short, Leo Strauss's work and its effects, as with Hannah Arendt's, can be related to his affiliation with two worlds.

The attitudes toward Strauss that we meet in the essays in this volume are quite diverse. In all of the essays, however, the challenge that radiates from the untimely message that Strauss proclaims becomes evident. Söllner attributes a half-philosophical, half-theological character to this message. It is philosophical at the core and theological primarily in the manner in which a binding tradition is proclaimed. But this character is also implicitly Strauss's in the way it treats "sacred texts," out of which answers to the really important questions are to be obtained, and in the style in which it condemns "heresies" – those modern developments of thought that have led away from the insights of classical philosophy.

In an essay that compares and contrasts Strauss and Heidegger, Horst Mewes also assigns Strauss's thought a place in the unstable intellectual space between philosophy and theology, although he takes an entirely different approach from that of Gebhardt. In a certain sense, Mewes's Strauss is also at once philosopher and theologian. Strauss interprets the irresoluble contradiction between reason, in the form of Greek philosophy, and revelation, in the form of the Bible, as being constitutive for Western culture, irresoluble because ultimately, reason cannot refute revelation, nor revelation reason. It is obvious that this is the portrait of a great outsider in the academic world, especially the American academic world of the twentieth century. The Strauss we encounter in Gebhardt's essay is similar. The search for truth in the essential Straussian sense can only be pursued in opposition to the modern understanding of science, that is, in opposition to the modern scientific project.

Is he, with his philosophical theology and theological philosophy, a great outsider, not only in the academic world of the twentieth century but also in the world of modern democracy? One cannot become involved with Leo Strauss, the political philosopher, without confronting this question. It appears in various guises in the contributions of George Kateb, Timothy Fuller, and Jürgen Gebhardt. Kateb treats it most explicitly and most skeptically, without of course reaching any final judgment. If it is characteristic of Hannah Arendt that the political is elevated and stylized, for Leo Strauss the political is rather relativized. For him, the highest level of life is the philosophical life of contemplation, not the political life of action. The positions of both of these thinkers appear to distance themselves from democracy. In Strauss's texts there is certainly much negative evidence. And if one sums up what the texts say, considers the philosophical position behind them and the manner of proclaiming the truth, it seems hard to think of Strauss as anyone but a man of Platonic aristocratic ideals, even though it remains obscure what that means in the twentieth century. Kateb nonetheless asks the question of whether one might read the philosopher in a different way, namely, the way Strauss himself taught students to read political philosophical texts, which he believed carried hidden messages that had to be deciphered. Following Strauss's own method, is it possible to read into his distanced attitude toward democracy a sympathy for democracy which has to be warned of its weaknesses? Kateb poses this question without answering it.

The emphases are somewhat different in Timothy Fuller's essay. Fuller's observations on what seems to be quite a different topic, "Leo Strauss's Defense of Liberal Education," can be read as well as a contribution to the discussion of democracy. Strauss's educational ideal is doubtless an aristocratic one. The study of the "great books," the dialogue with the masters, which for Strauss composes the nucleus of liberal education, forms a concern of the few and is intended only for the few. But this ideal of education is related to the idea of democracy. When Timothy Fuller describes liberal education, as Strauss means it, as "the necessary endeavor to found an aristocracy within democratic mass society," then it is presupposed in this description that democracy requires such an aristocracy as a counterweight – here Aristotle's mixed constitution surfaces as a distant memory. Possibly the connection between the aristocratic ideal of education and the democratic constitution is to be understood in such a way that, for Strauss, democracy deserves approval and support if and only if the democratic principle can be perceived as asserting the universalization of the aristocratic principle.

Finally, for Gebhardt the question of how Strauss regarded modern democracy seems less important than the question of what his philosophical project means for democracy. And here his answer is unambiguous: "The Straussian philosophical project is to be understood as a restitution of the historical form of Western civilization, that is, the city of man set against the modern project of the universal and tyrannical state, which aims to eliminate the city as well as man."

Be that as it may, Strauss's judgment of democracy is closely tied to his judgment of modernity as a whole. Thus, every discussion of the topic, "Strauss and Democracy," ultimately runs up against the question: How valid is the principled critique that Strauss levels at modernity? How well founded is his philosophical attack on modernity? This is the theme at the center of Robert Pippin's essay. His thesis that Strauss perceived modernity only selectively and did not really become aware of certain options inherent to the thinking of modernity bears significantly on our understanding of his views of democracy. Pippin illustrates this primarily by using Strauss's interpretation of Rousseau. Like no other thinker in the history of modern political philosophy, Rousseau joined a fundamental critique of modernity with the highly modern attempt to found a civil society consistent with the ideal of self-determination. Rousseau thus indeed represents a particular challenge to Strauss's thought.

In this contribution as in all the others in this volume the positions become clear from which further discussions of Leo Strauss's and Hannah Arendt's works can be pursued. The influence of these two thinkers has not yet reached an end, something that cannot be said of very many political thinkers of our century. Our findings suggest that the fruitfulness of their thinking is linked to the tragedy of their emigration.

# PART I

# Hannah Arendt

# 1

# *Hannah Arendt and the Theory of Democracy: A Critical Reconstruction*

HELMUT DUBIEL

## INTRODUCTION

*On Revolution* is Hannah Arendt's major contribution to political theory, and although the book's potential as a source of a theory of democracy is not immediately apparent, it is not necessary to dig very far to unearth the treasures this work contains. Arendt's notion of the secular foundation of political authority and of communicative power as well as her concepts of "public freedom" and the "founding act" have since been adopted as the standard components of numerous theories of democracy that are based on a philosophical approach. Yet it is true that the book's potential does not speak to theories oriented toward current issues. There are two reasons for this.

First, the parts of her work that can be related to systematic questions of a theory of democracy are mainly clad in the guise of a comparative reconstruction of the conceptual worlds of men who lived during and reflected upon the American and French revolutions. In other words, the reader is constantly forced to take the trouble of extracting a systematic political theory from a superbly presented history of ideas. The second reason why *On Revolution*'s potential for a theory of democracy is not immediately apparent is Arendt's idealization of the founding of the North American confederation, which she treats as though it represented a historical realization of the utopian democratic republic. This tendency, which determines the perspective she adopts throughout the book, compels her to conceive of all the political developments of the following two centuries as constituting a decline. The impression that Arendt's chosen form of presenting political history is based on a theory of decline has earned her the reputation of a "conservative utopian" or a "political antimodernist," and this impression is all the stronger when viewed in the light of other parts of her overall oeuvre.

11

In her famous *The Human Condition* Arendt constructs a retrospective model of Greek antiquity as a hierarchy of models of activity and then similarly traces its progressive decline over the course of occidental history. In the present context, however, this conception of a theory of decline by no means explains the passion with which Hannah Arendt followed ongoing developments in American democracy. Her public statements on the politics of racial integration, on the Vietnam War, on the civil rights and student movements, and on Watergate are not at all what could be expected from someone whose outlook on the course of the world was one of detached melancholia.[1] Thus there seems to be a contradiction between her theory of decline and her critique of contemporary society. Yet if we focus more closely on Arendt's understanding of her own methodology, we find this contradiction, if not resolved, then at least losing some of its starkness.

Arendt only comments sporadically and sparsely on the method adopted in her books, the most explicit instance being the foreword to *Between Past and Future*.[2] She likes to describe her method using the terse epithet of "telling a story." By this she means neither recounting a mere history of ideas nor providing a sort of idealist historiography that purports to grasp real history by reconstructing the most prominent documents of intellectual history. For Arendt, a thoroughly consistent postmetaphysical thinker, any form of historicophilosophical construction of the past has long since become impossible. Following the secularization of religious views of the world and the disintegration of absolutist traditions of interpreting the world, she believes not that the past as such but rather the inner band that gave it clear contours has dissolved. She expresses this modern experience of a past that is no longer accessible through substantive traditions with one of the aphorisms of René Char, the French poet: "Notre héritage n'est précédé d'aucun testament." To Arendt's mind – and here, incidentally, her thought resembles that of Walter Benjamin – writing history is only possible in the form of exploratory models. No longer is there a law connecting past and present. It is no more possible to explain the course of modern history conclusively by referring to constellations of the past than it is to preclude the incursion of something radically new in history. This radically antimetaphysical conception of history also proscribes any resort to some historicophilosophical surrogate. And it denies the validity of any evolutionary notion of progress or a theory of linear decline.

In a powerful image, Arendt characterizes the procedure she follows, which is both a form of conceptual history and at the same time a way of

---

1 In particular, see the collection Hannah Arendt, *Zur Zeit. Politische Essays,* ed. Marie L. von Knott (Berlin, 1986).

2 Hannah Arendt, *Between Past and Future* (Cleveland and New York, 1963 [originally 1961]).

conceiving of political theory, as "salvaging pearls under the rubble of history."[3] Indeed, in both *The Human Condition* and *On Revolution,* she reconstructs and arranges topically lost layers of meaning that have been sedimented conceptually and handed down in documents from classical Greece and the early modern revolutions. Her interest in these sedimented layers of meaning is not historical but rather arises with a view toward contemporary needs:

My assumption is that thought itself arises out of incidents of living experience and must remain bound to them as the only guide posts by which to take its bearings.[4]

In Hannah Arendt's eyes, the political theorist who focuses on intellectual history somehow keeps alive those extinct traditions that have rendered past experiences useful as a point of orientation in the present. Against the background of her critique of a philosophy of history, however, Arendt is compelled to assume that the connection between the layers of meaning reconstructed from the standpoint of conceptual history and the orientational potential they offer is itself historically arbitrary. The theorist him- or herself does not control the conditions under which the story told also conveys a message. Whether or not the lost potential of the past can really be unearthed depends also on the present:

The history of revolutions . . . could be told in parable form as the tale of an age-old treasure which, under the most varied circumstances, appears abruptly, unexpectedly, and disappears again, under different mysterious conditions, as though it were a fata morgana.[5]

Whether Arendt consistently adheres to this method in her own work is a moot question and one that cannot concern us here. For it is most certainly the case that the vantage point of a history of decline, which she herself criticizes, informs her political theory to a greater extent than does that method of exemplary mode of thought that allows history to be linked to current problems of orientation. Nevertheless, it is the latter method that we will follow in our reconstruction of the elements of a theory of democracy inherent in Arendt's work.

## THE MUNDANE LEGITIMATION OF POLITICAL AUTHORITY

Today it is still common among historians to posit a favorable connection between modern political revolutions and Christian tradition. In particular, they cite the rebellion of early Christian sects against the secular powers of

---

3 See Seyla Benhabib, "Models of Public Space – Hannah Arendt, the Liberal Tradition and Jürgen Habermas," unpublished manuscript. Benhabib is professor of philosophy at SUNY Stony Brook.
4 Arendt, *Between Past and Future,* 14.      5 Ibid., 5.

the day, their radical egalitarianism, and their promise of a heavenly realm as examples that demonstrate that modern revolutionaries are mere successors to a heritage that, although now given a secular form, dates back a thousand years. Arendt criticizes the notion of continuity in intellectual history inherent in this construct. In contrast she proposes a sharp rupture between Christian tradition and political modernity, an argument that she at the same time uses to prepare the way for her theory of a democratic revolution. She does not, however, refer to the complex of early Christian ideas just mentioned but rather to the phenomenon of how political authority is legitimized. To Arendt, the phenomenon of a secular legitimation of political rule is something radically new. Even though modern revolutionaries may have culled metaphors and images from the Christian tradition to describe what they thought and did, Arendt considers it wrong to view this as a mere secularization of an originally Christian doctrine. Instead, these thoughts and deeds were something objectively new in history. Given the burden of a tradition that had sedimented over two thousand years, the self-misunderstandings and misconceptions of revolutionary politics expressed in these borrowings were thus absolutely inevitable. The transcendental justification of political authority that has been prevalent in the Western world had its roots in the Roman trinity of religion, tradition, and political authority. The most recent form this took, and one that continued to have an impact well into modern history, was the absolutist doctrine of the divine right of kings.

The cover of the first edition of Hobbes's *Leviathan,* published in the seventeenth century, is best suited to illustrate the understanding of politics prevalent at that time. It is an understanding still steeped in the Christian tradition. It depicts the head and torso of the monarch. His crowned head, his scepter, and his sword touch the edge of heaven and the upper half of his vast body, large enough to encompass the globe, is composed of innumerable minute human figures. The lower half gradually merges with a portrayal of a spacious Renaissance landscape, decorated with castles and palaces. This picture gathers together all the elements of an image of politics that had emerged over a very long time. And it is only against this background that we can truly understand the rupture that the democratic revolutions in France and America constituted in this allegorically represented tradition, a rupture visible only retrospectively.

The absolute monarch justifies his absolute rule by appealing to a divine right. In the picture, crown, scepter, and sword appear to act like antennae conveying the transcendent message to the secular social order. At the same time, the monarch's physical self directly embodies the social unity. It is within the monarch's body that his subjects feel themselves united with the political community. In other words, the monarch was the pinnacle of the earthly pyramid of rulership, and as such drew together all secular power. This pinnacle was also the juncture where earthly power coalesced with the transcendental order, grounding once and for all the criteria for good and just rule on earth, unaffected by the passage of time.[6] The constituent elements of this image, namely, the religious framework of earthly rule and the monarch's embodiment of legitimation, are all invalidated by democratic revolution. With the beheading of the absolute monarch – for example, Charles I in England or Louis XVI in France – the this-worldly embodiment of an inviolable divine order is brought to an abrupt end. Beheading kings was an act that should also be understood metaphorically, paving the way for a modern, mundane understanding of politics.

Using Hannah Arendt's terms, we can now say that a public space based on religious legitimation is first constituted as a political space to the extent that secular power ceases to be sanctioned by religion and religious convictions become confined to the private sphere. An autonomous public sphere – that is, one that obeys a rationality and criteria of legitimation of its own – first comes into existence once the secular domain has freed itself from the immediate tutelage of the church. In other words, we can first speak of "politics" in the modern sense once absolute powers – be they clothed in religious or metaphysical guise – can no longer claim any authority in the public space.

Seen from the viewpoint of the history of ideas, it was Machiavelli who first reflected on the problematics involved here. Admittedly, his sole concern was the subordination of all political maxims for action to the imperative of the self-preservation of the state, an imperative that he posited as absolute. Nevertheless, this led him to anticipate the possibility of a type of state legitimation that did not actually take its place on the stage of history until traditional forms of arriving at a unified political will had been largely secularized. The type in question is the creation of state legitimacy that did not rely for its validity on some transcendental authority. Arendt is fascinated by the fact that the shift from a sacral to a secular foundation of legitimacy that occurred in the course of the French Revolution was not adequately understood by the very people who set it in motion. By continuing to search for some absolute authority, something that could at best be a mundane replica of complete divine authority, they failed to recognize the intrinsic logic and dignity of a purely mundane foundation of legitimacy.

6 See Ernst H. Kantorowicz, *The King's Two Bodies. A Study in Mediaeval Political Theology* (Princeton, N.J., 1957).

In his book *The Legitimacy of the Modern Age,* Hans Blumenberg tenders
the thesis that the development of systems of interpreting the world must
be conceived of as a slowly unfolding dialectic of questions and answers.
Epochs can be delimited within the flux of time in terms of the collection
of answers that can be given to a relatively stable, though not suprahistorical set of existential questions. Thus, a new epoch can never refrain from
answering questions bequeathed it by a previous epoch. Many problems
concerning the transition in modern history from one epoch to the next and
the secularization of the history of ideas in particular can, according to Blumenberg, be explained by referring to this phenomenon of the recurrence
of prescribed questions.[7] In our case, the search for an absolute source of legitimacy that transcended the here and now even after the Revolution was
the consequence of such a recurrent question. Hannah Arendt merely approaches this problem in a different way when she notes that the form and
course taken by the French Revolution were also shaped by the regime that
it brought to an end.[8] To Arendt, the nation-state that emerged during the
age of absolutism harbored the potential for a form of political organization
that could survive without the borrowed glory emanating from a transcendent sphere beyond politics. However, the absolutist state proved to be no
substitute for the lost religious sanctioning of the world. The dominion with
which the monarch was invested in the age of absolutism corrupted that
state, for, bereft of any transcendental ties, absolutism became tyranny. It
has always been a fundamental principle of divine law that its rules do not
apply to itself, and the absolute monarch inherited this logic. Hannah
Arendt points out that the ancient Greeks already regarded a ruler who was
not bound by his own laws as a tyrant. In the absolutist state the monarch
embodied the unity of the nation and God's will on earth. However, in the
French Revolution the throne vacated by the monarch was now occupied
by the "people," who were invested with the attributes originally accorded
to the former. Quasi divinity, infallibility, unity of will, and embodiment of
the nation now became attributes of the people. Like the absolute monarch,
the people were located outside the domain of politics. The burdensome
legacy of divine right thus carried over is also to be seen in the fact that the
revolutionaries in France regarded the people as the source of both power
and the law. Admittedly, the best-known symptom of this search for a transcendental source of authority, a foundation for legitimacy beyond the political domain is Robespierre's cult of reason.

7 Hans Blumenberg, *The Legitimacy of the Modern Age,* trans. Robert M. Wallace (Cambridge, Mass.,
   1983).
8 Hannah Arendt, *On Revolution,* (London, 1963), 154.

To use Blumenberg's terminology, it is the prescribed question of an absolute and transcendental foundation of legitimacy carried over into modernity that is the major theme addressed in Arendt's political philosophy. She addresses the quite incredible delay before the spirit behind such legitimacy, which seeks to provide mundane justifications for all systems of human order, manages to take root in the political domain. In her book *On Revolution,* Arendt does not cease to be amazed by the fact that the revolutionaries of the eighteenth, nineteenth, and indeed twentieth centuries were really unable to conceive of a radically this-worldly form of legitimation for political rule, one that was therefore necessarily fallible and constantly in need of revision. The world has seen a whole range of attempts to continue the transhistorical legitimation of the public sphere with secular means. One need think only of the cult of reason, the hypostatizations of nationalism, the proclamations of short-term historicophilosophical aims, the secular substitutes for religion known as Stalinism and fascism, or indeed the notion that remains influential today that politics should be determined by the overriding imperatives of growth and technology. All these legitimations of politics based on metapolitical quantities are evidence of the failure to establish a radically new source of authority commensurate with the spirit of modernity.

## THE FOUNDATION OF FREEDOM

Hannah Arendt draws a fundamental distinction between two models for founding politically integrated communities. The first corresponds to the social contract suggested by Hobbes in *Leviathan.* Its structure is vertical, with the people concluding a contract with their ruler. The term "foundation" is misleading, for what we have here is a contract between an extant society and a ruler located outside it. The hypothetical original contract envisaged here has the sole function of justifying a form of rule that is already being exercised. Every individual foregoes his or her chance to influence the course of public affairs. He or she also forfeits potential powers of solidarity that would result from voluntary alliances within society, instead bestowing all autonomy of action on the sovereign. To the extent that consent plays any role at all in this context, it is merely the generalized consent to allow oneself to be ruled. This vertical model presumes the structural division of rulers and ruled. Because the relationship between the two parties cannot be changed by procedures foreseen within the model itself, the only course open to those who are dissatisfied with the way rule is exercised is to seize power themselves by violent means. This model, having arisen during the transition from an absolute to a constitutional monarchy, has also not emancipated itself from the notion of divine right. Although religious sanctioning of secular rule no longer occurs in the authentic context of an intact Christian tradition, it nonetheless survives in the secondary, as it were, functional sense: as a means of stabilizing a system of rulership that no longer wishes to rely solely on the threat of violence. It shares one decisive characteristic with that older tradition which it puts to its own instrumental ends, and that is its location of the community's highest authority, and thus the source of that community's legitimacy, outside the framework of the polity as such.

Hobbes's model provides an admirably suited foil against which to contrast Hannah Arendt's concept of a democratic social contract. This latter contract is not concluded between a people and its ruler but rather within a group of private individuals who recognize each other as equals. They thereby tie their isolated capacity for action into one power structure based on solidarity. This horizontal rather than vertical contract centers on a reciprocal promise to stand up for each other in the shared knowledge that there can be no guarantee for the integrity of the community beyond the bounds of this contract. This horizontal model of a social contract is genuinely modern in that it dispenses with any form of religious or socially transcendent sanction. To the extent that authority is now invested in the politically united community, in other words to the extent that the community itself becomes the source of power, the authority to define the bounds of legitimate rule is transferred to those symbolic and institutional practices which keep alive that initial reciprocal promise. Furthermore, to Hannah Arendt the democratic social contract is not some hypothetical construct outside history that an established governmental structure utilizes to justify itself retroactively. Rather, as is prefigured in the French and particularly the American revolutions, it is a real historical occurrence in which the revolutionary pioneers of modernity become aware of the impetus driving them forward. In the horizontal model, the division into rulers and ruled is not completely abandoned, but is instead given a less rigid, procedural form. It is only with the advent of the image of democratic foundation that a distinction can be made between, on the one hand, a political authority that demands blind subordination and, on the other, a pragmatic obedience to the law born out of the rational recognition of functional imperatives.

Arendt reads this concept of a democratic social contract into the process of the foundation of the American Constitution and buttresses her argument by offering a communicative concept of political power. According to the latter, the existence of modern political institutions does not depend on either some (superimposed) transcendental guarantees that they shall persist, or on some police-based capacity for repression, but rather on the communicative energies of citizens who recognize each other as equals, energies that went into founding the institutions. In this conception, the stability of a political order no longer rests precisely on some nonspecific willingness of citizens to obey the state sovereign but instead on the reciprocal duty they have assumed to create a constitution and to stand up for it. Hannah Arendt sums up the essence of this concept in what has since become a classic and succinct statement:

In distinction to strength, which is the gift and the possession of every man in his isolation against all other men, power comes into being only if and when men join themselves together for the purpose of action, and it will disappear when, for whatever reason, they disperse and desert one another. Hence, binding and promising, combining and covenanting are the means by which power is kept in existence; where and when men succeed in keeping intact the power which sprang up between them during the course of any particular act or deed, they are already in the process of foundation, of constituting a stable worldly structure to house, as it were, their combined power of action.[9]

Throughout *On Revolution,* Arendt orients herself toward this notion of social power as something generated communicatively, preserved in "founding" institutions and repeatedly reiterated through symbolic acts. She explicates it by addressing the ambiguity of the concept of "constitution." The latter is ambiguous because it refers to the two separate aspects of the process of creating a constitution in that it regards this both as a completed act now extant in documentary form and as a process of reciprocal consultation, discussion, and debate that preceded the act. It is Arendt's theory of power that first enables us to grasp that this process of instituting a written constitution – which she describes by taking the example of the American Constitution – is at least as important as the document that attests to its completion. The document's political authority, something that has to assert itself, for example, in mediating in future conflicts is only as great as the communicative energy that went into it during the process of discussion prior to its codification. In this conception, a constitution decreed by professional politicians or indeed by a small group of constitutional experts can never become an independent source of legitimacy.

The problem that Arendt has to wrestle with at the end of *On Revolution,* and for which she finds no convincing answer, is brought to light by this identification of the founding act with the historically unique instance of

9 Ibid., 175.

the proclamation of the U.S. Constitution. The problem is how this public demonstration of a promise of reciprocal solidarity by the citizens in the
form of the unique act of proclaiming a constitution can be given enduring
form in political institutions and symbolic practices. It is unclear whether
Arendt sees herself merely as a historical reporter or is arguing as a political
theorist when she speaks of the way in which commemoration of the
founding act can become almost a cult, as witnessed in the case of the American Revolution. She describes, albeit without using the concept, the cryp-
toreligious worshipping of the Constitution in the United States. Without
clarifying for the reader whether she regards such a form of legitimation
founded on civil religion as desirable for the present, she goes on to portray
quite extensively the etymological origins of the word "religion," which in
the context of ancient Rome meant linking oneself back to a beginning.
She attributes the stability of the young American republic to the secular
holiness of the Constitution; that is, her point of orientation is again civil
religion. No doubt she would herself contest quite decidedly that this is an
expression of an incomplete process of secularization. The authority of the
young republic stems, she claims, precisely not from some "immortal leg-
islative" but rather from the phenomenon of a thoroughly secular founding
act. To shed light on the secret of such a mundane founding act she clearly
goes beyond the bounds of political science as a discipline and also abandons any clear, conceptually distinct historiographical line. She moves with
prophetic demeanor along the heights of existential anthropology when trying to solve the riddle of the mundane holiness of the Constitution:

What matters in our context is less the profoundly Roman notion that all foundations are reestablishments and reconstitutions than the somehow connected but different idea that men are equipped for the logically paradoxical task of making a new
beginning because they themselves are new beginnings and hence beginners. . . . [10]

She was well aware that her approach was fraught with this innate tension between a this-worldly communicative concept of social contract and
the historical uniqueness of the founding act itself, which can only be kept
alive by civil religious practices of public commemoration. Thus, many of
her concluding comments on the council system focus on the possibility of
perpetuating the founding act by means superior to ritual remembrance, although she never satisfactorily explains what the possibility may be. For example, she deliberates as follows: Once the revolution has reached its goal
with the founding act of the constitution the revolutionary mind then op-
poses some new beginning. An institution that accords with the spirit of this

10  Ibid., 213.

new beginning would continually cast aspersions on the revolutionary achievements of the founding act. It is a well-known fact that Thomas Jefferson proposed the following solution to the problem: The act of revolutionary foundation should be repeated by each new generation at approximately twenty-year intervals. In light of the approach she has taken, Arendt feels that this is an inappropriate suggestion. Yet she concedes that this proposal accurately reflects the problem involved, namely, that the people are given freedom by the revolution but are not given a place to exercise that freedom.

Arendt's almost romanticized description of the revolutionary act of founding a democratic republic prompts two objections. And they are both so obvious that Arendt herself tried to take them into account in a piece she wrote later on "civil disobedience." By according theoretical pride of place to the revolutionary big bang that generates a space for public freedom, she at the same time dramatically devalues those constitutional and institutional provisions for maintaining public freedom in the long term. And she seems to imply that for the generations that followed the Founding Fathers, the only available means of collectively reassuring themselves of the legitimacy of their own actions was the civil religious practice of ritual remembrance of a revolutionary new beginning that others accomplished. If these two premises are accepted, one is bound, not only in practice but on a theoretical level as well, to adopt a perspective from which the project of a democratic republic almost inevitably forgets its revolutionary origins and degenerates into the mere representations of private interests. It was precisely this phenomenon that Arendt, rightly or wrongly, believed she had identified in contemporary Western democracies.

A perspective that would have been commensurate with her own theoretical premises would have envisaged the revolutionary emphasis of the foundation of a democratic republic being preserved precisely in the practical utilization of those spaces for public freedom that the republic provided. This viewpoint would strip the act of "foundation" or "constitution" of its historical uniqueness and make it part of everyday life in a dynamic sense.

In her essay on civil disobedience, Arendt alludes to this conception of a founding act embedded in everyday life. Allude is the apposite verb here because she only develops the notion of a dynamic founding act *ex negativo,* that is, from the perspective of the consequences that could arise should the process of renewal be permanently disturbed. Civil disobedience is one possible way in which citizens can react to such a disturbance. Arendt speaks metaphorically of "internal immigration" when referring to the strange phenomenon whereby every new generation and every new individual has to be socialized in terms of the established political order, which is thus in turn repeatedly renewed. Certain conditions have to be met in order to ensure that this self-rejuvenation or perpetual renewal is permanent. For their part, the "newcomers" have to recognize the constitutional framework within which a change in the established order is permissible. Arendt uses the misleading concept of "tacit consent" to describe this acceptance of the constitutional framework. It is misleading because it can cause one to forget that recognition of the rules governing legitimate changes is in turn dependent on the availability of legitimate opportunities for dissent and change. From a political point of view, the so-called concept of tacit consent thus has two dimensions. On the one hand, a duty can be derived from it for dissenting minorities to accept (at least temporarily) decisions and institutions of the majority that have solidified in the course of time or at most to change them in terms of the constitutionally guaranteed rights to freedom of opinion and to free expression of will. On the other, for the respective majority and the public authorities, tacit consent implies the duty merely to represent the power of the people and not to assume it permanently as a possession. These two dimensions of tacit consent result quite logically from Arendt's model of a horizontal social contract which allows for no (legitimate) guarantees for the continuance of that contract other than the reciprocal pledge of the citizens to stand up for the integrity of a political order they have jointly established. If the public authorities, be it on their own initiative or at the behest of a strong majority, should revoke the second dimension to tacit consent by curtailing the space for public action, then this also affects the first dimension. For this amounts to a breach of the promise to stand up reciprocally for the integrity of a mutually supported order. However, this does not mean that the dissenting minorities are no longer obliged to remain within the constitutional framework. Rather, to the extent that the majority occludes access to the political realm, they now have the task of insisting, by means of symbolic political practices, upon open access to the political sphere. In this manner they repeatedly recreate the preconditions for the creative political activity of the founding act. Prompted by the contemporary examples of the civil rights movement and protest against the Vietnam War, Hannah Arendt interpreted the practice of civil disobedience in precisely this way.

Arendt's theory contrasts sharply with the work of Carl Schmitt, who maintained that the secret of the polity lay in the ability to use violence to enforce the law. For Arendt, however, "violence" is the opposite of "power"; that is, a political order will bring forth symptoms of a violent nature to the extent that it is no longer backed by the consent of its citizens.

Ever an Aristotelian, Arendt sees an inner connection between the political character of human existence and language, that is, the ability to coordinate individual plans for action by means of speech. Whoever conceives of politics in this manner must invariably exclude the phenomenon of violence from a definition of politics. "Violence," Arendt suggests, "is itself incapable of speech."[11] It cannot be an object of political theory because it can only be discussed in the technical logic of military and police experts. Violence is therefore related to the polity only externally and not intrinsically: It can only guard the latter's borders. This is, at the same time, the criterion for legitimating the use of violence. The state can legitimately deploy violent means to the extent that the responsible agents of that violence protect the communicative modus operandi of the political sphere. However, should the executive or other relevant social parties to a conflict start to conceptualize the controversies at hand in terms of the strategic logic of a potential civil war then the death knell of politics will have been sounded. Violence destroys the inner logic of politics. Taking this idea one step further, it would therefore make sense to replace the notion of the state's monopoly on violence with an equivalent drawn from a theory of democracy, namely, the public monopoly on violent means. Arendt's communicative concept of power would suggest that we strictly limit the authority of the police and the judiciary to those acts that protect those principles and rights of political communication that serve to ensure the integrity of the political sphere.

PUBLIC FREEDOM

In other words, for Hannah Arendt there is a direct and positive link between power and freedom. She repeatedly points out by references to the writings of the leaders of the American Revolution that they were concerned not just with freedom in the sense of the absence of compulsions on the individual – that is, the use of state power to guarantee the possibility of individualism – but rather with the establishment of "public freedom," a concept they defined positively. Although public freedom seems to stand in contrast to negative liberal rights on a conceptual level, this is in fact not true when viewed in terms of real history. The experience of totalitarian societies has taught even those who had not realized it earlier that the establishment of negative rights of freedom is the very precondition for the existence of a political space that could be said to embody public freedom. Following Arendt, we could distinguish between three stages in the real-

11 Ibid., 9.

ization of freedom conceived in this manner. The first stage is represented
by the existence of liberal negative rights of self-defense such as the basic
rights protecting life and property. This is merely a preliminary form of freedom because it is still limited in terms of the social classes to which it applies. The second stage is thus reached when those freedoms are extended
to "everything with a human face," that is, once liberal negative rights have
been raised by revolutionary means to the status of universal human rights.

It is not until the third stage is reached that public freedom is established,
that is, the public exercise of those institutions, politicocultural practices,
and legal principles that maintain the integrity of the political community
and give it a form that can stand the test of time. The distinction between
"liberation" and "freedom," frequently cited by Arendt in order to pinpoint
stages in a revolution, underlies this logic of the development of public freedom. Liberation solely involves struggling to gain negative rights; the establishment of freedom involves setting up those institutions and practices
that publicly embody freedom. Understood thus, freedom can by no means
be reduced simply to the unhindered pursuit of unpolitical activities, the
spaces for which are defined by the state. The concept of public freedom is
explained further by the concept of public happiness, which follows from
it. It is once more the example of the leaders of the American Revolution
that Arendt resorts to in order to demonstrate that in a democratic republic it is not a burden for the citizens to participate in public life. Nor does
such participation stem from a strategic intention geared toward securing a
private advantage but rather is enjoyable in a manner unlike any private activity. This enjoyment of things political is what she terms public happiness.
It is clear if seen against the background of her communicative concept
of power that this happiness by no means refers to some hedonistic by-
product of a Machiavellian striving for power but is rather that peculiar form
of enjoyment that can arise from opening up and participating in a political
domain. She thus maintains that the famous reference to the "pursuit of
happiness" by no means simply meant that each citizen was to be free to
pursue his or her own private happiness. Jefferson, at least in part, was also
thinking of establishing by political means a realm of public happiness. And,
she continues, it is only this concept of public happiness that explains the
reason for the founders' radical critique of the monarchy, for the latter system involved banishing the monarch's subjects from the public domain.
However, it is no accident that Arendt constantly reads the notion of public happiness into the history of the Greek polis or the American Revolution but not into any other historical phenomena. There is no other element
of her political philosophy on which the theory of decline mentioned at the

outset has more bearing than in the way she treats the phenomenon of the enjoyment of public life. It is always described in terms of its decline:

What remained of them in this country, after the revolutionary spirit had been forgotten, were civil liberties, the individual welfare of the greatest number, and public opinion as the greatest force ruling an egalitarian, democratic society, . . . and the ability to take a stand against one's own government if need be, to form pressure groups. . . . This is undoubtedly more than mere remnants, but it nevertheless signifies a sad decay and deformation of something that once really existed.[12]

Hannah Arendt explains the decline of the utopia of public freedom, which once took on concrete form in the creation of the United States, by referring to a figure of thought that remained in the background of her comparison of the French and American revolutions but nevertheless influenced her appraisal of them, namely, the separation of the political from the social along the lines of the classical Greek model. Arendt uses the term "political" to designate the space in which, given fortuitous historical circumstances, public freedom can be founded and lent a permanent institutional form. The "social" refers to the whole complex of social labor. Arendt transfers all the attributes that classical Greece and its contemporary philosophical self-interpretations reserved for the domain of the material reproduction of the family onto the modern form of organizing the satisfaction of social needs.

The reasons for the schematic nature of her approach are far from evident. The conflicts that arise from problems of social labor are thus, to Arendt, in the final instance not political, for they too are stigmatized as being purely private, as being tainted as belonging to the sphere of organic reproduction. It is as if she were saying that human self-preservation is a suprahistorical and in the final analysis an apolitical phenomenon – and that the basic anthropological pattern of this phenomenon was laid down conceptually once and for all in Greek times.

In *The Human Condition,* Arendt extensively outlines the theory of the relationship between the public and the private as prefigured in classical Greek thought. She accepted this theory as the normative blueprint for the two modern revolutions. In the case of *The Human Condition,* one frequently does not know whether Arendt is presenting her own opinion, is providing an affirmative description of someone else's opinion, or is simply reporting as an historian of ideas. This is true, for example, when she says that modern society is only a "family collective which understands itself as a gigantic super-family and the political form of organization of which is the

12 Ibid., 223, amended to include a passage from the German edition, *Über die Revolution* (Munich, 1986 [originally 1965]), 284.

nation."[13] Or, for example, when she states that "freedom is to be located exclusively in the political realm, that necessity is a prepolitical phenomenon characteristic of the realm of the private household, and that force and violence can only be justified in this domain, for they comprise the only means of overcoming necessity."[14]

She accuses modern Western thought as a whole, and its late variants of liberalism and Marxism in particular, of obscuring and inverting this ancient division and hierarchy because they only treat politics as a function of a society that is integrated in economic terms. It is in fact common today, both in scholarly and in lay discussions, to classify societies by reference not to their political constitution but to their form of economic organization. It has especially been the Western Left that has long tended to typify the conflicting Western and Eastern world systems in economic terms and less with regard to some political point of comparison, that is, the degree to which they provide opportunities for freedom. Arendt rejects the assumption implicit in this approach, namely, that the economy monocausally predicates political freedom. To Arendt, both the growth and the crisis-related weakening of productive forces always contain the danger of overburdening the political sphere with structural problems foreign to it, a danger that in economically developed mass societies takes the form of political apathy, privatism, and consumerism.

This division of the "political" and the "social" spheres, inspired by its predecessor in classical antiquity, is also the basis for her distinguishing between a "political revolution" and a "social revolution." She maintains that of all revolutions only the American one, promoted by economically favorable circumstances, truly generated freedom. By contrast, the French Revolution degenerated into a social revolution under the pressure of fast spreading mass poverty, as a consequence of which the natural compulsion, that is, necessity of physical survival, occupies the political space. Factual immiseration, now in a publicly visible form, turned the thrust of the French revolutionaries away from the goal of achieving political emancipation for the Third Estate, thus burdening the political space with a cluster of problems foreign to it.

The schematics of Arendt's theory of decline, based on the division in Greek antiquity between the political and the social, has an even stronger impact on the shorter excursus in which Arendt focuses on fully fledged capitalist societies, without admittedly using this designation for them. The self-correcting mechanism built into modern capitalism – be it in the shape

---

13 Cf. Hannah Arendt, *The Human Condition* (Chicago, 1958).    14 Ibid.

of the welfare state guarantees or types of state intervention – is always linked to a reduction in complexity in the relation between state and society. And Arendt is only able to understand the thrust of this loss of differentiation in one way on account of the interpretative blueprint she follows, namely, as the colonization of politics by society. She claims that the "overburdening" of the public space in which freedom can occur with problems that, by virtue of their (supposed) nature, resist political solution, reduces humans to silent reactors to economic compulsions.

Such an interpretation is both schematic and elitist. It is schematic because it accords a normative status to one historical form assumed by the relation between political and private reproduction, taking it as the yardstick – albeit one that is historically and sociologically unsuitable – for macrodevelopments in capitalist modernity. The normative status granted the strict separation of political and economic reproduction in societies in classical antiquity inevitably prompts the question as to what price from the modern point of view has to be paid for this separation. The polis as the space in which a form of public freedom could unfold was only possible because women, slaves, children, workers, and Greeks who had no civil rights were excluded from that space. And because the labor of the latter gave those free citizens the leisure to indulge in politics, which Arendt terms "public happiness" and the decline of which she bemoans in modernity.

Arendt's interpretation of modern societies is elitist, for she has not eradicated those traces of exclusiveness from her key concept of the "public sphere" that adhered to it in classical antiquity. The semantics attached to the concept precisely during the French Revolution – which Arendt after all described from a critical and distanced viewpoint – has nothing in common with the agonistic public sphere in which a select few citizens defy their own mortality in noble competition for moral stature and political honor. In the modern understanding, that exclusive character has been replaced by an awareness that the public sphere cannot be blocked off in one dimension or other; previously excluded social groups cannot be excluded who now push their way even into the space in which public freedom occurs. Nor can it be closed off to issues that were traditionally considered "pre-" or "unpolitical," or to culturally specific patterns that attempt to prescribe what the barriers between the private and public spheres are once and for all. A modern notion of the public sphere can be described at three levels, namely as a "factually," "socially," and "temporally" open-ended space in which the conflicts between citizens with regard to coordinating common affairs take place. By "factually open-ended" I mean that all issues are permissible as objects for debate in the public space. In societies of the type in which we live – unlike antiquity and also unlike the nineteenth century – a self-evident separation of the political and unpolitical spheres of life no longer exists.

The development of the welfare and interventionist state has undermined the liberal distinction, valid for so long, between a state-controlled public sphere and a private sphere clearly sealed off from this. No one today will still claim that the relation between workers and entrepreneurs is nonpolitical and is based on private law. At the same time, under the banner of "the private is the political," social movements, especially the feminist movement, have washed away the dam that hitherto concealed from the public eye the phenomena of structural violence within the intimate and family spheres.

A modern and democratic concept of the public sphere must continue to be understood to signify a socially open-ended space. "Socially open-ended" is used here to mean that no social group can continue to be denied access to the public sphere. The history of the idea of the public sphere has always been accompanied by the critique that it is only available to certain social classes or limited to one sex. The history of the struggle for political rights in Western democracies has always been a struggle – by no means ended – in which workers, women, subproletarian strata, ethnic minorities, and homosexuals have fought to gain equal access to the public sphere.

Finally, the model outlined here also has a temporal dimension. Because the conflict over the shape public affairs should take is permanent, the public sphere is truly an open-ended process. One particular citizen or social group cannot be allowed to occupy the terrain of public communication for long. The history of public communication also teaches us that the big do not stay big nor do the small remain small forever – if we view them through the wide-angle lens of the historiographer. In modernity, no single worldview, no single system of belief can hope to occupy the public sphere permanently in some hegemonial fashion. These three dimensions or levels of the political public sphere can be considered as a unity when viewed from the perspective of a completed process of Enlightenment, one that turns its back on any definition that lies beyond the public sphere of who or what can be banned from the domain of public discussion when and for how long.

# 2

# The Questionable Influence of Arendt (and Strauss)

GEORGE KATEB

The influence of Hannah Arendt and Leo Strauss on political theory in the United States has been considerable. I have no wish to deny that the great power of their work earned them their standing. Still, their influence is, to some nontrivial extent, worrisome. The nub of the matter is that both radiate disapproval of modern democracy. In a very selective way, I would like to take up the bearing of Arendt's work on modern democracy, and to a lesser degree, that of Strauss's on the same. My hope is to suggest that anyone committed to modern democracy should resist the influence of both these German–American philosophers while not being totally impervious to it. I therefore aim to question the unquestionable influence of Arendt and Strauss.

Now, it would be instructive to consider Herbert Marcuse alongside Arendt and Strauss. He was, for a time, even more prominent than they were. One can say that, in any case, Marcuse, Arendt, and Strauss were probably the three most influential émigré German political theorists in the United States. Marcuse provides yet another kind of hostility or skepticism toward modern democracy, to go with that of Arendt and Strauss. Their interrelationships can be a fascinating subject for reflection, all the more so because their common bond was Heidegger. Of the three, whose work will live on? Whose work will live the longest? No one can say. At the least, their reputations will have ups and downs.

## I

Let us stay with Arendt and Strauss, two whose love of Greece, inflamed and mediated by German philosophy, set them against modern democracy. My sense is that, of the two, Arendt may be the more serious enemy of modern democracy even though, and because, the cultural snobbism in her is much less than in Strauss. So is the cultural pessimism. Thus, the demos

29

do not offend her; indeed, she often praises ordinary people. This is not to say that she admired the culture of modern democracy. And nihilism (perhaps the main overt source of Straussian pessimism), construed as the philosophical or historical relativization of beliefs and principles, troubles her a good deal less than does zealous commitment. Despite the absence of conservative or authoritarian impediments to an appreciation of modern democracy as a culture, Arendt may nevertheless provide the greater antagonism. And her critique is decidedly political. Her target is the politics (what she saw as the false politics) of modern democracy. She reproaches modern democracy because it is not participatory. She celebrates Athens. It seems, then, that she reproaches modern democracy because it is not democratic, or not democratic enough. It seems that she is ultrademocratic. One wants to say that she reproaches modern democracy, not democracy as such.

Yet, on the matter of Athens, it is hard to say that she praises it as ordinary Athenian democrats praised it – namely for the fact that democracy rescued more than a few from oppression. The larger point, however, is that no lover of the polis can really appreciate modern democracy – constitutional representative democracy – except by a quite arduous effort. In *Considerations on Representative Government,* John Stuart Mill slides very easily from praise of polis democracy to the celebration of representative democracy as the "ideally best polity" in the present age. But the move is not defended at any theoretical length. Clearly, representative democracy is politically continuous with Athenian democracy only in some respects. It may be that one has to choose between reverence for polis democracy and appreciation of modern democracy.

The matter of Arendt and modern democracy is undeniably complex. A way to begin discussion is to say that Arendt never defends equal citizenship as a fundamental political right of every individual, despite her words in *The Origins of Totalitarianism* on the value of rights of membership in an organized nation.[1] Rather, she sees in citizenship an opportunity that belongs to those who welcome or seize it, no matter who they may be. She pays scant theoretical attention to those who have historically been legally or forcibly excluded from participation. Relatedly, she has no patience with those who, allowed to participate, choose not to do so or feel unable to. She reaches an extreme, if temporary, point when in *On Revolution,* she theorizes a new political scheme, based on Jefferson's idea of ward governments, that "would spell the end of general suffrage as we understand it; for only those who as voluntary members of an 'elementary republic' have demonstrated that they

---

1 Hannah Arendt, *The Origins of Totalitarianism,* 2nd ed. (New York, 1958), 267–302.

care for more than their private happiness and are concerned about the state of the world would have a right to be heard in the conduct of the business of the republic."[2] In her later essay, "Thoughts on Politics and Revolution," she puts her point less pugnaciously: "Anyone who is not interested in public affairs will simply have to be satisfied with their being decided without him. But each person must be given the opportunity."[3]

In Arendt's version of the ward system, participants would not function as representatives, with all the representative responsibilities. That must mean that they would form a self-enclosed world possessed of a sense of superiority to those who choose not to participate. They would live for each other, for their relationship, while the rest endured the consequences. Furthermore, all could not participate even if they wanted to since the numbers would be unmanageably great. The ward system, in Arendt's treatment, takes on the qualities of oligarchy, open as it may be. Yet representative democracy is devoted in theory to the rights and interests of the nonparticipants or the minimally participant.

In general, Arendt wants politics to be the monopoly of the admirable. Those worthy of admiration are the ones who want to "count and be counted upon,"[4] those who refuse the delight of passivity or the pleasures of private pursuits. They may come from any social class. They are admirable, she suggests, who follow Jefferson's lead in loving "your neighbor as yourself, and your country more than yourself."[5] She is intent on politicizing or repoliticizing the ideal of manhood, making virility indissociable from virtue, and finding in revolutionary councils and congresses and in insurgent movements in defense of constitutionalism the modern arenas in which men find, define, and spend themselves as men. She is a theorist out to make action shine, a woman intent on breathing new life, a new life, into men. Truly, real men would not have allowed Nazism to arise, and they were needed to resist it. She is haunted, in her ideal, by actual unmanly conformity and inertia, especially in Germany; though, of course, her ideal is a magnificent exfoliation; and only one of its seeds is her own need for psychological compensation. But such an outlook – namely, that politics should be the monopoly of the admirable – is not democratic, in any sense of the word. The modern sense, in particular, is that every individual, as a matter of right, should have at least that particle of power called the vote, and may use, not use, or mistakenly misuse that power. The dignity of each

2 Hannah Arendt, *On Revolution* (New York, 1963), 284.
3 Hannah Arendt, "Thoughts on Politics and Revolution" in *Crisis of the Republic* (New York, 1972), 233.
4 *On Revolution*, 257.    5 Ibid., 256.

(as it is an unearned dignity) rests on not being excluded; the dignity of all rests on being governed only by those they have chosen rather than by those who have, in some way or other, chosen themselves.

But the story of Arendt's relation to modern democracy has more ingredients. If one is committed to modern democracy, how does one respond to the heart of Arendt's political teaching as a whole – her theory of political action? I wish to suggest that, howsoever one responds, one should keep in mind two methodological points in order to avoid confusion.

She helps to supply the first one herself. In the very course of proposing a new interpretation of American experience, she warns the readers of *On Revolution* – putatively, American readers, for the most part – that political and social theories that have their roots in European experience, in the inextinguishable capacity of Europe's ethnic and religious rivalries and cultural-class system to engender tragic experience, cannot have the same sense or meaning for Americans. When she writes these words, she is, of course, an American citizen; and doubtless her writings after *The Human Condition* (1958) and *Between Past and Future* (1961) show a developing fascination with American politics and history. But she knows how European she must always remain, if in no other sense than that Europe's recent past, in which events, in their systematic evil, surpassed the repeated and all too familiar tragedy of the more remote past, must forever weigh on her, not as a Jew, but as a European; not as a victim, but as one who drew her life from a culture able to perpetuate systematic evil of a peculiarly deliberate kind. Let us remember that the title of *The Origins of Totalitarianism* in its British edition is *The Burden of the Past*.

She will try to instruct Americans about their history, especially those episodes when genuine political action manifested itself. But she, in effect, warns her American readers to be wary of her, just to the degree that she has to remain European. She says that theoretical writing has never flourished in America; but even Americans, blessed as they are in their material circumstances and the seemingly nontragic quality of their history, need theories to understand reality and "come to terms with it."[6] Americans, therefore, borrow from Europe. The frequent result is "strange magnification" and "distortion," which "may be due to the fact that these theories, once they had crossed the Atlantic, lost their basis of reality and with it all limitations through common sense."[7] She has uppermost in mind the ways in which Marxism damages American understanding of America. Is her own theoretical work, however, experiencing or suffering the same sort of

6 Ibid., 223.    7 Ibid., 222–23.

fate at American hands? Did she expect that it would? Did she take steps to warn American readers that they should make allowances for her European origins? The amount of deliberate self-undercutting she engages in, at the expense of her own theory, is hard to determine.

I think that we are faithful to her when we remember that she is fully sensitive to the intellectual consequences of the plain fact that she came to America as an adult, and that if she knows things about America as an adult, and that if she knows things about America that most natives do not and cannot, she also lives spiritually at a distance from her new home – productive of insight though such distance can be and is. She would not want us to say of her what Johan Huizinga said of Spengler: "He compels us to forget that we know better."[8] In particular, if we think that her theory of political action may omit some major considerations that are especially pertinent to modern democracy, and does so in part because of her belated acquaintance with the relevant experience, we have her blessing to try to repair that omission. The general lesson is that no one, whether American or European or both, should use, without appropriate adaptation, European theory about America or, naturally, American theory about Europe. (The lesson should apply to the reception of Strauss's work as well.) And if what she calls "an air of lightheartedness, a certain weightlessness" permeates American theory about American political life, about democracy in America, or about political and cultural life in general, and therefore eventually creates dissatisfaction among American theorists themselves, the remedy cannot for any purpose be the wholesale, unrevised, unadapted acceptance of any European theory, not even hers. This caution is needed even when or especially when the theory is not confined to the culture of its origin, but is instead, universal in the scope of its ambition.

It is incontestable that European political, social, and cultural theory has often been denser and more interesting than American theory. The trouble is that it may be too interesting: American scholars will try to find an American use for it because they are so aesthetically captivated by it. No doubt, a willed attempt by an American to use a European theory – unrevised or unadapted, or insufficiently so – can result in some insight. Even if distorted or exaggerated, the insight can nevertheless be stimulating. What I have in mind is not so much the value of watching with alienated eyes, but rather the possible value of recklessness; the value of, precisely, distortion or exaggeration; or, one may add, caricature. This is more like playing with perspectives than it is like managing them (in Nietzsche's sense). But I am afraid

8 Quoted from Huizinga's *Dutch Civilization in the Seventeenth Century and Other Essays* (1968) by William Dray in *Perspectives on History* (London, 1980), 100.

that the scholar thereby risks doing work that is even more lighthearted or weightless than Arendt thought the usual level of American theorizing to be.

Apart from fascination, another and equally questionable consideration may be at work. Some American scholars need to find European versions of ideas already formulated in the United States, as if authentication could come only from the outside. This sentiment is perhaps creditable, if too deferential. It is not creditable, however, when its adherents remain unappreciative of the American theoretical achievement. I would like to recall the words of D. H. Lawrence on the American capacity to get there first, so to speak. (I am willing to take authentication from an outsider, if only in order to be accommodating.) He has American literature in mind, but I believe that what he says can sometimes be applied to American political, social, and cultural theory. In his Foreword to *Studies in Classic American Literature,* he writes:

The furthest frenzies of French modernism or futurism have not yet reached the pitch of extreme consciousness that Poe, Melville, Hawthorne, Whitman reached. The European moderns are all *trying* to be extreme. The great Americans I mention just were it. Which is why the world has funked them, and funks them today.[9]

Nothing that I say is meant to disparage the penetration or validity of observations made of the American scene by Europeans. Tocqueville, Lawrence, Arendt herself, and numerous others say striking things that ring true. American self-understanding would be impoverished without these writers. They frequently serve to rescue American experience from the native observer's boredom, condescension, or obliviousness. It is caution I urge, especially caution in the use made by Americans, for understanding America, of theoretical frameworks devised by Europeans, but most especially, frameworks devised by them for European conditions and experiences or under the influence of European trauma. With due caution, European theory can be domesticated profitably, and this need not be the same as being deradicalized.

The second methodological point is that commentators should not conflate what a political theorist says about politics at its best and what he or she says about the rest of political life. Arendt herself is careful, for the most part, to indicate the applicability of her ideal conceptualization. She looks for evidence of the best politics and finds it in only a few times and places. She then draws out the fullest possible meaning of such uncommon actuality; she theoretically enhances or perfects it by inspired interpretation or reconstruction. There are only a few unimportant occasions in her work

9 D. H. Lawrence, *Studies in Classic American Literature* (1922) (New York, 1964).

where she seems to ignore the distinction between the best politics and the usual sort. The upshot is that, as her commentators, and in her name, we should not extend to political life in its entirety the glory, the grandeur, the existential supremacy, the life-redemptive quality, that she reserved for politics at its best. Concerning most of political actuality, she left almost all the work of judgment to be done – except, of course, when politics ushered in the systematic evil of totalitarian extermination. About evil, she made and elaborated powerful judgments.

When these two methodological points are disregarded, some strange results can follow. If the first is disregarded, and we look at constitutional representative democracy dominated by her theory of political action, an idle and irritable romanticism may ensue. There then can follow a rather dazed and secondhand critique – of the sort she would have spurned – of what may turn out to be, for all its appalling deficiencies, the best practicable political system in the conditions of modern life.

If the second methodological point is disregarded, one can come to adopt the view that it is always better to be political than apolitical and that every political system is deserving of allegiance. Additionally, one may accord all political life an autonomy or separateness, and an immunity from moral judgment, that Arendt seems to bestow on politics at its best, but only on it. We must resist the notion that we are true to Arendt's spirit when we simply affirm the prestige of politics.

Even more, we cannot allow any political agencies and actors – no matter what their form of purpose or policy – immunity from moral judgment. We must not think that political life has its own special morality different from everyday morality (no one is proposing a pure ethic of intention or ultimate ends as a standard), or that political life should be held to a lower standard than everyday morality, or that there is some unspecified value that is entitled to subordinate considerations of everyday morality when we come to assess political life. All these versions of realist immorality are antithetical to the foundations of modern democracy; but they are also foreign to Arendt's teaching.

Yet, even when due methodological caution is observed and Arendt's thinking is more or less accurately received, her influence is not all to the good. Especially on the interconnected matters of the nature of modern constitutional representative democracy and the place of moral judgment in the assessment of genuine political action is her influence sometimes to be regretted. My belief is that when two of her texts – her two most Greek texts – *The Human Condition* and *Between Past and Future* dominate one's reception of Arendt, then her influence is not unequivocally welcome.

All that she is able to make of constitutional representative democracy is that "representation is no more than a matter of 'self-preservation' or self-interest."[10] But this political system is vastly more complex than that, even when viewed from the perspective of the ordinary and largely inactive citizen. Though she rejects all Marxist reductions and perceptual obliterations, she has no feeling for the tonic psychological (perhaps spiritual) effects on individuals of being included as equal citizens. This effect may occur even when inclusion is only formal or minimal, without having been "merited," and even though actual politics is deformed by elitism, secrecy, mendacity, and injustice, and even though constitutional protections seem to have more reality than democratic participation. (This is not to say that it is less democratic in order to be more constitutional.) And until the essays collected in *Crises of the Republic* Arendt has little sense of the enormous encouragement that the constitutional representative system gives to those eager for genuine though episodic political experience, as if, by democratic episodes, to make up for the system's scarcely correctable undemocratic structures. The system, as an ensemble of moral and existential effects, eludes her. If that is the price she has to pay in order to be able to see deeply into the polis or councils or movements, then so be it. It is not wise, however, for us to imitate her one-sidedness: We do not have her genius to excuse us.

Arendt's sketchy skepticism toward, or tepid praise of, modern constitutional representative democracy can incite reflection. But we cannot remain enclosed within her work if we are to take in the phenomenon of modern democracy. In fact, we adhere to her spirit of inquiry when we are driven to revise or reject her teaching. Her passionate sensitivity to the evil of totalitarianism never leads her to anything like an equally passionate affirmation of the only political alternative in modern life, constitutional representative democracy, that has a chance to aspire to decency, or at least to the avoidance of systematic oppression.

Particular aspects of her theory of political action also tend to lead us away from constitutional representative democracy. As an example, I would mention her tender concern for political authority, which, she says, employs neither persuasion nor coercion.[11] Why apparently regret the loss of such a nonrational, mystified, reflexively obedient element? It is excellent to say, as she does, that the American Constitution knows no theory of governmental sovereignty and knows no European-style state. But why worry

---

10 *On Revolution*, 63.
11 Hannah Arendt, "What Is Authority?" in *Between Past and Future*, 2nd ed. (New York, 1968), 93. But see her rejection of the appropriateness of authority for the governance of adults, "The Crisis in Education," in *Between Past and Future*, 195.

about authority instead of legitimacy? Further, her romantic republicanism does not bring out the democratic and brawling qualities of the American Revolution and the founding period. Then, too, her theorization of kinds of social contract in *In Revolution* and later in "Civil Disobedience,"[12] while subtle and immensely instructive, is too insistent that the praiseworthy kind of social contract looks to the creation of a bond whose maintenance becomes the reason for being of all those who explicitly or tacitly enter into it. Heroic solidarity is not the aim of the actual social contract that is the American Constitution. In all these respects as well as others, the politics of constitutional representative democracy in America is submitted to an alien perspective that provokes but may not always illuminate.

On the place of moral judgment in the assessment of what she deemed genuine political life, I think that her work is fundamentally unsatisfactory. It is unsatisfactory from many perspectives, but surely from the perspective of one who is morally committed to modern democracy. If human conduct has consequences for individual members of the group itself or for people outside it, then it must be liable to moral judgment, no matter how many allowances for either greatness or desperation one is tempted or compelled to make. She admired the New Left for its genuine politics before it turned Marxist or violent. But she distorts the phenomenon: She pays only slight attention to its moral nature. The New Left in its prime was morally driven, not amorally energized. And then she is always praising Greece and Rome; but why choose to forget the rapacity that was Greece and the inhumanity that was Rome? All the recent work on Arendt's concept of judging cannot rescue her theory of genuine political action from an affinity to immorality, though of an existential rather than a realist kind. For Arendt, political judgment means either taking into account the views of others by seeing things "in the perspective of all those who happen to be present"[13]; or assessing, as part of a public of spectators, the existential or aesthetic worth of actions[14]; or acting with an anticipation of how one's deeds will be judged by spectators.[15] None of this need provide adequate moral restraint, if it provides any at all.

Arendt deplores the ruthless pursuit of substantive political goals, but she does not sufficiently weigh the moral costs of pursuing politics, not in order to attain a goal, but for the very reasons she endorses: politics for its own sake as a pleasure, or the sake of freedom, or creativity, or experience, or an

---

12 *On Revolution,* 169–70; Hannah Arendt, "Civil Disobedience" in *Crises of the Republic,* 85–88.
13 Hannah Arendt, "The Crisis in Culture" in *Between Past and Future,* 221.
14 Hannah Arendt, *Lectures on Kant's Political Philosophy,* ed. Ronald Beiner (Chicago, 1982), 63.
15 Ibid.

immortal name, or personal identity. All these pursuits can proceed without any moral motive or perhaps much of a sense of moral limits.

Any kind of immorality or disregard for moral concerns, any degree of it, any even faint approach to it on principle and with deliberateness, is incompatible with the presuppositions of modern democracy, a system that means nothing unless it means that no consideration, not even an existential one, no matter how sublime, can ever take priority over plain everyday morality. Modern decency is supposedly the politics more thoroughly permeated by everyday morality than any other, the politics that resolutely does not seek to transcend morality and create a nonmoral reason for its being.

Arendt is a great writer; her lifework is probably one of the most valuable in the fields of moral psychology and political theory in this century. She reads texts and she reads experience with tremendous power. I believe, however, that she is best taken, not as a monitor of the deficiencies of modern democracy and an evangelist of new political forms, but as the creator of what in *The Life of the Mind* she calls "thought trains,"[16] which we may understand as conceptualizations that are worthy objects of contemplation, with nonliteral and unpredictable effects on one's soul. I would thus extend to her and other political theories the status she posits for metaphysics. In serving her readers best when held not too closely, when (in fact) mistrusted as a guide to practice, she is like all real political theorists, most of the time. They must be refracted and resisted by us if they are to bestow their benefits.

II

What is Leo Strauss's relation to modern democracy? He did not produce a direct political theory, or a systematic exposition of political principles upon which a political position could be sustained. Rather, he produced a rich body of work that seems primarily concerned to explain what rules should be used in the interpretation of texts of philosophy and political theory, and to offer an interpretation of many of them with the help of these rules. In comparison to this immense achievement, how much could a political position matter?

It is clear, however, that people think it matters. Perhaps the main reason they do is that there is an undeniable affinity between conservatism and Strauss's students and sympathizers – in fact, Strauss appears to call himself a conservative.[17] Could it be, then, that his interpretations (and his

16 Hannah Arendt, *The Life of the Mind,* 2 vols. (New York, 1978), vol. 1: *Thinking,* 160.
17 Leo Strauss, Preface to *Liberalism Ancient and Modern* (New York, 1968), viii.

rules of interpretation) are meant to serve, if only indirectly, a particular political intention? I do not think that an unequivocal answer is possible. But let us suspend our uncertainty for the moment. Assume that both his interpretations and his rules of interpretation are indeed politically or ideologically interested. Working with that assumption, we would find that what often gives power to his readings is not only adherence to his rules and his consequent skill at interpretation, but his general outlook, which is political to an appreciable extent. One could even propose that his outlook determines his interpretations by giving them a strategy, which the rules in turn serve. By rules, I mean such precepts as: Read between the lines; expect meaning to be disguised; sometimes expect to find that a writer says the opposite of what he believes; and sometimes expect to find the writer's true sentiments expressed briefly and in an out-of-the-way region of the text.[18] By strategy, I mean a characteristic way of interpretation, of ascribing meaning to complex and disputed writings. I think that a case could be made for saying that Strauss's strategy of reading is not merely at the service of some local or temporary conservatism; rather – and far more important – it is at the service of an inveterate antidemocratic outlook, an authoritarian antidemocratic position.

Now Strauss includes himself among the "friends and allies" of democracy.[19] But the fact is that he almost never praises democracy, whether ancient or modern. In contrast, he gives voice clearly and simply to crucial antidemocratic sentiments so that, if one followed ordinary rules of reading, one would say that Strauss is not a friend or ally of democracy. He is at most a reluctant and disdainful supporter; a tactical supporter. Then, alerted by these antidemocratic sentiments, one would begin to notice that a certain pattern emerges in Strauss's interpretations of various texts. More precisely, one would, like Strauss, become an interested reader – of Strauss; but ideally, one would not simply be partisan, just as Strauss is not simply partisan.

I believe, finally, that the only way of repelling or just qualifying the claim that Strauss is an authoritarian antidemocrat is to follow his rules of interpretation in interpreting him, and to follow them with one strategic aim, among others: to ask whether it is possible that Strauss is a good and true friend of modern democracy.

But before coming to that last point, the merest of possibilities, let us sketch the case for claiming that Strauss is, in truth, an authoritarian antidemocrat. Throughout his writings, he says or unmistakably suggests that the people, the greater number, the many, need ruling, not just governing (they are not politically competent); that the people need a constant, an

18 See Leo Strauss, *Persecution and the Art of Writing* (Glencoe, Ill., 1952), esp. the title essay, 22–37.
19 Leo Strauss, "Liberal Education and Responsibility" in *Liberalism, Ancient and Modern,* 24.

almost desperate, curbing or restraining (they are licentious); and that in the modern age, they dominate society to such an extent that they produce, or are given by expert technicians, a mass culture of such philistine vulgarity that all standards of quality tend to disappear.[20]

No friend and ally of democracy could say or suggest these things and mean them. The democratic reader, made adversary to Strauss by these sentiments, would be sensitized to the possibility of a general antidemocratic outlook in Strauss, even when present not explicitly but only inferred by one's ordinary but interested reading. Finding expressions of an outlook, one can go on to attribute to Strauss the following strategy: He wishes to overcome one of the most frequently recurrent tendencies in the long sequence of political theories, namely, the tendency to think that the people, the greater number, the many, are likely to be morally better than the few, whether the few are defined by reference to superior intelligence or social status, or to the possession of official or unofficial power. The tendency, frequently in evidence in political theory, is to think that the people's vices are milder than those of the few, that the people are less cruel, less disposed to oppress, less in need of curbing and restraining than any of the elites. When the people are errant, one or more of the elites has or have seduced them. What is more, repression engenders licentiousness, not the other way around.

This tendency of sentiment in political theory is obviously not sufficient to turn into democrats most of the theorists who espouse it. But it is enough to spare the people the sort of horrified contempt present on the surface of Strauss's writing – even while he claims that he is a friend and ally of democracy. In pursuit of this strategy of interpretation, determined by his political outlook, Strauss works to disparage those writers like Hobbes and Machiavelli who are too outspoken in their advocacy of the view that favors the superior decency of the people, and to slant his interpretation of those writers in whom this espousal is much more muted (Plato and Aristotle, as the greatest examples). This is not to deny that some theorists – Rousseau and Mill are instances – fear the people more than their professed radicalism or liberalism would indicate that they should. But that is another story. And, in general, Strauss condemns modern philosophy because he claims that it serves modern democracy and the connected project of improving the material human condition.[21]

---

20  All these sentiments find a place in, among other writings, four essays in *Liberalism Ancient and Modern:* "What is Liberal Education?," "Liberal Education and Responsibility," "The Liberalism of Classical Political Philosophy," and "Perspectives on the Good Society."

21  "Liberal Education and Responsibility," 19–20.

Furthermore, the specific rules of reading commonly known as Straussian are used by Strauss himself to make us believe that most of the great philosophers and political theorists wrote circumspectly, not only, not primarily, because they feared that they would be persecuted for subversion, but mainly because they feared their own power to subvert. Popular enlightenment would only erode social order and intensify the innate popular will-to-licentiousness. Strauss disregards the fact, however, that there are surely other principal reasons for writing circumspectly; self-doubt or heuristic cunning, for example.

Pervading Strauss's work, consequently, is the sense that everything must be done to enhance the prestige of what Strauss claims is the classical position. The people need gentlemen to rule them; the classical aristocratic virtues of gentlemen are what we now would see as almost totally devoid of connection to the democratic (as well as radical Christian) understanding of what goodness consists of;[22] and gentlemen need the assistance of circumspect philosophers who do not carelessly or fully expose their doubts about religion and tradition, but instead help to sustain the established order by creating and manipulating certain myths. These are myths of Founding Fathers; myths of political authority; myths of the necessity for divine or metaphysical authentication for morality; and myths of authentication for particular systems of both gentlemanly virtue and popular discipline in which full discretionary permissiveness for "statesmen" is joined to rigid moral constraints for the "masses." The culminating Straussian injunction to all practitioners and students of political theory is, then, to defend and promote a so-called classical position in the modern age, as if one could improve modern democracy by viewing it in the light of Plato's or Aristotle's ideal conceptions. Strauss's dread is that otherwise, there will be democratic disorder with or without egalitarian "drabness."[23] His dread has been infectious and has sponsored a great deal of cant about modern democracy's dependence on classical virtue (in the few) and devoted allegiance (in the many).

If I am correct, Strauss's impact may be to emphasize the need to qualify democracy by elements thoroughly extrinsic to itself, and to impede the desire to see democracy as a moral system whose aim is not to level and cheapen but to effect a transcendence of aristocratic and gentlemanly notions and a transformation of the nature of the philosophical quest. This composite aim can be judged in a way wholly distinct from Strauss's (not Platonic but Nietzschean) way. This other way is ambivalently celebratory and reaches its highest point so far in work Strauss conveniently ignores, the

22 Ibid., 24.    23 Ibid., 12.

writings of Emerson, Thoreau, and Whitman. (At least Nietzsche took Emerson seriously.) Strauss never seems to have looked at American democracy or any modern democracy (unless it be Weimar), and he directs the gaze of others away from their reality. An inappropriate European theory, with both local and universal ambitions, blocks both observation and useful criticism.

This (counter-) strategy for reading Strauss can be repelled only by applying some of Strauss's rules of reading to Strauss. We could concentrate especially on those few sentences scattered here and there that go in a more positive democratic direction. For example, he says or suggests that only a democracy (perhaps only an imperial democracy)[24] could have prepared a mind as supremely daring and innovative as that of Thucydides[25]; that only democracy among the imperfect polities as a matter of principle tolerates and encourages philosophy[26]; that conservatism of an authoritarian sort could never have originated any tradition it cherishes, because only revolutions and sacrileges could have begun it and can sustain it[27]; and (satirically) that the perfect gentleman is merely the true Pharisee "who is not ashamed of anything or does not repent anything he has done because he always does what is right or proper."[28] Perhaps most important, Strauss says that

[the] only thing which can be held to be unqualifiedly good is not the contemplation of the eternal, not the cultivation of the mind, to say nothing of good breeding, but a good intention, and of good intentions everyone is as capable as everyone else, wholly independently of good education. Accordingly, the uneducated could even appear to have an advantage over the educated: the voice of nature or of the moral law speaks in them perhaps more clearly and more decidedly than in the sophisticated who may have sophisticated away their conscience.[29]

What is one to make of these thoughts? Are they only the eruption of feelings that an honest man, somewhat like Saul Bellow's Mr. Sammler, simply could not repress, but that do not essentially disturb the tenor of his life's work? Or does Strauss want us to find his deepest beliefs in them? Perhaps the latter. I hope so. I would rather be on Strauss's side than against him. But what would explain his subterfuge? Why nearly conceal a position that is obviously so much more popular — in both senses of the word — than the antidemocratic position an interested adversarial reader elicits?

At one point, Strauss says that we understand our own thoughts better when we seriously entertain alien thoughts. Was he trying then to strengthen

---

24 Leo Strauss, *The City and Man* (Chicago, 1964), 159.     25 Ibid., 159, 229 – 30.
26 "The Liberalism of Classical Political Philosophy" in *Liberalism Ancient and Modern,* 35.
27 "Preface to Spinoza's Critique of Religion" in *Liberalism Ancient and Modern,* 253.
28 Ibid., 268.     29 "Liberal Education and Responsibility," 22.

democracy by avoiding flattery and inducing democrats to undergo an asce-sis that would make them better democrats?[30] If that was his strategy, I am afraid it miscarried. Too many who came under his influence, even if they think they are democrats, and especially when they write about the creation and meanings of the American constitutional democracy, are, rather, literal and artificial authoritarian antidemocrats, without any saving hesitation like his. Instructed by him to preserve the polity, the tendency of their work is to misrepresent it and spread dislike of it.

## III

The value of Arendt and Strauss should not be defined exclusively by their relation to modern democracy. They have much to teach, apart from their views on our political system, and if need be, in spite of these views. But the fact remains that none of their power goes to improving the theory of modern democracy. I am in doubt as to whether that theory is even tested by its encounter with either of them. The failures and inconsistencies of modern democracy are not, in my judgment, addressed by Arendt or Strauss in a manner that feeds the imagination of democratic amelioration. I would therefore conclude this brief survey by saying that Arendt and Strauss do not strengthen modern democracy by their challenge. Rather, it is a sign of modern democracy's strength (strength of appetite, if nothing else) that some of its citizens give philosophical hospitality to their challenge. One of democracy's characteristic features is, after all, to be able to entertain self-rejection. The point is to find more serious reasons for self-rejection than Strauss (or Arendt) ever gives.[31]

30  Ibid., 24.
31  For instructive discussions of European theory and American practice, see Leon Bramson, *The Political Context of Sociology* (Princeton, N.J., 1961); and John G. Gunnell, *Political Theory: Tradition and Interpretation* (Cambridge, Mass., 1979) and *Between Philosophy and Politics: The Alienation of Political Theory* (Amherst, Mass., 1986).

# 3

# Hannah Arendt:
# A German-American Jewess Views the
# United States – and Looks Back to Germany

ERNST VOLLRATH

Hannah Arendt came to the United States as a refugee from the racial persecution and racial genocide being practiced by the totalitarian regime in
Germany and eventually became an American citizen. This experience continued to influence her view of the U.S. political system. And although, toward the end of her life, she leveled harsh criticism against specific political
practices, Arendt never altered her fundamental agreement with the principles of the American Constitution and the political perceptions upon which
these were based. Her entire political thought can be understood as an attempt to contrast and even reconcile the basic principles of the American
political system with European, above all German, traditions. In this attempt, she was guided by the principles of classic American political thought
that she discerned in the ideas of the Founding Fathers.

In a letter to Karl Jaspers, dated January 29, 1946, one of the very first
letters of their renewed correspondence following the Second World War,
Hannah Arendt tried to explain her view of the United States to her former teacher.

> With good reason you say "Happy America" – for here, in virtue of the essen-
> tial soundness of the political structure, the so-called society has not yet become so
> overwhelmingly strong that not many exceptions are tolerated.
> Much could be said about America. Here there really exists something like free-
> dom and a strong feeling in many people that without liberty one cannot live. The
> republic is no void chimera, and the fact that there exists no national state and no
> really national tradition – although there is an enormous need for coteries in the
> different national minorities and the "melting-pot" for the most part is not even an
> ideal, let alone a reality – has created an atmosphere of freedom or at least of non-
> fanaticism. What is more is that here people feel responsible for public life to such
> an extent as I do not know of from as many European countries. . . .
> On the other hand here a great practical-political sense exists, the passion to put
> things right – "to straighten things out" – , not to tolerate needless misery, to see
> to it, that in the midst of a sometimes cutthroat competition, everybody's "fair
> chance is preserved. . . .

45

The fundamental contradiction of the country is that of political liberty and so-cietal servitude [*politische Freiheit und gesellschaftliche Knechtschaft*]. The last one does not dominate completely, as I have already told you. But it is very dangerous since the society is organized in terms of races. This happens to be true regardless of any exception in society from bourgeoisie to the labor force. Naturally this is due to the situation of a country of immigrants. Unfortunately it is aggravated by the problem of the Negroes. There really exists a "race" problem in America not merely an "ideology."[1]

Although this picture of the United States later became somewhat darker, due to the McCarthy era, the Vietnam War, and the Nixon administration, Arendt held it until her death in December 1975. Now the clear-cut dis-tinction between a sphere of the political and an area of the societal is taken from the German experience. It originally mirrors the structure of a state-society, that is, of a society that is organized and dominated by the institu-tion of the "state," set over and against society as a sphere of nonpolitical relations of its subjects. It is highly doubtful whether this structure can be ap-plied to a civil society, that is, a self-organizing society where there is no such dominating institution set over and against that society. The United States, it should be noted, belongs more to that type of political structure called the civil society, if in reality such ideal types can be distinguished at all.

But in contradistinction to the traditional use made of the two spheres in German politicocultural perception, Arendt never identified the political sphere with the state. Her intention is to provide a criterion, in view of the perversity of politics present in totalitarian domination, to distinguish between what is authentically political and what is not. In actual politics we rarely, if at all, can meet an example of the political pure and simple. Arendt was never able to make clear the intention behind her use of that distinc-tion, maybe because she never distinguished between the pure concept of the political and the sphere of politics where social questions without any doubt can play an important political role. One may say that she constantly mixed up these two levels. This can be attributed to the problems of Ger-man political perception during the Weimar period, which for their part represented a particular sharpening of traditional political perceptions. Arendt could never completely free her thinking from the adherence to this perceptional framework. And if she succeeded at all in deviating from it, she did so only in regard to its conceptual part.

Her use of the traditional distinction of the political and the social – or preferably one should say the societal – in German politicocultural percep-tion may indicate the way in which her political thinking worked. She took

1 Hannah Arendt and Karl Jaspers, *Briefwechsel 1926–1969* (Munich and Zurich, 1985), 66f. For a cri-tique of her picture of the United States, see Nathan Glazer, "Hannah Arendt's America," *Commen-tary* (1975): 61–67.

the categories at hand, those she knew from her own cultural background together with those taken from her philosophy teachers, and transformed them in the face of those experiences with which she was confronted, above all the experience of totalitarian domination as the most perverted form of politics, an apolitical politics. But from where could she take that criterion or yardstick to measure this distinction almost completely ignored by traditional political thinking?

Arendt was not trained as a political scientist or a political theorist. This by no means is meant to represent an argument against the judiciousness of her political discernment.

On the contrary, lacking that *déformation professionelle* which too often blinds the specialist in his of her proper field, she exhibited a freshness of thought that made old things look new, new things unprecedented, and – to the common understanding – even absolutely irrational things intelligible.

During her years at the university from 1924 to 1929 Arendt had studied the treasured canon of German *Bildung* (literally "cultivation"): philosophy, theology, and classical studies. It may well be said that "politics" or "the political" did not play any decisive role in her intellectual development. German *Bildung* itself may without exaggeration be characterized by its nonpolitical self-perception. But it has to be admitted that this nonpolitical attitude includes grave political implications.[2] In 1933, with the Nazi rise of power, Arendt was virtually thrown into and confronted with the political in its most perverted form. As she later told Günther Gaus in an interview, it was this event – that is, no theoretical motive whatsoever – that completely changed her original indifference toward the political.[3] She now did not simply want to do something – collaborate with the Zionists, with Youth Aliyah, and so on – but to understand the significance of these events.

From now on, and in the presence of completely perverted politics, Arendt was in search for an authentic concept of the political. But where to find it? Not in philosophy! As she told Karl Jaspers in another letter:

This occidental philosophy never has had a pure concept of the political [*einen reinen Begriff des Politischen*] and never could have one since by necessity philosophy has spoken of Man in singular, and has simply neglected the fact of plurality.[4]

Furthermore, in her eyes the rise of totalitarianism had exploded the traditional framework of understanding and of judging the political.

2 Fritz Stern, "Die politischen Folgen des unpolitischen Deutschen," in Michael Stürmer, ed., *Das kaiserliche Deutschland, Politik und Gesellschaft 1870–1918* (Düsseldorf, 1970), 168ff. Originally: "The Political Consequences of the Unpolitical German," *History* 3 (1960): 104–34. See my article "Die Kultur des Politischen, Konzepte politischer Wahrnehmung in Deutschland," in V. Gerhardt, ed., *Der Begriff der Politik, Bedingungen und Gründe politischen Handelns* (Stuttgart, 1990), 268ff.
3 Günther Gaus, "Hannah Arendt," in G. Gaus, ed., *Portraits in Frage und Antwort* (Munich, 1963), 13ff.
4 Letter of March 4, 1951, *Briefwechsel*, no. 109: 203.

Totalitarian domination as an established fact, which in its unprecedentedness cannot be comprehended through the usual categories of political thought and whose "crimes" cannot be judged by traditional moral standards or punished within the legal framework of our civilization, has broken the tradition of occidental thinking. The break in tradition is now an accomplished fact. It is neither the result of anyone's deliberate choice nor subject to further decision.[5]

But for Arendt, the task remained to understand what had happened, to understand the complete breakdown of tradition, that is, of that horizon that formerly provided the means for understanding. This task remained all the more pressing since totalitarianism threatened to become not something unique and singular that had once been, and was vanishing into the past, but something that would remain a danger in the present, as long as mankind had not found the means to understand it correctly.

An insight into the nature of totalitarian rule, directed by our fear of the concentration camp, might serve to devaluate all outmoded political shadings from left to right and, beside and above, to introduce the most essential political criterion for judging the events of our time: will it lead to totalitarian rule or will it not.[6]

This is the constellation into which her thinking has to be brought: on the one hand, the complete decline of the traditional framework of political categories, caused not by theoretical exhaustion but by the factuality of events; on the other hand, the ongoing task to understand exactly these events in their proper factuality. What Arendt had discovered might be called, in contradistinction to the Heideggerian "ontological difference," "the political difference," that is, the difference between politically authentic politics and politically perverted politics, that is, apolitical politics as political apolitics. To assess this essential political difference, a criterion is necessary, and as such a criterion only a "pure concept of the political" can serve. What, than, did Arendt take to serve as this yardstick and measure for a pure concept of the political?

It has often been said that Arendt took as her model of authentic politics the polis of antiquity.[7] She has been heavily attacked for allegedly doing so.[8] Taking the ancient polis as the model for modern politics certainly would be totally inadequate. If Arendt simply had taken the ancient polis, that "sunken city," as her model she would have severely neglected the very

5 Hannah Arendt, "Tradition and the Modern Age," *Between Past and Future, Six Exercises in Political Thought* (New York, 1961), 26.
6 Hannah Arendt, "The Concentration Camps," *Partisan Review* 15, no. 7 (1948): 63.
7 Dolf Sternberger, "The Sunken City, Hannah Arendt's Idea of Politics," *Social Research* 44, no. 1 (1977): 132 – 46.
8 N. K. O'Sullivan, "Hellenistic Nostalgia and Industrial Society," in A. DeCrespigny and K. Minogue, eds., *Contemporary Political Philosophers* (New York, 1975), 228 – 51.

conditions of modernity. It is true that she constantly referred to Greek antiquity. "The Greek polis will continue to exist at the bottom of our political existence . . . for as long as we use the word 'politics.' "[9] This should not be taken as being yet another example of what has been called "the tyranny of Greece over Germany."[10]

Around 1750 the German perception of antiquity – at least in those intellectual circles that represented German culture – became divided. Roman antiquity as the paradigm of the political, in the sense of power politics, is to be distinguished from Greek antiquity as the paradigm of authentic culture. This discrimination is still visible in Hegel's characterization of the Roman world in his *Lectures on the Philosophy of History*.[11] The discrimination even has become broader under the impact of Napoleonic imperialism and its identification with Roman power politics.

The political implication of this discrimination is that the lack of a unitary national state in Germany is balanced against its cultural authenticity. Taken in this way, the discrimination of the two ancient models points to an apolitical self-interpretation in German cultural perception, an interpretation that has strong political implications. Speaking in terms of the ideal type approach in the Weberian sense, that is, admitting for variations and exceptions, one may, out of this precarious constellation, identify a twofold perception of the political in German culture: an affirmative perception of the state as the subject of domination (*Realpolitik*), and a critical and negative perception of that very institution together with the idea of its replacement by a voluntary association of people (*Meta-* or *Idealpolitik*).[12]

Arendt originally may have shared some of the implications of that cultural awareness. But when she was confronted with the totalitarian perversity of the political she decided to respond to that challenge in political terms, and consequently she was also confronted with the inadequacy of the traditional framework of political categories. For there was no place for the notion of an apolitical politics or political apolitics within the traditional framework of categories, particularly not within the specific German framework, where there existed a tendency – in *Realpolitik* – to legitimize all kinds of rule or domination as such.

How Arendt escaped this dilemma is not easy to say. She became and remained highly critical of the traditional categories. But it seems as if an am-

9 Hannah Arendt, "Walter Benjamin," in *Men in Dark Times* (New York, 1968), 204.
10 E. M. Butler, *The Tyranny of Greece over Germany* (Cambridge, 1935). Butler's book is confined to the aesthetic dimension. But her thesis holds true for the political dimension as well.
11 G. W. F. Hegel, "Vorlesungen über die Philosophie der Geschichte," in *Theorie Werkausgabe* (Frankfurt/Main, 1970), vol. 12, 339.
12 Vollrath, "Die Kultur des Politischen."

bivalence that went unnoticed is built into her critique. This can be demonstrated by taking one of the categories with which she authentically identified the political, namely, the category of rule or domination, that is, of the
power to coerce.[13] She blamed Plato and Aristotle, that is, philosophy, for
having introduced the category of *arche* thus understood, into the political
discourse of the occident. But is that true? She is certainly right in pointing
to Plato's mistrust of *peitho,* persuasion, as being sufficient for the guidance
of men, due to the trial and the condemnation of Socrates by the polis. She
is right, too, in her interpretation of Plato's replacement of persuasion by
reason and truth.

It was after Socrates' death that Plato began to discount persuasion as insufficient
for the guidance of men and to seek for something liable to compel them without
using external means of violence. Very early in his search he must have discovered
the truth, namely the truths we call self-evident, compels the mind, and that this
coercion, though it needs no violence to be effective, is stronger than persuasion
and argument. The trouble with coercion through reason, however, is that only
the few are subject to it, so that the problem arises of how to assure that the many,
the people who in their very multitude compose the body politic, can be submitted to the same truth.[14]

But can it really be said that "the political philosophies of Plato and Aristotle have dominated all subsequent political thought?"[15] Not to mention
Aristotle's clear differentiation between domination (*arche*) pure and simple,
that is, despotic domination, and politically qualified rule (*arch politike*), that
is, governance based on active consent and support by the ruled combined
with the rule-governed change in the respective positions of those who rule
and of those who are ruled.

It is, I would argue, in a very specific context that Arendt took the category of "domination" to be a universally valid political category. For there
is no culture where this very category of domination (*Herrschaft*) plays a
greater role in defining the concept of the political than traditional German
culture. Here the political sphere almost exclusively has been identified with
the state, that is, with the state's domination over its subjects, who owe it
submission and obedience. Much evidence could be given for the primacy
of the category of domination in German politicocultural perception. Only
two examples, both very characteristic, will be mentioned here. Germany's
most influential sociologist, Max Weber, whose thinking is deeply imprinted
by the particularly German field of *Staatslehre* and the problems of that

---

13 E.g., Arendt, "What Is Authority?," in *Between Past and Future,* 104ff., a translation of "Was ist Au-
torität?" in *Fragwürdige Traditionsbestände im politischen Denken der Gegenwart* (Frankfurt/Main, 1957),
130ff., is somewhat more precise. Here, she uses the German term *Herrschaft,* which has a specific
connotation. See notes 18 and 19 below.
14 "What Is Authority?," n. 14, 107f.      15 Ibid., 106.

discipline,[16] defined *Herrschaft* as the "authoritative power of command" (*autoritäre Befehlsgewalt*).[17] And one of the leading figures of German *Staatsrechtslehre*, Carl Friedrich von Gerber, simply expressed a common assumption held within this very important discipline for the formulation of German political perception when he wrote: "the legal nature of the power of the state, that is, of the state's power of will, [resides] in the concept of domination" (*Die rechtliche Natur der Staatsgewalt, also der Willensmacht des Staates, [beruht] in dem Begriff des Beherrschens*).[18]

When Arendt came to reflect on the elements and conditions of totalitarian domination, she found it necessary to get rid of the equation of the political sphere with the state. She knew quite well, however, that it had been totalitarian domination that had misused and destroyed the state in order to encourage its own dynamic. The state, at least this "state," was obviously unable to resist the new "Behemoth," to whom even the greatest "Leviathan" would fall victim. Therefore, she was led to regard the category of domination as basically exposing an apolitical character. Thus she universalized a concept stemming from and bound to German culture, with its state-centered perception of the political. To Arendt, the political sphere is defined – inauthentically – through the specific institution of the abstract state. It would necessarily be set apart from the notion of "the people" who would support the political framework through active assent. In her judgment, this separation formed one of the preconditions for the powers of totalitarian domination to overwhelm and pervert the political sphere. When she tells us, again and again, that "the" tradition has come to a definite end, it has to be said that this certainly holds true for the specific tradition of German politicocultural perception.

Where else could Arendt turn to find new and more adequate political categories? To be sure, she might have turned – and she certainly did – to the Greek origins of the political. But she knew far too well that a simple renewal of the Greek polis was doomed to fail under the conditions of modern age. Turning to these Greek origins could only serve to sharpen her political perception and intensify her search for a modern analogy of the Greek polis. What could – perhaps – be renewed was not the Greek polis, but its *politeia,* its politicality, so to speak.[19]

16 See my article "Max Weber: Sozialwissenschaft zwischen Staatsrechtslehre und Kulturkritik," *Politische Vierteljahresschrift* 31, no. 1 (1990): 102ff.
17 Max Weber, *Wirtschaft und Gesellschaft, Grundriss der verstehenden Soziologie*, 5th rev. ed. (Tübingen, 1972), 544.
18 C. F. von Gerber, "Über die Theilbarkeit deutscher Staatsgebiete," *Zeitschrift für Deutsches Staatsrecht und Deutsche Verfassungseschichte* 1 (1867): 9.
19 Dolf Sternberger, who first had pointed to Arendt's adherence to the outmoded model of the Greek polis, later came to interpret her thinking as being a renewal of the *politeia* concept: "Politie und Leviathan, ein Streit um den antiken und den modernen Staat," in his *Herrschaft und Vereinbarung*

Arendt found this modern analogy of the polity of the Greeks in the American republic. During a conference devoted to her work, one of the participants pointed out to her the paradigmatic role that the Constitution of the United States played in her thinking – and she did not object.[20] She then added a remark that may elucidate her interpretation of the American experiment.

You see I went back to Greek and Roman [sic!] antiquity only half because I like it so much – I like Greek antiquity but I never liked Roman antiquity. I went back, nevertheless, because I knew that I simply wanted to read all the books that these people [the Founding Fathers of the American republic] had read. And they all read all these books – as they would have said – in order to find a model for this new political realm which they wanted to bring about, and which they called a republic. The model of man of this republic was to a certain extent the citizen of the Athenian polis. After all we still have the word from them, and they echo through the centuries. On the other hand the model was the *res publica,* the public thing, of the Romans. The influence of the Romans was stronger in its immediacy on the minds of these men.[21]

In other words, she had given up the traditional disregard for Roman political institutions and perceptions in German politicocultural awareness. By the way, this may be contrasted with Thomas Mann's statement in his *Observations of an Unpolitical Man* where he says:

Whose aspiration it would be to simply transform Germany into a civil democracy [*ein bürgerliche Demokratie*] according to the Roman-Western sense and spirit, he would take away from her best thing and her most difficult thing [*sein Bestes und Schwerstes*], her problematic, wherein her nationality most properly resides.[22]

Thomas Mann's essay can be read as the expression of German cultural self-interpretation originating from one of the most intimate representatives of that culture. The essay points to a weakness in and even deficit of political judgment in German culture, and it may well be said that this deficit pertains likewise to the two modes of political perception, *Realpolitik* and *Metapolitik,* into which this perception is split. In their respective complementary antagonism both modes are not altogether free from an apolitical character.

Confronted with an utmost perverted form of politics, to which the rise of German culture's "unpoliticalness" certainly had contributed, Arendt was

(Frankfurt/Main, 1986), 188ff. This could well be connected with the specific sense of "constitution" in American political thinking. See Gerald Stourzh, *Wege zur Verfassungsdemokratie* (Vienna and Cologne, 1989), passim. The term "politicalness" is borrowed from S. S. Wolin, *Politics and Vision, Continuity and Innovation in Western Political Thought* (Boston, 1960), 431.

20 See M. A. Hill, ed., *Hannah Arendt. The Recovery of the Public World* (New York, 1979), 328ff. The conference took place in November 1972 in Toronto.
21 Ibid., 330f.
22 Thomas Mann, *Betrachtungen eines Unpolitischen,* in *Gesammelte Werke* (Frankfurt/Main, 1983), 53f.

looking for an authentic concept of the political and finally identified it with her conception of the American republic. This led her to her interpretation of the Roman threefold unity of tradition, religion, and authority in her essay "What Is Authority."[23] For it is, as she said, the Roman paradigm rather than the Greek one upon which the American republic has been modeled. One of the consequences is the replacement of the (Greek) relation of "to rule / to govern" and "to be ruled / to be governed" (*archein kai archesthai*) by the (Roman) relation of "to found / to establish" and "to preserve / to continue" as the basis from where to structure and understand the political in an authentic way. It is in this context that she approvingly quotes Cicero's statement, that "there is nothing in which human capability comes closer to divine hands than either in founding new commonwealths or in preserving those already founded" (*neque enim est ulla res in qua proprius ad deorum numen accedat virtus humana, quam civitates aut condere novas aut conservare iam conditas*).[24] Arendt put all stress on the first act of establishing and founding, that is, of "constituting." As to the second act, the act of preserving and continuing, she was rather skeptical and tried to fill in her favorite idea of the wards and councils, to which I shall shortly return. Might she have known the political thinking of Abraham Lincoln, which centrally is concerned with the problem of preserving the republic, or might she have remembered Alexis de Tocqueville's interpretation of the role of what he calls *les associations politiques* in America, she might have seen other possibilities.[25] In any case, it is the American republic that served as her paradigm of an authentic political institution.

Her agreement with the American experiment does not include an agreement with the actual politics of any government of the United States – on the contrary. Her correspondence with Karl Jaspers is filled with very critical, even acidly harsh comments on governmental policies. Her assessment of President Eisenhower, both the person and his performance, during the McCarthy era is only one example. She compared Eisenhower to Hindenburg and drew analogies to the German situation of 1933.[26] She later summarized her judgment in these words:

The republic becomes decomposed by democracy [sic!], for which the republic should prescribe its frame and its boundaries. One might even say society has overwhelmed the republic. This process has been loosened and it is very, very ques-

---

23 See note 14.
24 Hannah Arendt, *Über die Revolution* (Munich, 1963), 259. The Ciceronian statement is to be found in *De re publica* I 7, 12.
25 H. A. Rau, *Demokratie und Republik, Tocquevilles Theorie des politischen Handelns* (Würzburg, 1981).
26 Letter to Gertrud Jaspers of Nov. 1, 1952, in *Briefwechsel*, no. 137, 239. Since her husband, Heinrich Blücher, had been a former member of the German KPD, Arendt avoided public comment on

tionable whether it can be stopped, even if McCarthy will suffer defeat. Nevertheless this defeat will be decisive, the condition sine qua non; for then, at least, we
could start again to fight for the republic.[27]

And when McCarthy eventually was defeated she wrote triumphantly:

Here in America, the reversal within a few weeks at the beginning of the year is
one of the most interesting and most terrific phenomena belonging to the chapter "public opinion" I know of. Only Tocqueville could have imagined such a
story. . . . Today the atmosphere of the country is as we always knew it, hardly different; very pleasant and reasonable. Even Eisenhower, who as an individual truly
is an idiot, is as reasonable as can be hoped for. The political tradition of the country has, once again, prevailed, and we, God be praised ["Gott sei's gedankt, getrom-
melt und gepfiffen" – an expression from Berlin slang], were mistaken.[28]

It is in this context that Arendt recorded her newfound love of the world
and tells Jaspers that she will name her book on political theory "Amor
Mundi," a phrase borrowed from Saint Augustine on whom she had written her doctoral dissertation – it became *The Human Condition.*[29]

   This is a good example of the pattern according to which Arendt looked
at the United States, its factual policies, and its political structure. "Oh,
how this country has declined if it is measured against its very own standards."[30] Even in her last essay, "Home to Roost,"[31] which was a contribution to the Boston Bicentennial Forum and which she gave as a speech
on May 20, 1975, she never changed this perspective. On the one hand,
she always was and remained highly critical of the actual policies of the diverse administrations, even reproducing some of the prejudices of the
New York intellectual clique among whom she had to take refuge following the uproar after the publication of *Eichmann in Jerusalem.* On the
other hand, and more important to the framework of her political thinking, she had discovered an institutional political form – together with the
intellectual origins of this form – accompanying and even helping to generate it – that was different from the traditional German framework of political categories and institutions.

   In a lecture given at the Rand School in 1948, Arendt spoke of the
United States as a "twentieth-century (and in some respects a nineteenth-
century) society [that] lives and thrives on the solid basis of an eighteenth-

the McCarthy era. There is only one article by her on that problem: "The Ex-Communists," *Commonweal* 57, no. 24 (1953): 595–99.

27  Letter to Karl Jaspers of Dec. 21, 1953, *Briefwechsel,* no. 152: 272.
28  Letter to Karl Jaspers of Aug. 6, 1955, *Briefwechsel,* no. 169: 300f.
29  Letter to Karl Jaspers of Aug. 6, 1955, *Briefwechsel,* no. 169: 301.
30  Letter to Karl Jaspers of Jan. 31, 1959, *Briefwechsel,* no. 235: 398.
31  Originally in the *New York Review of Books,* June 26, 1975, reprinted in Sam B. Warner, ed., *The
American Experiment* (Boston, 1976), 61–77.

century political philosophy" and believed it had "a form of government that . . . is among the few survivors of true political freedom, and among the ever few guarantors of that minimum of social justice without which citizenship is impossible."[32] To her, the political institutions of the United States, and the intellectual framework of the categories connected with these institutions, formed a model of a polity wherein one could hope for the preservation of the public realm and of political freedom – even in the face of the threat posed by the rise of totalitarian movements. She always became very upset whenever she believed that this could become endangered from within the society itself. Nevertheless, the American experiment remained an existing paradigm for what she constantly was looking for: a "pure concept of the political."

This idea is most clearly documented in *On Revolution*. Written during a critical period in Western politicointellectual development, when the very institutions of Western political culture seemed to have gone down a path of self-destruction and were confronted with the counterparadigm of revolutionary Marxism, Arendt went back to the original meaning of "revolution." In this she took the founding of the American Republic as her basic paradigm. To her, revolution means the political realm of freedom wherein men are bound together by common promises. They thereby establish a worldly space within which their common power to act together resides and may be preserved. In this context she speaks of the "healing power of institutions," namely, of the institution of the republic, thus overcoming the anti-institutional bias of several of the most influential critics of Western political culture.[33]

Arendt was very anxious about the possibility of preserving this space of freedom and tried to entrust its preservation to wards and councils. This was one of her favorite ideas, which she had learned from her second husband, Heinrich Blücher. He had been a member of the Brandler group of the German Communist Party (KPD) and had been exorcised during the Bolshevik takeover of that party. From him she inherited a mistrust of the party system, which she generalized into a critique of Weimar politics. What she may have had in mind was the idea of a constitutional and representative republic of wards establishing a paradigm of the political, pure and unimpaired.

Another aspect of her interpretation of the American Revolution is the clear distinction between the American and the French revolutions, based on her discrimination between the political and the social or the societal.

---

32 From a yet unpublished manuscript in the Library of Congress, quoted in E. Young-Bruehl, *Hannah Arendt: For Love of the World* (New Haven and London, 1984), 209f.
33 In translation, *Über die Revolution* (Munich, 1965), 226.

She attributed the failure of the French Revolution to culminate in a permanent constitution to the invasion of the social question into the political mission of founding the republic. For holding this view, Arendt has been heavily attacked.[34] Again, the purpose of her sharp distinction is her concern for the preservation of the political, pure and unimpaired.

But the most important and the most remarkable parts of *On Revolution* are those concerned with the intellectual origins of the American Revolution. Here, Arendt encountered a type of political thinking completely different from that type of political thinking she knew from her German experience. It is this type of political thinking that she judged to be authentically connected with an experience of the political as such. It is in this context that she discovered the politically decisive role of "opinion," that is, of the plurality of opinions, so strange to any kind of philosophical speculation that always prefers unity to plurality. The text to which she refers is the Federalist Papers, particularly those parts written by James Madison.[35]

Although it may well be said that her reading of the founders is highly selective – it is basically confined to some writings of Thomas Jefferson, John Adams, and James Madison, together with a certain knowledge of the English and early American forerunners – she nevertheless discovered a distinctively "new science of politics," to use a phrase of Tocqueville's. In her interpretation, this new science of politics had risen not out of philosophical speculation but out of the very experience with the political. And she could trace these ideas back to their origins in Roman experience and in the continuation of this type of political thinking in certain strands of the European tradition. She took this whole bundle of conceptions and ideas as offering a perceptional horizon for gaining an authentic concept – or at least understanding – of the political.

Arendt knew that a comparable type of political thinking hardly existed in the tradition of German culture. Whereas in the context of the American experience this perceptional horizon is embedded in a long tradition and fortified by its incorporation into the existing institutions of the republic, nothing of that kind could be found in the German tradition of political thinking, which is governed by the concept of the state as an entity superior to but at the same time abstracted from the community of its people. This holds true even for those conceptions that do not affirmatively refer to the state, but on the contrary proclaim the necessary withering away

---

34  Jürgen Habermas, "Die Geschichte von den zwei Revolutionen," in same, ed., *Kultur und Kritik* (Frankfurt/Main, 1973), 365–70.

35  *Über die Revolution* (see n. 34), 292ff. See my article, "That All Governments Rest On Opinion," *Social Research* 43, no. 1 (1976): 46–61.

of the state and its replacement by a community of those who freely associate with one another without interference of any institutional measures. The two conceptions are related to each other in an antagonistic as well as a complementary way by their common reference point, that is, the state as an entity that possesses a personality of its own above, over, and against its citizens, either affirmatively or negatively.

The only place in German culture where she could discover at least some kind of resemblance to the perceptional horizon of the republican political culture in the United States was in Kant's *Critique of Judgment.* "Here," she told Karl Jaspers,[36] "the true political philosophy of Kant lies buried, not in his *Critique of Practical Reason.*" It would lead us too far astray to elaborate more fully the implications of her interpretation of Kant's *Critique of Judgment,* namely, that it represented his true political philosophy.

Two remarks need to be made here. First, since German culture possessed neither a strong republican tradition nor strong republican institutions, a substitute could only be found where German culture traditionally had its strength. Philosophy was certainly one such place of strength. At the same time, these cultural strongholds had to be transformed and their traditional nonpolitical character likewise had to be reformulated into political terms. It is exactly this reformulation that Arendt saw in Kant's *Critique of Judgment.*

Second, Kant's *Critique of Judgment* can be regarded in two very different ways. It is absolutely correct to base the interpretation of this work on the problems Kant himself developed in the two "introductions" of the *Third Critique,* that is, particularly the problems of how the two other "Critiques" are related to one another and how the endangered identity of "reason" (*Vernunft*) can be safeguarded. But it is likewise possible to put the *Third Critique* into a different tradition, one that yields a different answer to the problems of modernity than those offered by scientific rationality and eventually to the Aristotelian concept of "phronesis" as the kind of rationality that is related to a world of men and thus in itself politically qualified.[37] When Arendt began to reinterpret Kant's *Critique of Judgment* as

36  Letter to Karl Jaspers of Aug. 29, 1957, *Briefwechsel,* no. 209: 355.
37  Part of this tradition has been specified in Alfred Bäumler, *Das Irrationalitätsproblem in der Aesthetik und Logik des 18. Jahrhunderts* (Darmstadt, 1975); see also my *Die Rekonstruktion der politischen Urteilskraft* (Stuttgart, 1976), 83ff. It could be argued that within occidental culture there are to be found two types of rationality, both responding to problems arising from the optional character – as against a ceremonial-mythical character – of occidental culture (Aristotle, *Nichomachean Ethics* VI 7, 1141b3ff.): a noetic-scientific type of rationality and a prudential – or "political" – type of rationality. The latter, although highly important, has never been elaborated to its full extent. A cluster of concepts belongs to this type, among which are to be counted, together with the whole range of the rhetorical tradition, such concepts as "common sense." It is this tradition that broke down with totalitarianism, a breakdown prepared not by science itself, but by the imperialistic invasion of science into the worldly space. Hannah Arendt has shown this breakdown in her *The Human Condi-*

offering the principles of a theory of the political, she did not merely restore a tradition that had been destroyed or at least gravely endangered by
the rise of modern scientific rationality. Her restoration of this tradition
happened in the face of its complete breakdown. The Kantian concept of
"reflective judgment" enables people to judge reasonably even if all other
standards have broken down. This parallels a situation in which totalitarianism becomes a distinct possibility.

It is quite understandable that, after the Second World War, Arendt's
view of Germany was very critical and rather skeptical. Her correspondence
with Karl Jaspers is filled with sharp comments on the politics of the German government and of the attitudes of the German people. It would be
interesting to identify the specific topics to which her attention, and Jasper's,
was directed. Two remarks may suffice. Arendt's attitude toward the politics of the German government was influenced by her disagreement with
the politics of the Israeli government. Sometimes she also indicated her disagreement with Jasper's political assessments, but, out of veneration for her
old teacher, she almost never insisted on elaborating her deviation.

In two articles in particular, Hannah Arendt publicly addressed the problems of Germany after the Nazi rule.[38] Both articles were written shortly after the defeat of the Third Reich and both are centered around her fear that
the continuity of nihilistic and passive attitudes in Germany that had contributed so much to the rise and the success of the totalitarian movement
would not and could not lead to a revival or founding of a truly republican
form of the political sphere. What she was able to see in the Federal Republic was a continuation of traditional pattern rather than a truly new
foundation and new beginning. She measured this against her understanding of the innovative spirit of the American Republic. She always looked
at the German problem as exposing – certainly within particular deficits of
traditional German culture – universal threats arising from the challenge of
modernity itself.

---

tion (*Introspection and the Loss of Common Sense*) (Chicago, 1958), 254ff. In her understanding, "reflective judgment," in the Kantian sense, could heal this loss since it did not, as was the case with
"ancient prudence," presuppose the existence of a true polity, but only that capability which is common to all humans as humans: thinking. But this capability to think is not one peculiar to the professional philosopher, *Denker von Gewerbe,* as she called them, but to everybody, even you and I! See
Kant, *The Life of the Mind* (New York and London, 1977), vol. 1: 3, and Kant, *Critique of Pure Reason,* trans. Norman Kemp Smith, (New York, 1963, B 871).

38  Approaches to the "German Problem," *Partisan Review* 12, no. 1 (1945): 93–106; "The Aftermath
of Nazi Rule, Report from Germany," *Commentary* 10, no. 4 (1950): 342–53.

PART II

*Leo Strauss*

# 4

# *Reflections on Leo Strauss and American Education*

TIMOTHY FULLER

What follows are reflections on Leo Strauss's role in and contribution to the debates over American education, particularly the character of his defense of liberal education. In entering the American educational scene, Strauss entered a forum in which a revolution in education had been underway since the second half of the nineteenth century, parallel in its own way to educational changes in Great Britain and Europe. Strauss did not invent, and did not claim to invent, the issues about liberal education in a democratic culture on which he spoke. But he did present himself as both a critic and a friend of American democracy and, in so doing, clarified his conception of the role of the philosopher in the polity. His views on both liberal education and the philosopher's role were indicative also of how he understood the practical implications of the issue of natural right and history.

My reflections were stirred not long ago when, as I was composing this essay, I attended the annual August conference of all faculty and staff at my college which starts the new academic year. It is customary on that occasion to introduce new faculty. Among those introduced there were a geologist who specializes in the dynamics of sand dunes, a professor of dance, a specialist in eighteenth-century French literature who also studies contemporary Francophone literature of the Caribbean, a computer scientist, a topologist, specialists in Asian and Middle Eastern politics, Byzantine art, physiological psychology, Soviet history, contemporary U.S. history, eighteenth-century English satire, and genetics, and a philosopher who has translated and written a commentary on Plato's *Sophist*.

This array, astonishingly broad for a liberal arts college of 1,900 students, but thought by most to be stimulating and exciting in its diversity, would be far exceeded in variety by any large university in the country. Higher education has long since become, to put it mildly, highly specialized and very diverse. This is one of the clearest results of the reform movement in education, begun in the latter half of the last century, that sought, successfully, to transform universities into research institutions dominated by research professors and their research programs as opposed to teachers whose principal task was to transmit the shared heritage of our civilization to undergraduates. Throughout this century institutions of higher learning have accepted that their role is to accumulate and organize knowledge, and to advance the power of science and technology, thus "contributing to society" by fostering progress and enlightenment understood in large measure as the improvement of material life. Daniel Coit Gilman, the first president of Johns Hopkins University – a leader in the late nineteenth century in creating a university that was entirely a research university – laid it down that "in selecting a staff of teachers, the Trustees have determined to consider especially the devotion of the candidate to some particular line of study and the certainty of his eminence in that specialty; the power to pursue independent and original investigations, and to inspire the young with enthusiasm for study and research."[1]

The old concerns for the development of moral character or virtuous conduct are not mentioned in this statement. Johns Hopkins University thus was committed explicitly from its founding to the primacy of graduate research studies leading to the Ph.D. as the symbol of academic success and fulfillment. It solidified by its unequivocal commitment a development that had been emerging since the early 1860s when institutions such as Harvard, Yale, Columbia, Michigan, and Wisconsin began to remake their traditional structures to accommodate the new emphasis.

Consider, by contrast, this statement of John Henry Newman, written in the midnineteenth century (1852) just as these changes were about to get underway in earnest:

I have said that all branches of knowledge are connected together, because the subject-matter of knowledge is intimately united in itself, as being the acts and the work of the Creator. Hence it is that the Sciences, into which our knowledge may be said to be cast, have multiplied bearings on one another, and an internal sympathy, and admit, or rather demand, comparison and adjustment. They complete, correct, balance each other. This consideration, if well-founded, must be taken into account, not only as regards the attainment of truth, which is their common end, but as regards the influence which they exercise upon those whose education consists in the study of them . . . to give undue prominence to one is to be unjust to another. . . . There is no science but tells a different tale, when viewed as a portion of a whole, from what it is likely to suggest when taken by itself, without the safeguard, as I may call it of others.[2]

---

1  Daniel Coit Gilman, *The Launching of a University* (New York, 1906), as quoted in David M. Ricci, *The Tragedy of Political Science, Politics, Scholarship and Democracy* (New Haven, Conn., 1984), 42.

2  John Henry Newman, *The Uses of Knowledge. Selections from The Idea of a University*, ed. Leo L. Ward (Arlington, Ill., 1948), 8–9.

Newman's pronouncement appeared alongside the very changes that would undermine his idea of the university, and the academic reformers in Oxford were not sorry when he departed Oxford upon his conversion to Roman Catholicism. For Newman had argued that, while the university's object is the study of literature and science and not religious training, the university:

cannot fulfill its object duly, such as I have described it, without the Church's assistance . . . it still has the office of intellectual education; but the Church steadies it in the performance of that office.[3]

Today the nationally recognized liberal arts colleges in America – colleges that remain officially institutions for undergraduate teaching and that were founded mostly by religious denominations – not infrequently refer to themselves as "research colleges." The term means that, while the faculties of these liberal arts colleges may still devote much of their time to teaching, they expect to compete and to be judged and rewarded by the standards President Gilman announced at Johns Hopkins for the research university a century ago. It is normal today to say that research is essential to good teaching. This reflects both the orientation new faculty bring with them from their graduate training and the tendency to define undergraduate studies as preparation for graduate research. Teaching institutions increasingly offer incentives and special rewards to those of their faculty members who publish scholarly material and engage actively with their professional counterparts outside their home schools.

Moreover, as specialized studies proliferate – a natural outcome of establishing the criteria of original and innovative research buoyed by the belief in the progressive accumulation of useful knowledge – the desire and ability for faculty members to converse with each other, inspired by confidence in a common bond of understanding, shrinks. The "crisis" of higher education is now a central topic of debate, although the crisis has been underway for some time.

It is true that there has been a countervailing movement in higher education. From the 1920s at Columbia, later at Chicago and St. John's College, Annapolis, among others, efforts were made to establish a great books curriculum and courses in the history of Western civilization. Some large universities have created small, alternative liberal arts programs within the larger university structure in which a few students may elect to enroll. We are informed, nevertheless, that only about 20 percent of the institutions of higher learning in the United States require their students to take Western

3 Ibid., 1.

civilization courses. Insofar as this countermovement has succeeded, what it has achieved is the insertion of survey courses into curriculums, alongside the more specialized courses and research programs, available to students but not necessarily required of them and often not urged upon them. This amounts to a two-track educational program: Students can divide their time between something called "general education" and specialized studies.

Academics are acutely aware of public skepticism about the character of higher education; they feel the loss of a commonsense bond between themselves and the larger world of which they are a part; they are simultaneously defensive and haughty about both the separation and the criticism. They have a great deal invested in the current concept of the university. They have gotten used until recently to being left free to evolve their intellectual interests in an uncontested way, as they have for the last generation been used to a regularly expanding financial investment in higher education. Now they can no longer be confident that the public will be content either to refrain from questioning them or to continue to invest larger and larger sums of money in their undertakings. It has become fashionable to expose scandals and absurdities in the conduct of professors and academic administrations, most recently in the uncovering of the misuse of large government grants in our most prominent research universities. The defining of the university is less and less formulated out of a commonly held academic tradition in which teachers and scholars engage in continuous reflection and conversation, and more and more influenced by those extrinsic sources who wish to mine the "mental resources" of the academy. Academic institutions are, it is widely asserted, disintegrated communities of scholars; to be in their midst no longer necessarily means we will encounter a self-understanding and commitment that bespeaks a distinctive activity. The idea of a university is contested and unclear.

The basic uncertainty was quickly apprehended by Strauss. He connected it to the peculiar difficulties of scholarship and teaching in a democratic age, while also insisting that the full dimensions of the problems involved could not be appreciated unless and until a comprehensive reexamination of the central issues of Western philosophical and political thought were undertaken.

The motto on Harvard's seal is "Veritas," or Truth. The motto on the building in which I myself work at Colorado College is, from the Gospel of John, "You shall know the truth, and the truth shall make you free." But in both of these places of learning, and in many others, there is a great debate over whether there is any truth. The debate calls into question not alone the commitment made by Gilman of Hopkins and others a century ago, but also the ancient commitment to searching for wisdom of which the modern scientific quest may be understood to be a particular interpretation.

A century ago there was little hesitancy to believe that the techniques of modern scientific research would be deployed with growing success to enlighten civilization through the dissemination of truth. A century before Gilman, in a remarkable essay called "What Is Enlightenment?" (1784), Immanuel Kant had urged that we "dare to know," that we make use of our intelligence in order to pass from the interim stage of becoming enlightened, or civilizing, into a condition of full enlightenment, that we pass on from the childhood to the maturity of the race. The modern research university has seemed to be the institution through which the Kantian affirmation of the project to enlighten ourselves would be brought to concrete fulfillment. For Kant had also argued for the role of the thinker as a critical analyst of society's assumptions as a means to social progress. The pattern of criticism in the service of reconstruction and presumed advancement seemed to fit well with the growing confidence in the advancement of knowledge through scientific inquiry.

In his *Logic of the Moral Sciences* (1843), John Stuart Mill projected the symbiotic relation between a science of society and the art of political decision making through which many of the predicaments of social life would be transformed into problems for which well-designed solutions could be devised. While admitting that the contingencies of life could not be completely eliminated, Mill did assert that the aim of practical politics would be

to surround the society which is under our superintendence with the greatest possible number of circumstances of which the tendencies are beneficial and to remove or counteract, as far as practicable, those of which the tendencies are injurious.[4]

And, in his celebrated essay *On Liberty* (1859), Mill argued that promoting absolute freedom of thought and discussion would in time bring about a convergence of what is true and best for humanity in what he imagined as the spontaneously improving society. But what has come to the fore is an argument over whether the term "truth" is of use to us. Is it not the case, we are asked or told, that truth is relative to the discourse of particular

4 J. S. Mill, *A System of Logic in Selected Writings of John Stuart Mill,* ed. with an intro. by Maurice Cowling (New York, 1968), 345. Mill defended the primacy of intellectual progress while binding it tightly to material improvement: "The impelling force to most of the improvements effected in the arts of life is the desire of increased material comfort; but . . . the state of knowledge at any time is the impassable limit of the industrial improvements possible at that time; and the progress of industry must follow and depend upon, the progress of knowledge." Ibid., 374. Here "knowledge" is not being used to refer to what Strauss refers to as liberal education, even though Mill was steeped in the elements of liberal education and wrote about them. Mill identifies the fundamental problem of social science to be "to find the laws according to which any state of society produces the state which succeeds it, and takes its place." Ibid., 360.

groups and that while there can be views treated as true within a group, beyond the group's boundaries their truth can sustain no special status in the
midst of competing alternatives. This is not by any means a novel argument.
It is as old as philosophy itself, but it seems currently to have compelling
force in the universities, and its emergence was foreseen by Strauss in his
discourses on education.

Mill's faith in the ultimate convergence of ideas is in doubt today. The
academic institutions that were to foster enlightenment appear to many now
to generate more heat than light, often disdaining the very bases upon which
they previously solicited the support of the larger public, which they
claimed to serve and to enlighten.

The issue is stated dramatically by Alasdair MacIntyre in his book, *Three
Rival Versions of Moral Inquiry,*[5] wherein he distinguishes the "encyclopedic"
from the "genealogical" definitions of knowledge, showing that "enlightenment" has come to have both a negating and an affirming connotation.
The former definition, the encyclopedic, describes the older, positivistic
confidence in the method of accumulating information and expanding the
power of human self-regulation through the systematic gathering and organizing of the data, symbolized by the great dictionaries and encyclopedias
of the Enlightenment. The latter definition, the genealogical, describes the
revolutionary undertaking, inspired by Nietzsche's demolition of values
through revealing their dirty origins, to expose the concealed subjectivity
and struggle behind what presents itself as scientific knowledge, and thus to
deconstruct the encyclopedic enlightenment. MacIntyre asserts that these
rivals are locked in a battle of mutual destruction that might permit a different and, as MacIntyre sees it, superior form of the university to emerge,
addressing itself specifically to the conflict of traditions in a way reminiscent
of the method of Scholastic disputation.

Hovering over these concerns is the much-used term "modernity" and
the question whether modernity is good or bad for us. As the argument has
developed, one discerns some of the salient features that inevitably enter
into any discussion of the modern situation:

Modern life is characterized by "abstraction," in the sense that large-scale
technical, economic, and bureaucratic institutions have taken precedence
over smaller, relatively cohesive communities who share a way of life in
concrete form. We encounter this in the complicated structures of the modern university, or "multiversity." It reveals to us the degree to which the
university today has come to reflect the world it inhabits, the world of the
mass to which the managerial revolution is a response. The university's dis-

5 South Bend, Ind., 1990.

tinctiveness as an institution among other institutions has diminished. Periodic calls for renewal of community issue from academics. It is not obvious, however, that many of them would accept the alterations in academic life that would be necessary to bring such renewal to fruition, even if they retain some residual memory of what that was like. To do so would be also to question the democratization that has affected all modern institutions. The democratizing of the universities has ensured a dizzyingly swift expansion that has produced a chaotic proliferation of motives and aims, and disputes over "standards."

Discussions of the "technological society" or of the rationalism of modern life, document how lives are redefined as careers, and societies reinterpreted by would-be social engineers as raw materials for designs and plans for the future. The capacity to enjoy and to make use of the present has been demoted. By contrast, the felt need to move on, to be productive, to justify oneself as a contributor to some supposititious program to lead society to an alleged promised land, and the incapacity to achieve repose, dominate. This is reflected in the university's loss of confidence in the idea of learning for its own sake, the pursuit of wisdom as an intrinsic reward, not to mention its growing dependency on and desire for the largesse of governments and foundations.

This, in turn, encourages both greater preoccupation with and uncertainty about what it means to be a self and how that self is to relate itself to others. Traditional understandings of conduct are called into question and rejected; the art of moderating conduct in relation to others becomes more difficult. Civility comes to be seen as a repression of the self rather than as an essential feature of the collegiality and conversationality through which the self might develop without suffering isolation.

The inability to sustain collegiality and conversationality is related to the cult of liberation, the desire to experience everything as a matter of choice, to multiply options, thus rendering the resources of traditional inquiry invisible and perhaps finally inaccessible. But this also calls forth the experience of choice without a destiny, and the question, choice for what end? Education in the service of what? As Strauss put it:

There is a tension between the respect for diversity or individuality and the recognition of natural right. When liberals became impatient of the absolute limits to diversity or individuality that are posed even by the most liberal version of natural right, they had to make a choice between natural right and the uninhibited cultivation of individuality. They chose the latter.[6]

---

6 Leo Strauss, *Natural Right and History* (Chicago, 1953), 6th Impression, 1968, 5. One may well ask if Strauss's "they" is not far too broad a categorization. It is not the case that all "liberals" would choose diversity as an end in itself. Nor can we define liberals fairly as merely those who do prefer diversity

In Strauss's terms, the choice of diversity as good in itself is a distortion and restrictive even while proclaiming the expansion of freedom. For

liberal education is concerned with the souls of men and therefore has little or no use for machines. If it becomes a machine or an industry, it becomes indistinguishable from the entertainment industry unless in respect to income and publicity, tinsel and glamour.[7]

The preceding prepares the way to consider Leo Strauss's position in American education or, more broadly, in the education of a democratic age. It is essential to remember that Strauss entered an American academic culture that had a history parallel within its own idiom to the history of modern higher education in Europe; that the transformation of the universities had American and British versions as well as a continental European one. The transformation is Western, not merely European – and Strauss understood it so. We can see this in the following remarks of Strauss on the difficulty of defining liberal education today:

"Liberal education is education in culture." In what culture? Our answer is: culture in the sense of the Western tradition. Yet Western culture is only one among many cultures. By limiting ourselves to Western culture, do we not condemn liberal education to a kind of parochialism, and is not parochialism incompatible with the liberalism, the generosity, the openmindedness, of liberal education? Our notion of liberal education does not seem to fit an age which is aware of the fact that there is not *the* culture of *the* human mind, but a variety of cultures.

And, he remarks, paraphrasing Heidegger, that today it is insisted "that every comprehensive view is relative to a specific perspective, or that all

as an end in itself. Indeed, academic debates over the limits to diversity indicate that the choice of unalloyed diversity is by no means uncontested among liberals. It is true that liberalism makes a strong commitment to diversity as a good in keeping with the diversity of goods for human beings to pursue. Thus, it is not easy for liberals to insist on limits to diversity without questioning their own motives. However, this is often as likely to reinforce their sense of legitimacy in drawing a limit, when they are convinced that they have drawn it correctly, as it is to do otherwise. This naturally exposes them to the charge of hypocrisy on both left and right, but especially among those "progressives" who think there is an obvious goal in life which is inhibited only by the inhibited. The academic version of this debate is unlikely to recede unless and until a consensus on the distinctive character of the university and its engagement is restored. This would require a depoliticization of education, but many today deny that any human undertaking can be detached from politics. This belief, if it persists, will prove in the long run to be a great misfortune for universities and for other activities as well. But it is a mark of the current difficulties that many are hard pressed to mount an argument in favor of the transpolitical character of some of the most important human engagements.

7 Leo Strauss, "Liberal Education and Responsibility," in *Liberalism Ancient and Modern*, ed. with a foreword by Allan Bloom (Ithaca, N.Y., 1989 [1968]), 25. This essay first appeared in 1961. Here Strauss is saying that what is missing is the clear vision of the idea of liberal learning as a distinctive undertaking, shaped not by the prevailing culture but by the reflections on the experience of liberal learning accessible to its practitioners. The latter might very well have a deeper connection to their antique predecessors in regard to their experience of teaching and learning than they do to professional "educators," or the sociologists of education.

comprehensive views are mutually exclusive and none can be simply true.[8] Strauss wrote this in 1961, but a generation later American academics cannot be unaware of or untouched by the point.

Because the academic surroundings in America were, though not identical, also not unfamiliar, Strauss succeeded both in offering a distinctive but recognizable voice on education and in creating a major impact in particular on the American political science profession. He had the advantage of being an ally to those who sought to recover a lost understanding of education and, at the same time, one who had experienced directly the intensity of the crisis of civilization in Europe, the crisis Strauss referred to as the "crisis of the West."

Strauss was not unique in this. There is no doubt, however, that his impact in the post–World War II world of American political science is equal to any. The impact was concrete and remains visible in the numerous students and students of students who have been inspired by and carried on his work. The first part of his career in the United States, the period of the 1940s and 1950s, saw the triumph of the "behavioral revolution" in political science. But throughout this period there were the stirrings of the countermovement that was to issue in the revival and current flourishing of new interest and vitality in the study of political philosophy. *Natural Right and History* (1953) was an important harbinger of this restoration. In the 1950s it was common to debate the question whether political philosophy still existed. But there can be no doubt today that it both exists and even has some claim to dominating the consciousness of the political science profession.

In his stalwart defense of the great books, Strauss offered a philosophical justification for their centrality and related that defense to his understanding of the fundamental problem of our democratic age and hence also of the study of politics in that age.

There exists a whole science . . . political science – which has so to speak no other theme than the contrast between the original conception of democracy, or what one may call the ideal of democracy, and democracy as it is.[9]

8 "What Is Liberal Education?" 4, 8. Strauss here adapts the issue posed in modern philosophy to a question posed by every thoughtful undergraduate who is exposed for the first time to the world's variety. His intention is to show that certain skeptical questions will arise as an inherent part of the educational undertaking, if they are permitted to arise. They are, of course, permitted to arise in a democratic age where the consideration of all questions is, in principle at least, permitted. But the posing of the skeptical questions is the acknowledgment of knowing that we do not know which is the start of the quest for wisdom. Education does not end with the celebration of diversity; on the contrary, that is the stimulating beginning from which the hard and longer, arduous but not always stimulating, journey must begin. The recognition of the latter is a prerequisite experience and without it one can hardly be said to have begun serious thought on the issues.

9 "What Is Liberal Education?" 5. Here too we may ask whether this is an adequate characterization of the political science profession's aspirations. Alternatively, for example, we might say, following

However, political science, to the extent that it adopted the meaning of the word "science" associated with the modern natural and physical sciences, allowed the split between philosophy and science, or between the philosopher and the scientist, to continue. The philosopher might criticize democracy, but the scientist might be inclined either only to study its features or to increase its power to do what it will.[10] Strauss, speaking as philosopher against the scientist, argues that modern democracy is principally not a regime but a mass culture managed by elites.

Thus we understand most easily what liberal education means here and now. Liberal education is the counterpoison to mass culture, to the corroding effects of mass culture, to its inherent tendency to produce nothing but "specialists without spirit or vision and voluptuaries without heart." Liberal education is the ladder by which we try to ascend from mass democracy to democracy as originally meant. Liberal education is the necessary endeavor to found an aristocracy within democratic mass society. Liberal education reminds those members of mass democracy who have ears to hear, of human greatness.[11]

The recollection of human greatness in an age that denies it and in which those who could have it conceal it, is to be accomplished through the reading of the great books. Strauss here quotes the indictment of modernity voiced by Max Weber in *The Protestant Ethic and the Spirit of Capitalism* as a sign, since Weber, in elaborating the postulates of modern social science, pointed insistently to the limits of what this social science could do as well as to what it could claim to achieve. Strauss thought that this implied the need of a philosophical critique of the methodology of the social sciences, and reconsideration of the aims of traditional political science, that is, political philosophy in the classical sense.

The philosophical questioning of the modern social sciences meant recovering the arguments of the great books. By great books Strauss meant works written by those who had surpassed the status of pupil.

The teachers themselves are pupils and must be pupils. But there cannot be an infinite regress: ultimately there must be teachers who are not in turn pupils . . . the greatest minds. Such men are extremely rare. We are not likely to meet any of them in the classroom. We are not likely to meet any of them anywhere. It is a piece of

Hegel and today Michael Oakeshott, that the fundamental object of investigation has been to define the categorical distinctiveness of the "modern liberal state" in contrast to the "ancient city." Looked at this way, it would not restrict modern political studies to issues of democratic culture.

10  "Liberal Education and Responsibility," in *Liberalism Ancient and Modern,* 22. See also Leo Strauss, "An Epilogue," in *Essays on the Scientific Study of Politics,* ed. Herbert J. Storing (New York, 1962). There Strauss showed what moderation of speech could include by saying: "Only a great fool would call the new political science diabolic: it has no attributes peculiar to fallen angels. It is not even Machiavellian, for Machiavelli's teaching was graceful, subtle, and colorful. Nor is it Neronian. Nevertheless one may say of it that it fiddles while Rome burns. It is excused by two facts: it does not know that it fiddles, and it does not know that Rome burns," 327.

11  "What Is Liberal Education?" 5.

good luck if there is a single one alive in one's time. For all practical purposes, pupils, of whatever degree of proficiency, have access to the teachers who are not in turn pupils, to the greatest minds, only through the great books. Liberal education will then consist in studying with the proper care the great books which the greatest minds have left behind – a study in which the more experienced pupils assist the less experienced pupils, including the beginners.[12]

I confess to an inclination toward Strauss's argument, but there are questions we cannot avoid if we are to do the argument justice. First, can a human being cease to be a pupil? Is learning not an endless engagement, coterminous with human beings such that it has no specifiable starting-point or end? It may be that a few inquirers in reduced intellectual circumstances will cease to find others around them from whom they can learn much. Could such individuals transcend the dependence on dialogue that classically characterizes the philosophical pursuit? Would the quest for wisdom cease to be problematic? Can there be individuals who somehow go beyond being pursuers of wisdom and simply *have* wisdom? Does not even a human being who is not a pupil still have to be a learner, perhaps a self-moved seeker?

Strauss's statement also suggests that the writers of great books show their greatness through those books. Implied is a demand for a reader capable of appreciating the achievement manifested in such books, a great reader or, at any rate, a reader who senses the need of greatness without yet knowing exactly its features. Strauss attaches greatness to great philosophical achievement. But greatness is also necessarily associated with superiority in the sense of heroic action in the military field and in politics, and in enjoying a right to rule that is insulated in some degree, though not entirely, from the opinions of the many about one's qualifications to rule.

It is, for Strauss, the philosophical achievement that must constitute the saving grace today because the dominance of the democratic culture cannot be overthrown or significantly moderated in the foreseeable future, and the efforts to do so in our time have been corrupted by the misunderstandings of our time, which have called for an even more radical rejection of the past instead of a recovery of it.[13]

---

12 Ibid., 3. It should be clear that this definition of what a great book is does not specify a list or canon, although it is not hard to construct the list of books important to Strauss. Rather, this is the hint of a connoisseur to initiates as to what to look for. The fact that we do not know ahead of time, and cannot predict, what those initiated will choose to honor is nonetheless compatible with the conviction – and, indeed, the demonstration by the true teacher – that such books do exist. There is, in short, a tradition of teaching and learning that goes with being truly educated but, sadly in our time, this is regularly caricatured as a doctrine and a program rather than as an adventurous quest for self-understanding in which the journey is no less relevant than the destination.

13 Horst Mewes has expressed this point very clearly in an unpublished paper, "Critics of Modern Rationalism: Strauss and Heidegger." In it he writes: "Whereas Strauss's view of the crisis of Western civilization can be called a modified Platonic perspective which affords a genuine alternative to the modern crisis, Heidegger regards Plato in the most crucial respects as the very source of the

Nor need the real philosophers have any interest in political activism. They can be content so long as they are left free to philosophize in the midst of current events.

We are not permitted to be flatterers of democracy precisely because we are friends and allies of democracy. While we are not permitted to remain silent on the dangers to which democracy exposes itself as well as human excellence, we cannot forget the obvious fact that by giving freedom to all, democracy also gives freedom to those who care for human excellence. No one prevents us from cultivating our garden or from setting up outposts which may come to be regarded by many citizens as salutary to the republic and as deserving of giving to it its tone. . . . We are indeed compelled to become specialists, but we can try to specialize in the most weighty matters or, to speak more simply and more nobly, in the one thing needful.[14]

The pursuit of greatness, then, demands the contemplation of the greatness of the past as recorded in those books that competently preserve an account of greatness. The question of doing more in light of the study of the greatness of the past is not clearly answered, except that one is to allow oneself to be a witness to the study of the great books. To do this is to unify the inner disposition to greatness with one's manifest conduct in a moderate, politically respectful, fashion.[15]

It was always Strauss's intention to portray the philosopher as a seeker who passes between dogmatism and radical skepticism. Such a person does not claim either to have overcome Socratic ignorance or to know that it is impossible to attain wisdom. In his argument with Alexander Kojève, for

beginnings of that crisis. For Strauss, Platonic philosophizing (or Socratic philosophizing) discovered certain basic problems and alternatives of human thought which provide permanent standards by which to judge the 'obfuscations' of modern enlightenment philosophy. For Heidegger, however, Platonic philosophy is already under the 'coercive yoke' of the type of human thought that hides the very source and prerequisites of all truth. Since Plato contains the seeds of all subsequent Western metaphysics up to and including Nietzsche, it is unable to provide any standards by which to judge or resist nihilism and 'homelessness' that due to modern variations of Platonism blossomed forth from those seeds."

14  "Liberal Education and Responsibility," 24.
15  To take diversity seriously in academic debates would be to take up the aristocratic critique of democratic culture as a legitimate voice emergent in democratic freedom. Such freedom is, ambiguously, both a condition urging voices to speak, and a cultural determination of what they may say. This aristocratic voice is not inherently in opposition to the "liberal tradition" even if it refuses to honor uncritically the democratic culture that has come to characterize the world of liberalism in our time. Among the safeguards against the dangers of such a critique would be the traditional criteria of philosophical and academic inquiry, the principles of Socratic ignorance and conversationality. The radicalization of the universities, in undermining these traditions, looks to be a self-destructive tendency in a democratic culture. When Strauss says he is critical of democracy because a friend to it, he means to say that democracy should be praised for its virtues and challenged on its vices. Unfortunately, there is a democratic tendency to want simply to be praised, or worse, flattered, and that, in effect, is likely to mean being praised for its faults or excesses. The diversity of human goods is real. Thus, the appearance of excellence or greatness in our midst should be responded to so as to appropriate its contribution opportunely, not vilified because it embarrasses a concealed desire for a diversity that is actually a uniformity.

example, Strauss admitted that there can be no simple refutation of historicism. The claim of natural right or natural law presupposes the existence of natural right or natural law. Likewise, historicism presupposes its own historical assumptions defining natural right or natural law as refuted. The modern political philosopher is thus forced to live in the tension between "natural right" and "history." To live in that tension is to acknowledge the obstacles to making up one's mind once and for all, not adopting either the opinion that natural right is simply true or the opinion that it has been superseded by historical fate, but struggling toward the knowledge that would come only by transcending these alternatives. At the highest level, then, there would still be a conversation of political philosophers – even intense disagreements – wherein each of them would reveal their inclinations toward one or the other of the alternatives in full awareness of what can be said against them. *Natural Right and History* constituted Strauss's "observations on the problem of natural right."[16]

For Strauss the Socratic quest continues to be a real, present possibility. Holding the options open is the starting point for the possible refutation of historicism, and thus the basis for the critique of democracy presented as our historical fate. There is no decisive insight in the Hegelian sense, the alternatives are not decisively disposed of by the movements of history. Strauss can choose to think unhistorically, but in so choosing, he cannot choose innocently. It is a historical issue knowingly to live unhistorically. In this respect, we may remain within the Hegelian ambiance: We are in ourselves what we are for ourselves, or our essential character is what we understand it to be. Even if learning is natural to human beings, the argument of natural right must be learned. The choice of a way of life, as Max Weber said, is the choice of a way of knowing. By choosing within the tension specified, the political philosopher becomes exemplary for the critique of the positive social sciences. If to choose a way of life is to choose a method of knowing, then conversely to choose a method of knowing is to choose a way of life.

In Strauss's outlook, these choices are the catalysts for analyzing alternative interpretative frameworks, and the political philosopher must become the diagnostician of these alternatives, including the one that he self-consciously chooses for himself; he must create the dialogue. There emerges a characteristic range of alternatives in relation to each of which there may be associated conceptions of the best regime. As to these alternative possibilities, the political philosopher can neither simply be a positive social scientist nor a resolute activist.

16 *Natural Right and History,* vii.

The philosopher's dominating passion is the desire for truth, that is, for knowledge of the eternal order, or the eternal cause or causes of the whole. As he looks up in search of the eternal order, all human things and all human concerns reveal themselves to him in all clarity as paltry and ephemeral. . . . Chiefly concerned with eternal beings, or the "ideas," and hence also with the "idea" of man, he is as unconcerned as possible with individual and perishable human beings and hence also with his own "individuality," or his body, as well as with the sum total of all individual human beings and their "historical" procession.[17]

This liberal education moves us toward a dimension of reality obscured under current conditions because such education will proclaim that historical knowledge is not identical to wisdom. This is not because we do not understand our own age and conditions, but because we understand them very well. We are led by our very historical sophistication to perceive the limits of historical knowing. Thus liberal education requires us to live for ourselves, and living for ourselves in the deepest sense means pursuing the philosophical life. But the liberal education, insofar as it carries with it the duty to perpetuate the opportunity of liberal education for the future, means that we cannot abandon altogether the paltry and ephemeral conditions of earthly existence. "Education to perfect gentlemanship, to human excellence, liberal education consists in reminding oneself of human excellence, of human greatness."[18]

There is, then, a tension between concern for human greatness and for the greatness of the whole that far surpasses human greatness. The heart of the philosophical aspirant lies above even as he remains below. The boldness of the aspiration curtails and transforms the initial enthusiasm for worldly successes. Such an individual becomes educated in the sense of becoming the intersection of the divine and the human things without being able to identify simply with either pole, without being certain to which pole one truly belongs.

The desire for eternal things weakens attachment to other human beings, but the detachment from typical material desires also dissolves the motives to antagonize and compete with others. Yet the natural sociality of human beings, together with the need of conversation to check the sanity of one's convictions, forces the philosopher to be attached to others. Beyond this, there is the urge to improve others by conversation as a check on the sanity of their convictions.[19]

Strauss thus fastens his attention on the question of what the "proper care" in reading great works means, for this means to take proper care in

17 Leo Strauss, *On Tyranny* (Ithaca, N.Y., 1968), 211–12.   18 "What Is Liberal Education?" 6.
19 Strauss, *On Tyranny,* 214–16.

educating oneself. Proper care in educating oneself necessarily requires concern for the question of education in general, and thus concern for others.
Taking proper care, however, will show that the "community of the greatest minds is rent by discord."[20] Thus there can be no independence from
the necessity of dialogue; the pursuit of wisdom cannot cease to be problematic. Since "wisdom is inaccessible to man, and hence virtue and happiness will always be imperfect," liberal education must be an activity which
is capable of becoming an end in itself for serious human beings.[21] The serious cannot simply identify themselves with the regimes of the democratic
culture – or with any regime on earth – which is not to say they cannot live
lawfully within them. In Strauss's view, living lawfully – including paying
respect to prevailing opinions – within a democratic regime is nearly all that
such regimes require of one. But merely to live lawfully is not to explore,
or to be required to take seriously, the matter of fulfilling one's humanity.
One's humanity and one's citizenship are not identical.

To learn to be human, then, is not to center one's attention on current
political and social issues as if they were a set of problems for which solutions are to be devised, and which thus define one's duty. Rather, to learn
to be human is to acquaint oneself with the universal human predicament
(in part no doubt illustrated by the current issues) by seeking greater con-
versancy with that predicament's dimensions and the classic alternative re-
sponses to them. In this sense, the philosophical pursuit of greatness
necessarily detaches itself from the pursuit of greatness as that could be defined – inadequately – in the politics of our time. Greatness as defined today would too easily mean celebrity or vulgar recognition. Greatness then
almost inevitably is associated with self-assertion or self-promotion.

Liberal learning engenders modesty about political things as it directs us
to boldness in philosophical things. The pursuit of political boldness may
well be only political rashness.

The responsible and clear distinction between ends which are decent and ends
which are not is in a way presupposed by politics. It surely transcends politics. For
everything which comes into being through human action and is therefore perishable or corruptible presupposes incorruptible and unchangeable things – for instance, the natural order of the human soul – with a view to which we can
distinguish between right and wrong actions.[22]

This opens up – indeed, demands – an active role for us as philosophical
pupils since even we who are the less than greatest minds must assess the alternatives presented to us. Not all will be satisfied merely to take notes and

20 "What Is Liberal Education?" 4.     21 "What Is Liberal Education?" 7.
22 "Liberal Education and Responsibility," 13.

develop a catalogue, or to become philosophical pedants. For this reason liberal education, properly speaking, cannot become indoctrination and the responsibility for working out one's self-understanding cannot be relinquished.

Strauss elaborates on the character of the task to achieve self-understanding in discussing the difference between "liberal education" and "responsibility." Strauss observes that we regularly now speak of individuals as "responsible" where once we spoke of them as "just," "conscientious," or "virtuous." To be held responsible, Strauss points out, is merely to be in the position of being either virtuous or vicious; murderers can be responsible for their criminal acts just as teachers can be responsible for imparting knowledge to their students. Responsibility is closely associated with accountability. In general, apart from the issue of criminality, responsibility is used to signify anyone who carries out an appointed task.

In this sense, the term "responsibility" equalizes us because there is a common denominator of responsibility that can be imputed to the widest range of jobs without distinguishing among them with respect to the effect they may have on the development of the lives of the jobholders, the goals, purposes, or talents they encourage. To be responsible in this sense is to acquire the praise most easily granted in a democratic culture. It becomes plausible to associate the responsible discharge of one's task with maturity or fulfillment. It permits open-ended broadening and thus, in Strauss's terms, a lowering of the idea of fulfillment. Numerous educational experts today encourage us to translate the engagements of teaching and learning into "behavioral objectives," in order to rationalize responsibility in expressions of quantitative measurement. By such measurements, philosophical undertakings, because they are not amenable to behavioral specification, might easily seem less responsible than many if not most others. Behavioral standards of accountability replace the conversational with the apparently commensurable. Finally, the paradigmatic experiential meaning of liberal education is lost from sight. Philosophical conversation must resist this trend.

How is this resistance to be carried out? If "liberal education consists in listening to the conversation of the greatest minds," we nevertheless "must bring about that conversation. The greatest minds utter monologues even when they write dialogues."[23] We must re-create in ourselves a dialogue that is suppressed in the democratic ambiance. That it remains possible to do this shows that there is something here natural to the human condition which the ethos of the age cannot eradicate.

---

23  Ibid. I take it by monologue Strauss means "argument" or the expression of the position one has found persuasive. The expression of an argument is, of course, the invitation also to a response from others.

That there are great works is a position I willingly defend. Moreover, I think Strauss helps us to respond to contemporary critics of the great books or those who deny there can be such books.

Responsible teaching, according to the analysis of responsibility before us, cannot be a sufficient standard. According to it, responsible teaching need not, perhaps is not even encouraged to take account of differences of superior and inferior in the works studied or the subjects chosen for study. According to that same analysis, the task of the learner suffers the same fate. All efforts at liberal education in the original sense can then easily be made to look arbitrary, narrow, and elitist.[24]

Strauss's endorsement of the intellectual power of great works does not deny our freedom to respond to them. Indeed, it promises that sort of freedom related to the original meaning of the word "liberal" against the contemporary meaning, which is satisfied with responsible conduct regardless of the aims or content of the undertaking. But if we must create the dialogue to which the "monologue" (argument) of a great book is the invitation, then the great books do not oppress but rather liberate us in this sense of the word. They expand the horizon of our imagination without dictating the conclusions to which we are obliged to submit.

Liberal education, which consists in the constant intercourse with the greatest minds, is a training in the highest form of modesty, not to say of humility. It is at the same time a training in boldness: it demands from us the complete break with the noise, the rush, the thoughtlessness, the cheapness of the Vanity Fair of the intellectuals as well as of their enemies. It demands from us the boldness implied in the resolve to regard the accepted views as mere opinions, or to regard the average opinions as extreme opinions which are at least as likely to be wrong as the most strange or least popular opinions. Liberal education is liberation from vulgarity. The Greeks had a beautiful word for "vulgarity"; they called it *apeirokalia,* lack of experience in things beautiful. Liberal education supplies us with experience in things beautiful.[25]

Thus the great books, while inciting us to bold thought, will also make it less easy for us to want liberation in the sense of becoming current in the received "wisdom," the intellectual fashions of the day. We will not be liberated from skeptical second thoughts, and thus we will not be fluent participants in the current scene.

24  To say responsibility cannot be a sufficient standard is not to say we are free to be irresponsible in discharging our daily duties and obligations. Nor does it mean that officeholders are not to be held accountable for how they discharge the duties of their offices. It is to say that after all this has been done there remains something more. Human beings are different from any other beings in the inexhaustibility of the undertaking to be human and the incompleteness of all formulas of completion.
25  "What Is Liberal Education?" 8.

The facile delusions which conceal from us our true situation all amount to this: that we are, or can be, wiser than the wisest men of the past. We are thus induced to play the part, not of attentive and docile listeners, but of impresarios or lion-tamers. Yet we must face our awesome situation, created by the necessity that we try to be more than attentive and docile listeners, namely, judges, and yet we are not competent to be judges. As it seems to me, the cause of this situation is that we have lost all simply authoritative traditions in which we could trust, the *nomos* which gave us authoritative guidance, because our immediate teachers and teachers' teachers believed in the possibility of a simply rational society. Each of us here is compelled to find his bearings by his own powers, however defective they may be.[26]

To defend liberal education today is thus to engage in an exercise of retrieval or recollection in a world hostile to the undertaking. It is a peculiarity of our time to be estranged from our past even as we collect more and more detailed information about it.

In the academic debates this means to insist upon the distinction between the superior and the inferior. Strauss informs us that the current trends in education are, if the tradition of liberal learning is a guide, antithetical to liberal learning. The founding idea of liberal learning contradicts the prejudices of the modern democratic culture. Strauss thus unfolds an argument that distinguishes his own view from the historicist view he rejects. According to the historicist view, the idea of liberal education evolves in accordance with the changes that mark each historical epoch. Strauss's view, in contrast, is that there is a permanent insight into the character of liberal education. Moreover, Strauss held that his idea is philosophically discernible and accessible to inquiry even in the midst of changing historical circumstances. To learn what to look for in the midst of all that goes on historically, one must consult those works that articulate the experiential foundation and with the help of which one can attempt to distinguish liberal education from other activities. Without knowledge of those works, one will very likely lose confidence in the task.

Thinking about education is thus at the heart of thinking philosophically. And since education cannot but be at the heart of the way of life of a society, and a central factor in fashioning the coherence of a society's way of life, thinking philosophically about education is an act that takes the political life seriously. To take the political life seriously means to take to heart the differences between classical and modern philosophy.

According to classical philosophy the end of the philosophers is radically different from the end or ends actually pursued by the nonphilosophers. Modern philosophy comes into being when the end of philosophy is identified with the end which

26  Ibid.

is capable of being actually pursued by all men. More precisely, philosophy is now asserted to be essentially subservient to the end which is capable of being actually pursued by all men . . . the modern conception of philosophy is fundamentally democratic. The end of philosophy is now no longer what one may call disinterested contemplation of the eternal, but the relief of man's estate.[27]

On this basis, it is easy to see why today the discussion is largely about education for democracy instead of what Strauss is taking up: What is the educational task in facing democracy?

Education for democracy meant and means altering the attitudes of the many who initially distrusted science and technology to make them willing believers in its infinite power for improvement, and also persuading us that egalitarianism is a standard or vision of order from which all societies' departures are to be seen as unfortunate distortions of a "true" order of human relationships. Education in the face of democracy would mean questioning the vast achievements of the scientific-technological culture as though they were a "lowering" rather than a "raising" of standards, while insisting on the need to confront the diversity of human accomplishments. This would be the Socratic reversal necessary in our time. If everyone thinks we are raising ourselves, it becomes the task to ask in what sense we might be lowering ourselves. We would be showing in what way our enlightening is really a darkening. At the same time, as a recollection, it is not the nihilistic revolt against enlightenment. It is quite different.

Enlightenment came to mean a universal project to improve health, longevity, income while expanding "trade which unites all peoples," in order to take precedence over religion "which divides the peoples."[28] Responsibility, Strauss argues, we can now see is a term at first encouraging, of necessity, only enlightened self-interest, but not necessarily an idea of virtuous fulfillment. Later, however, with the hope of eliminating scarcity from the world, responsibility comes to include compassionate concern for maintaining minimum universal material standards for all. It cannot be ignored that the pursuit of liberal education in the classic sense will be taken as evidence that those who pursue it are incapable of the requisite compassion, and thus are inadequate contributors to the democratic project. The result is "hardly more than the interplay of mass taste with high-grade but strictly speaking unprincipled efficiency."[29] But since mass taste precludes

27 "Liberal Education and Responsibility," 19–20.     28 Ibid., 20.
29 Ibid., 23. The efficiency is unprincipled "strictly speaking" because its aim is to satisfy the widest range of demands through the multiplication and expansion of resources so that as few decisions about what to support as possible will need to be made. The criterion for refusing a demand will then not be based on an idea of virtuous human fulfillment, but only on what is available to satisfy desires because they are desires. We are born in possession of IOUs.

holding anyone in particular responsible in any meaningful way, the ultimate ground of self-understanding in a democratic culture is a kaleido-
scopic, continuous transformation of day-to-day opinions and beliefs.
Everyone and no one is responsible for our situation.

At the heart of modern inquiry we must confront the question of natural
right and history. Our views will presuppose a stance on this question. This
requires taking seriously antidemocratic arguments without seeking to form
an antidemocratic party or a revolutionary movement.

For we cannot expect that liberal education will lead all who benefit from it to understand their civic responsibility in the same way or to agree politically. Karl Marx,
the father of communism, and Friedrich Nietzsche, the stepgrandfather of fascism,
were liberally educated on a level to which we cannot even hope to aspire. But
perhaps one can say that their grandiose failures make it easier for us who have experienced those failures to understand again the old saying that wisdom cannot be
separated from moderation and hence to understand that wisdom requires unhesi-
tating loyalty to a decent constitution and even to the cause of constitutionalism.
Moderation will protect us against the twin dangers of visionary expectations from
politics and unmanly contempt for politics. Thus it may again become true that all
liberally educated men will be politically moderate men. It is in this way that the
liberally educated may again receive a hearing even in the market place.[30]

Thereby we may fortify ourselves to elevate the sense of being responsible – in dramatic terms, the life of relative existential commitments – toward
the forming of a vision of the life of virtue. Whatever the boldness of that
vision, Strauss will not permit its beholder to separate it from political modesty or the virtue of moderation, the virtue that is virtuous in relation to all
intellectual stances. But moderation need not be a sign that the best lack all
conviction; it will be a sign, rather, that importance does not reside only in
or even depend primarily on universal acclaim of it.

30 "Liberal Education and Responsibility," 24.

# 5

# Leo Strauss: The Quest for Truth in Times of Perplexity

JÜRGEN GEBHARDT

In the aftermath of the breakdown of the Marxist-Leninist empire in Eastern Europe, fundamental questions about politics force themselves on the public discourse of the peoples who are trying to reconstruct civil society. What was rightly called the theme of political philosophy by Leo Strauss has once again been put on the agenda of European political debate: "mankind's great objectives, freedom and government or empire – objectives which are capable of lifting all men beyond their poor selves."[1]

As a consequence of the collapse of socialist orders, reflections on the good society, good life, and common good emerge. These thoughts raise some doubts about accepting the liberal-capitalistic system hook, line, and sinker insofar as the totalitarian systems are "a convex mirror of all modern civilization and a harsh, perhaps final call for a global recasting of that civilization's self-understanding." Václav Havel, the author of these lines, goes on to say that the totalitarian systems are "most of all, a convex mirror of the inevitable consequences of [modern] rationalism, a grotesquely magnified image of its own deep tendencies, an extreme outcropping of its own development and an ominous product of its own expansion." Being "a symbol of a civilization that has renounced the Absolute, which ignores the natural world and disdains its imperatives" the totalitarian systems "are a deeply informative reflection" of the crisis of Western rationalism itself.[2] Havel "cannot avoid the impression that many people in the West still understand little of what is actually at stake in our time."[3] In all probability the warnings of Western complacency and the concomitant hypocrisy won't obtain much hearing, either by a triumphant right or by a left shattered by defeat. But the critical voices in the East, few as they may be, prove that. "In an

---

1 Leo Strauss, *What Is Political Philosophy?* (Glencoe, Ill., 1959), 10.
2 Václav Havel, "Anti-Political Politics," in John Keane, ed., *Civil Society and the State* (London, 1988), 381–98, 389.
3 Ibid., 393.

hour of crisis, when the order of a society flounders and disintegrates, the fundamental problems of political existence in history are more apt to come into view than in periods of comparative stability," as Eric Voegelin states in his *New Science of Politics*.[4] Whoever enters into serious conversation with sensible people in the formerly socialist countries can't avoid addressing substantive questions of politics, that is, questions of a philosophical nature. Those questions emerge from the immediacy of political life marked by an all-pervading feeling of crisis, and they are certainly not considered exercises in academic theorizing that is of bookish irrelevance to the life of real people. With these preliminary remarks I hope to prepare the ground for a fresh understanding of the original intentions that formed the philosophical project of Leo Strauss and other émigré scholars who came to the United States in the 1930s.

According to the critical account of John G. Gunnell, this philosophical enterprise was transformed into political theory "as not only a distinct academic discipline but a profession."[5] The "invention of political theory" as a subfield of political science and as of "a wider interdisciplinary enterprise" can be traced back to "a quarrel that originated in the challenge to the values of American political science initiated by émigré scholars during the 1940s."[6] Gunnell's reading of the discourse history of academic political theory of the United States is part of this discussion. Centering around some idée fixe, which signified the "myth of the tradition," a "Europeanized political theory in the United States"[7] developed and led to "the constitution of a paradigm that provided both a subject matter and an approach to study and research."[8] According to the émigré scholars, political theory was "a response to a crisis, as a diagnosis of disorder and a critique of contemporary politics, . . . a search of a truth of political order and human nature, and . . . the construction of a vision of a new political society."[9] Gunnell, who is primarily concerned with the internal dialectics of a disciplinary history of American political science, will not let himself be drawn into a discussion about the objectives of a philosophical approach to politics on their own merits. He correctly notes that the "institutionalization of the idea of political theory as a distinct field of study and subject matter" subjected the philosophical project to the process of becoming more literal, doctrinal, academic, and departmentalized.[10] But Gunnell never asked himself whether

---

4 Eric Voegelin, *The New Science of Politics* (Chicago, 1952), 1–2.
5 John G. Gunnell, *Between Philosophy and Politics* (Amherst, Mass., 1986), 116.
6 John G. Gunnell, "American Political Science, Liberalism, and the Invention of Political Theory," *Archiv für Rechts- und Sozialphilosophie* 82, no. 1 (March 1988), 71–87, 71.
7 Gunnell, *Between Philosophy and Politics*, 116.     8 Ibid., 21.
9 John G. Gunnell, *Political Theory: Tradition and Interpretation* (Cambridge, Mass., 1979), 89.
10 Gunnell, *Between Philosophy and Politics*, 119.

this institutionalization had by any chance eclipsed the very intentions of the originators of the philosophical project in question. Instead Gunnell states that the "academic activity of political theory" alienated itself from political science as well as from politics and that, in consequence, "political theory became at once little more than a ritual plea, an entreaty, unheard, except fortuitously and indirectly, in the world of politics and a curiosity in the world of academe."[11]

Be that as it may – there is no doubt that the project of a philosophical inquiry into politics, as Leo Strauss and many a confrère of his introduced to American intellectual life, has been absorbed into a highly organized and routinized system of teaching and researching practiced within the framework of the well-established academic discipline of political or social science. Gabriel A. Almond, a leading figure of mainstream political science, recently offered a classification of the schools and sects in the discipline based on an ideological and methodological dimension. In terms of ideology he distinguishes between the Right and the Left, and with regard to methodology the extremes of hard and soft. By combining these two dimensions he comes up with four schools in political science. Leo Strauss and his students figure prominently under the heading of soft Right.[12] Almond acknowledges the impact of the European émigrés, and he is also doubtful as to Straussian political philosophy. But his view of the discipline is presented in a conciliatory mood in that he claims Greek origins for all political science, notes that the "hard science – soft science polarity . . . has . . . been endemic to the discipline since its origins," and, last but not least, welcomes "all methods that illuminate the world of politics and public policy" to the discipline.[13] When studied from a different angle, Almond's picture of political science seems to confirm Gunnell's findings in some respects: The philosophical quest for understanding human existence in history and society, which motivated Leo Strauss, is apparently lost on the professional practitioner of political science.

Harry V. Jaffa argues along these lines and criticizes some of Strauss's former students, who hailed the award that had been established in honor of Leo Strauss by the American Political Science Association "for the recognition it has given to political philosophy 'as one of the important traditions within the discipline.' " He comments on the absurdity of this language, and in particular on that aspect of it which implied that political philosophy was " 'one of many' subdivisions or branches of political science." He points out that "the very idea of political philosophy, as a practical science, was

11 Ibid., 222.
12 Gabriel A. Almond, *A Discipline Divided* (Newbury Park, Calif., 1990), 14–15, 21–22.
13 Ibid., 24–25, 29.

inextricably connected with the idea of an architectonic science," which, in the Aristotelian sense, guides all other practical sciences.[14] Jaffa puts forth that Strauss's concept of political philosophy is concerned with the very foundations of the science of politics itself, but he questions whether philosophizing about politics, as practiced by Leo Strauss, can be reconciled with the institutional realities and the practice of professional political science at all. It may be possible to adapt organized Straussianism to the exigencies of the profession, but does this hold true for the philosophy of politics as well? Maybe this question touches on the predicament of "normal" political science, that is, political science in times of stability, which feeds on conventional wisdom to the extent that the search for the truth of human existence seems to be superfluous. I don't know whether we should speak of "political science's tragic condition" in view of this situation, as David M. Ricci suggests.[15] It depends on whether we still or again share Strauss's suspicion that political science "fiddles while Rome burns" without knowing that it is fiddling and that Rome is burning.[16]

Strauss, in any case, was convinced of the enduring crisis of the West. He had started on his philosophical project in response to this crisis, and the persistence of the crisis required that the project, that is, the quest for truth, be continued. It does not promise answers or solutions to the perennial fundamental problems of human life, but brings forth those excellent human qualities that – in some way – make up the good life, in other words; it has a humanizing effect. Up to now the Straussian enterprise has been discussed in a rather general way and from the point of view of an outside observer. However, an assessment of Strauss's philosophical intentions, of how they fit to American intellectual life, and, finally, of the significance of the philosophical project today requires an analysis of Strauss's self-understanding and a study of its experiential roots. Obviously such an undertaking is beyond the scope of the present investigation, because it would demand a comprehensive interpretation of Strauss's rich, multifaceted, multilayered, and in itself often contradictory oeuvre. Upon closer study, however, his thought and his life, considered a unity in this respect, reveal certain intellectual key elements that play a decisive part in the formation of the philosophical project. The discussion of those key elements will not fulfill the requirements that Strauss himself has set for "historical understanding" and I am afraid that we will fall short of understanding Strauss "exactly as he understood him-

14  Harry V. Jaffa, "The Legacy of Leo Strauss's Defended," *The Claremont Review* 4, no. 1 (Spring 1985), 20–24, 22.
15  David M. Ricci, *The Tragedy of Political Science* (New Haven, 1984), 315.
16  Leo Strauss, "An Epilogue," in Herbert J. Storing, ed., *Essays on the Scientific Study of Politics* (New York, 1962), 307–27, 327.

self."[17] But it is some consolation to know that even the people who are undoubtedly the most attentive and exacting readers Strauss could have wished for, namely, his students, seem to quarrel a lot about how their teacher is to be understood. The heated exchange between Thomas L. Pangle and Harry V. Jaffa as to what constitutes the legacy of Leo Strauss's points in this direction.[18] The hermeneutical problems involved in this controversy cannot be resolved by constructing two Straussian philosophies that contradict each other fundamentally. Reasoning along these lines, Shadia B. Drury suspects that Strauss literally taught different people different things. On the one hand, there were students to be "initiated" into an esoteric philosophy that "has refuted faith and *has* an absolute right to rule unhampered by law, even if these are 'truths' that must be kept hidden." On the other hand, Drury states, there are those who are instructed on the honorable and right life of the city, that is to be gentlemen in accordance with those standards of civilization that are illusionary to philosophers.[19] From this point of view, Strauss formulates both an exoteric philosophy that is concerned with the good order of the society and an esoteric philosophy that subverts any conception of the good society by celebrating and enacting the Nietzschean superman "beyond good and evil." By this hermeneutical sleight of hand, Leo Strauss turns out to be "the quintessential 'modern.' His radical depreciation of morality embodies the very 'crisis' of the West that he describes."[20] In the face of Drury's interpretation, it should be noted that those scholars who come from the same cultural background as Strauss and were not at all in agreement with his thought, for example, Helmut Kuhn, Hans-Georg Gadamer, Karl Löwith, or Eric Voegelin, never suspected Strauss of secretly subscribing to the Nietzschean philosophy of superman. Understanding the occasionally opaque and contradictory writings of Strauss may not always be easy, but they do not contain a secret doctrine destined to form a Nietzschean sect of "heroic Epicurians" bound to corrupt American youth. The present more prosaic approach intends to heed Strauss's advice while studying the formative elements of his philosophical project: to ask for "the conscious and deliberate intention of its originator."[21] Our "guiding question," therefore, "must become . . . the question as to what question was uppermost" in Strauss's mind.[22] For the time being, I will not

---

17 Leo Strauss, *The Rebirth of Classical Political Rationalism,* ed. Thomas L. Pangle (Chicago, 1989), 208.
18 See Thomas L. Pangle, "The Platonism of Leo Strauss," and Jaffa, "The Legacy of Leo Strauss's Defended," *Claremont Review,* 16–24.
19 Shadia B. Drury, *The Political Ideas of Leo Strauss* (New York, 1988), 188.
20 Ibid., 200.    21 Strauss, *Classical Political Rationalism,* 209.
22 Leo Strauss, "On Collingwood's Philosophy of History," *Review of Metaphysics* 5, no. 4 (June 1952), 559–86, 581.

discuss the vexing question as to whether the distinction between esoteric and exoteric teaching, which is so important to the Straussian way of studying historical texts, applies to Strauss himself. This exoteric/esoteric complex implies several interrelated aspects of the connection between philosopher and society, but the crucial point for gaining understanding in this regard is Strauss's self-assessment, since esoteric teaching in his opinion is the privilege of only the philosopher in the true meaning of the word.[23] To what extent there is a Straussian esoterism depends on how Strauss judged his own philosophical project in the light of his conception of philosophy. This problem will be dealt with presently.

Although Strauss would have accused me of historicist leanings, it seems necessary to sketch the historical context of the intellectual biography of Strauss in order to understand the conscious and deliberate intentions that are at the roots of his thinking. No matter how inadequate a summary of the essentials may be with respect to the complexity of the subject, it must suffice for our telescopic approach. Whereas Gunnell is less concerned with the motives of authors like Strauss than "with their contribution to the myth of the tradition and entailed notions,"[24] he, like other observers, knows "that this literature can be understood only within the tradition of German historical philosophy and hermeneutics and that the approach is not simply an instrumental choice in that it is merely one way of doing philosophy and thinking historically."[25] But, since he is occupied with the trivialities of academic political theory, he never gets round to discussing the theoretical relevance of this German intellectual experience on its own merits. From the perspective of Gunnell's American-centered view, the German émigré scholars illegitimately interpreted their practical experience of the Weimar Republic and totalitarianism in terms of a general crisis of civilization in the West that had to be coped with intellectually, spiritually, and politically. In reference to Havel, my paradigmatic Eastern European political philosopher, one might at least take seriously Strauss's argument that "the crisis of our time has its core in the doubt of what we can call the 'modern project.' "[26]

Indeed, this deep-seated conviction of an ongoing "crisis of modernity" marks all of Strauss's writings. To American professors like Gunnell or Stephen Holmes, another critic of Strauss, he seemed obsessed by the contemporary crisis of the West. "No run-of-the-mill scholar," Holmes claims, "would have suggested that he could help us vanquish our civilization's en-

23  Strauss, *Classical Political Rationalism,* 66–68; Strauss, *Political Philosophy,* 222 and 227; Leo Strauss, "Persecution and Writing," *Social Research* 8, no. 4 (Nov. 1941), 488–508, 502–504.
24  Gunnell, *Between Philosophy and Politics,* 113.      25  Ibid., 111.
26  Leo Strauss, "Political Philosophy and the Crisis of Our Time," in G. J. Graham and G. W. Carey, eds., *The Post-Behavioral Era* (New York, 1972), 217–42, 217.

emies and remedy our century's ills. No average professor would have suggested that he could answer the burning question left untouched by modern science: How should human beings live?"[27] Irrespective of whether reflecting on the ills of our century and on living a good life is considered a duty of a person determined to educate young men and women who raise those questions in class, Strauss felt obliged to do so because "modern western man no longer knows what he wants" and "he no longer believes that he can know what is good and bad, what is right and wrong." In his view, the crisis of modernity consists in this very fact and, consequently, a political philosophy that seeks "the best social order" is deemed impossible and unnecessary in our time.[28] Thus, the crisis of modern culture is "primarily the crisis of modern political philosophy" in that it has lost "its faith in reason's ability to validate its highest aims."[29] In Strauss's opinion, meeting the crisis of modernity first of all involves restituting the dignity of the fundamental question about right and wrong, about the just and the good, that is, to restore political philosophy in its true sense. For political philosophy rightly understood is not to be considered an "academic pursuit," but should be viewed as a cultural enterprise concerned with the principles of societal order.

To many Americans Strauss's judgment smacks of the self-delusion of the politically impotent intellectual: "To say that the crisis of the West has philosophical origins is to imply that it has a philosophical cure. To intellectualize the origins of society's problems is to enhance the social prestige of intellectuals."[30] This ad hominem argument certainly does not disprove Strauss's inference that the socially relevant beliefs of the citizens, which sustain the society in existence, involve certain truths about the meaning of human life which originated in the minds of concrete persons. Insofar as those truths are an essential component in the structure of any political society, one might correctly assume that sociocultural crises and the ensuing social problems are rooted in the intellectual and spiritual life of society.

These remarks are not the last words of wisdom on Strauss's specific cultural interpretation of the modern crisis, which would require more extensive exploration beyond the scope of this essay. Some general remarks, however, have to be in this respect. First, it should be noted that this notion of the cultural crisis was characteristic of the German intellectual community, the "mandarin intellectuals," as Fritz Ringer defines, in terms of an ideal type, the German "cultural and social elite which owes its status pri-

27 Stephen Holmes, "Truths for the Philosophers Alone?" *Times Literary Supplement,* Dec. 1–7, 1989, 1319–24, 1319.
28 Leo Strauss, "Three Waves of Modernity," in Hiail Gildin, ed., *Political Philosophy* (Indianapolis and New York, 1975), 81–98, 81.
29 Ibid., 82.     30 Holmes, "Truths for the Philosophers Alone?" 1323.

marily to educational qualifications, rather than to hereditary rights or wealth."[31] The emergence of the German mandarins and their prominent role within German society is closely linked to the specifics of the political, cultural, and social development in Germany in the nineteenth and early twentieth centuries. This is also true for the decline of the mandarin tradition, which ended with the failure of the Weimar Republic in 1933.

Ringer maintains that the mandarins were only able to play their part "as a functional ruling class" in an intermediate stage of the socioeconomic evolution of modern society, which ended with full industrialization.[32] Without underestimating this social precondition of the rise and fall of the mandarins, one should not forget that their functional role was intrinsically dependent on the overall success of the state-sponsored university system in Germany in the nineteenth century. Based on the revolutionary principle of unified research and instruction, this new university system produced novel organizational forms of scholarship which resulted in a differentiation and professionalization of the natural sciences as well as the humanities. Guided by the concept of *Wissenschaft* and *Bildung,* which defined higher learning in terms of searching for truth and self-cultivation, the university aimed at the scholarly education of a cultural elite. After German unification in 1871, the universities were the unquestioned social and intellectual centers of the cultural life of the nation, and the professoriat operated as the guardians of the national culture.

I may be forgiven this rather hasty excursion into the sociohistorical world of the German Mandarinate, but I maintain that Leo Strauss's personal style and intellectual outlook reflect the habitudes and the intellectual vision of the German mandarins. Even if Ringer's picture of the mandarin borders on being a malicious caricature, it features some important aspects of the mandarin's self-assessment:

They demand to be recognized as a sort of spiritual nobility, to be raised above the class of their origins by their learning. They think of themselves as broadly cultured men, and their ideal of personal "cultivation" affects their whole conception of learning. Seeking spiritual ennoblement from education, they tend to reject "merely practical" knowledge and the pursuit of morally and emotionally neutral techniques of analysis. Instead, they regard learning as a process in which contact with venerated sources results in the absorption of their spiritual content, so that an indelible quality of spiritual elevation is conferred upon the student.[33]

Most German émigré scholars more or less shared this attitude. Once they were transplanted from German universities to the world of American col-

31 Fritz K. Ringer, *The Decline of the German Mandarins* (Cambridge, Mass., 1969), 5.
32 Ibid., 7.      33 Ibid., 9.

leges, this attitude acquired an exotic flavor and was met with enthusiasm as well as disgust. Leo Strauss was most successful at infusing this vision of scholarship into the American academic community. A good deal of the persisting controversy about Strauss and his school, in my opinion, has to do with this aspect of his work. It is not so much specific scholarly results as the idea of scholarship proper that is at stake.

The implication that the humanities were concerned with true knowledge as much as the natural sciences is crucial to this idea of scholarship. In German terminology, the humanities claimed their *Wissenschaftlichkeit*. According to Ringer, the natural scientists were as much mandarins as their colleagues in the humanities. However, he had good reasons for equating the mandarin intellectuals primarily with German academic humanists and social scientists.[34]

Since Ringer does not elaborate on these good reasons, they are described below. The natural sciences and the applied sciences produced impressive results and effected Germany's formidable economic progress. They did not, however, influence that country's cultural makeup in the late nineteenth century. In the aftermath of the decline of the idealist philosophies, the unfolding system of history-based humanistic disciplines increasingly played the leading role in society's self-interpretation. These empirically oriented interpretative sciences of man in society and history postulated "that they – and not a philosophical system – ascertained and revealed the truth about the world, indeed the truth of the world."[35]

This idea of the intellectual leadership of the interpretative sciences of man gave rise to two alternative conceptions: neo-Kantian *Kulturwissenschaft* and Dilthey's *Geisteswissenschaft*. These two approaches intended to lay out, both in terms of epistemology and methodology, the fundaments of the historical and philosophical disciplines in order to guarantee their theoretical status as *Wissenschaften* and to demarcate them from the natural sciences at the same time.

The mandarins, however, being by and large culturally liberal Protestants (with a certain dislike for Catholics and Jews, and a strong attachment to the Bismarckian state), burdened the philosophical and historical disciplines with the mission to stem the emerging forces of social and cultural change in Germany, so as to cope with the attendant cultural crisis and to provide a rapidly modernizing society with the badly needed cultural as well as social cohesion in terms of the specific German ideal or order, namely, the cultural and legal state.

---

34 Ibid., 8.    35 Thomas Nipperdey, *Deutsche Geschichte 1815–1866* (Munich, 1983), 532.

As much as the neo-Kantians and the Diltheyans differed on their concept
of science, they agreed that the cultural crisis was a crisis of European civilization and, furthermore, that order had to be reconstructed under scholarly guidance. According to Dilthey, the movement of the natural sciences
and the historical-critical *Wissenschaftslehre* had reached their conclusion:

The following effects would be encountered. First, the dissolution of dogmas and,
second, the dissolution of metaphysics. Third, in the course of the mechanical era,
psychology would achieve a mechanical construction of emotional life, social
democracy would constitute a political mechanism: every person is but a small machine part. Fourth, there would be naturalism in art; fifth, rule of the press; and
sixth, the dissolution of the social basis due to luxury, female rule, salons etc.,
which, seven, would find a political analogy in the universal and equal right to vote.

In the face of this situation, the task of the day was

to construct a social epoch which includes the valid features of individualism in a
socially oriented social order. Such a task requires the participation of philosophy,
which increases the ability to solve such problems.[36]

In a similar vein, the neo-Kantian Wilhelm Windelband believed that the
duty of his ideographic science of culture was to preserve the consciousness
of human culture and to defend the educational principle of the cultured
person (*Kulturmensch*). Windelband maintained that this was dangerously
undermined by the force of natural sciences, technology, and the emergence
of the masses, which led up to the democratization of the cultural, social, and
political life. The ultimate purpose of the cultural sciences consisted in em-
bodying the transempirical cultural values of humankind in society in order
to create a spiritual basis for all social estates and all individuals, because the
lack of such a basis is the ultimate cause of the ills of modern society.[37]

Following Germany's defeat in 1918, the feeling of an all-pervading cultural and sociopolitical crisis intensified. The notion of crisis spurred the
quest for some kind of synthesis between learning and the realities of life in
the deeply troubled Weimar Republic. Like the whole generation of young
scholars in the early 1920s, Leo Strauss, who had been academically socialized into the neo-Kantian paradigm, fell under the spell of a thriving intellectual culture that absorbed Nietzschean radicalism, French vitalism,
scientific positivism, traditional historicism, phenomenology, critical realism, revised classical idealism, Freudianism, and, last but not least, Heideggerian existentialism. In his obituary for Kurt Riezler, Strauss wrote that

36  Wilhelm Dilthey, *Gesammelte Schriften,* eds. Helmut Johach and Frithjof Rodi (Göttingen, 1982),
vol. 19: 303–04.
37  Wilhelm Windelband, *Die Philosophie im deutschen Geistesleben des 19. Jahrhunderts* (Tübingen, 1909),
109–14.

there was a strong dissatisfaction with the established academic positions "and a groping for a new way of thinking, that is, a feeling that a return from those academic positions to the great epoch of German thought (the epoch from Kant to Hegel) would not suffice. There was awareness of the general direction in which, as was believed, one had to move but there was no clarity and certainty about the way."[38] The impact of Heidegger on a whole generation of young sensitive minds evolved from this intellectual situation. Heidegger gave "expression to the prevailing unrest and dissatisfaction because he had clarity and certainty, if not about the whole way, at least about the first and decisive steps."[39] How Strauss himself was affected by his encounter with Heidegger will be discussed in due course.

Leo Strauss was a marginal mandarin, and as a believing Jew, he did not stay with the university but joined the *Akademie für die Wissenschaft des Judentums*. Thus, his experience of the intellectual world of the mandarin was considerably influenced by what Strauss called the Jewish problem. Born and raised in Germany, Strauss "found himself in the grip of the theological-political predicament"[40] insofar as it grew out of the specific "predicament of the German Jewry."[41] As George L. Mosse pointed out, the German-Jewish *Bildungsbürgertum* derived their postemancipatory identity from the very concept of self-cultivation (*Bildung*) based upon German classical culture which was at the root of mandarin worldview. "The new self-identity of the German Jews was expressed within a framework that gave it form and discipline and served to transcend Judaism and Christianity." In the course of the profound sociocultural change in German society, the ideas of classical culture and with them the concept of *Bildung* vanished. Thus, the "common ground between the German and Jewish *Bildungsbürger* which had once seemed so certain and promising" was eroded. "This erosion of the classical concept of *Bildung* was not sudden but gradual and never complete; it gained its full momentum only after World War I. . . . On the surface, this was the Indian summer of the bourgeois world and Jews never lived more comfortably. In reality, their isolation and their role as 'outsider' were being prepared."[42] Young Leo Strauss sensed that the tentative association between the "spirit of Goethe" and liberal democracy in the Weimar Republic was fragile and he did not share the belief of the German Jews "that their problems had been solved in principle by liberalism: German Jews were Germans of the Jewish faith, that is, they were no less German than the Germans of the Christian faith or of no faith. . . . This assumption was not accepted by

---

38 Strauss, *Political Philosophy*, 241.    39 Ibid., 246.
40 Leo Strauss, *Spinoza's Critique of Religion* (New York, 1965), 1.    41 Ibid., 3.
42 George L. Mosse, *German Jews beyond Judaism* (Cincinnati, 1985), 14.

the strongest part of Germany and hence by Germany."[43] Reflecting on de Lagarde's view of Judaism in 1924, he sums up de Lagarde's demand for a Reich policy toward the Jews (*Judenpolitik*).

The German people – in view of their negligible national strength cannot tolerate a foreign people in its midst, least of all a people exhibiting such national solidarity and intellectual danger as the Jewish people. For this reason, the state has to either assimilate . . . or drive out the Jews. The second option particularly is a possibility with regard to the Eastern Jews when a leading nation of Germans is established in Central Europe in the event of a war on two fronts against France and Russia.[44]

Why did Strauss deem it necessary to study "Judaism in German thought" in the polemical writings of Paul de Lagarde (1827–91) at that time? De Lagarde, an excellent Orientalist had become notorious for his antibourgeois, antiliberal culture critique (*Kulturkritik*) of the Wilhelmine society that was to be reformed by a future German popular religion based on an anti-Judaistic (that is, anti-Pauline) Jesus. Strauss obviously felt that the prophets of nationalism were moving from the fringe to the center of German society. Reading de Lagarde would not only dispel the liberal illusions of the German Jews but also clarify the ultimate meaning of assimilation: the renunciation of Judaism. In 1962 he wrote that in the course of their cultural emancipation, the German Jews "opened themselves to the influx of German thought, the thought of the particular nation in the midst of which they lived – a thought which was understood to be German essentially: political dependence was also spiritual dependence. This was the core of the predicament of German Jewry."[45] And he voiced the implication of what he called "assimilationism": "Full social equality proved to require the complete disappearance of the Jews as Jews – a proposition which is impractical, if for no other reason, then at least for the perfectly sufficient one of simple self-respect. Why should we who have a heroic past behind and within us, which is not second to that of any other group anywhere on earth, deny or forget the past?"[46]

As early as 1923, Strauss maintained that Zionism was not a viable alternative to assimilation since "Zionism continues and intensifies the anti-Judaizing tendency of assimilation."[47] In retrospect Strauss pointed out that the basic idea underlying strictly political Zionism was not Zionist at all, and for this reason had to accept Jewish culture, which had its roots in the Jewish heritage.

43 Strauss, *Spinoza's Critique,* 4.
44 Leo Strauss, "Paul de Lagarde," *Der Jude* 8, no. 8 (1924), 8–15, 15.
45 Strauss, *Spinoza's Critique,* 3.    46 Strauss, *Classical Political Rationalism,* 232.
47 Leo Strauss, "Der Zionismus bei Nordau," *Der Jude* 7, nos. 10/11 (1923), 657–60, 659.

[But] one could not have taken this step unless one had previously interpreted the Jewish heritage itself as a culture, that is, as a product of the national mind, of the national genius, presents itself not as a product of the human mind, but as a gift, as a divine revelation. . . . When cultural Zionism understands itself, it turns into religious Zionism. But when religious Zionism understands itself, it is in the first place Jewish faith, and only secondarily Zionism. It must regard as blasphemous the notion of a human solution to the Jewish problem.[48]

This holds true for the foundation of the state of Israel, which has been such a great blessing for the Jews. And the American experience does not invalidate this statement either: The hope for and the faith in America "cannot be of the same character as that faith and that hope which a Jew has in regard of Judaism and which the Christian has in regard to Christianity," which are based on "explicit divine promises."[49]

Having reflected on the whole range of attempts to adapt Judaism to modernity, Strauss recalls his intellectual stance in those early years. He was to "wonder whether an unqualified return to Jewish orthodoxy was not both possible and necessary – was not at the same time the solution to the problem of the Jew lost in the non-Jewish modern world and the only course compatible with sheer consistency or intellectual probity."[50] Those early notions about returning to orthodoxy seem to have arisen from the encounter with the work of Martin Buber and Franz Rosenzweig. Their philosophical attempts at rejuvenating biblical faith implied a "qualified return to revelation" as Strauss maintained, insofar as they treated the relationship of reason and revelation still within the confines of modern philosophy. In the face of modern philosophy and the ensuing modern weltanschauung, an unqualified return to orthodoxy seemed to be out of the question and Spinoza was the principal witness to this claim. "Orthodoxy could be returned to only if Spinoza was wrong in every respect."[51] In an article entitled "Das Testament Spinozas," which was written in 1932 and accompanied his book on Spinoza, Strauss explicated his reasoning. The modern weltanschauung has become doubtful and the foundations laid out by Hobbes and Descartes require critical examination in themselves. Spinoza's critique of the Law depends on the grounding of modern philosophy. "If these fundamental ideas have become doubtful, then Spinoza's criticism of the Law has also become doubtful and, consequently, it also has become doubtful whether he can be considered a teacher of Judaism."[52] Being one

---

48 Strauss, *Spinoza's Critique*, 6.     49 Strauss, *Classical Political Rationalism*, 233.
50 Leo Strauss *Spinoza's Critique*, 15.     51 Ibid., 15.
52 Leo Strauss, "Das Testament Spinozas," *Bayerische Israelische Gemeindezeitung* 8, no. 21 (1932), 322–26, 324.

of the Nietzschean "good Europeans," Spinoza broke with Judaism without becoming a Christian. He maintained "neutrality towards the Jewish
nation" and supported the "assimilationist" solution of the Jewish problem
more than the "Zionist" one which he had also discussed.

   This contestation must be seen in conjunction with the specific situation
of German-Jewish scholarship. The liberal Jewry founded the "Science of
Judaism," the historical-critical study of Jewish heritage by Jews. It was the
Jewish variety of the previously described empirical sciences of man and, in
particular, of German historicism. This science of Judaism purported a *Bibelwissenschaft* (Biblical sciences) that was incompatible with any theological
conception of biblical history: "The atheism of today's Biblical sciences is
evident," wrote Strauss in 1925.[53] Strauss's study of Spinoza was commis-
sioned by the *Akademie für die Wissenschaft des Judentums* and the subject matter of the research was to be the establishment of modern biblical sciences
in terms of a special discipline that treats the Bible like any other object in
accordance with the methods of *Geisteswissenschaft*. However, Strauss shifts
the focus of the investigation to the premises of Spinoza and shows that
there is no "unconditional" science (*voraussetzungslose Wissenschaft*) of the
Bible since it is premised by the critique of revelation in particular and critique of religion in general that transforms the Scripture into an inter-
pretable literary document of a purely human making. In this respect the
science of Judaism operated on the rational concepts of *Kulturwissenschaft*
and *Geisteswissenschaft*. It was this "atheistic" implication of the science of
Judaism that made Strauss adopt a critical appraisal of the theoretical and
methodological paradigm of modern *Kulturwissenschaft* and *Geisteswissenschaft*. They historicize religion, degrading it to an ingredient of "culture," "spirit," or "life" in terms of weltanschauung, and direct their
scientific efforts toward achieving a synthesis of religion and philosophy that
would in itself be the embodiment of the rational and empirical science
dealing with culture and history respectively.

   Modern *Bibelwissenschaft* emerged from the struggle of enlightenment
against orthodoxy. Although enlightenment was not able to refute orthodoxy, it did circumvent it by creating the world of modern culture that excluded orthodoxy on the grounds of its incompatibility with the scientific
weltanschauung of modern rationalism. Strauss's critical reading of Spinoza
proved to him that even a powerful philosopher like Spinoza could not refute orthodoxy on its own terms, as Strauss was to explain in his later writing. "Philosophy, the quest for evident and necessary knowledge, rests itself

53 Leo Strauss, "Biblische Geschichte und Wissenschaft," *Jüdische Rundschau* 30, no. 88 (1924),
    744–45, 745.

on an unevident decision, or an act of will just as faith does."[54] To the extent that the rationalist assault on orthodoxy was successful, it was based on belief "and, being based on belief, is fatal to any philosophy." In this sense, however, rational philosophy was theoretically self-destructive and Strauss began "to wonder whether the self-destruction of reason was not the inevitable outcome of modern rationalism."

This self-destruction of reason becomes evident when the enlightenment loses its scientific basis by turning into modern "idealism" and discovering the aesthetics of human creativity and historicity of the human world. This modern idealism proclaims the relativity of all interpretations of the world and throws open the door for rehabilitating the premodern "natural world view" that is defined by the Bible[55] and "the premodern Rationalism, especially Jewish medieval rationalism and its classical (Aristotelian and Platonic) foundation."[56]

It should be noted that, from this point of view, the "Jewish problem" involved the fundamental issue of human philosophy versus divine revelation, a question that could never be solved by political or human means as modern rationalism insinuated. It is but "the most manifest symbol of the human problem as a social or political problem."[57] The conflict between philosophy and revelation reflects the irreversible dualism in man, the dualism of deed and speech, of action and thought that is part of man's constitution. The human solution to this conflict would imply the creation of a society that is free of contradictions, and that is beyond human capacity.[58]

Strauss's analysis of the Jewish problem had to be generalized once a position was found that would allow bringing modernity into focus as a project of self-destructive rationalism in its entirety. This required a change of orientation that reflects the possibility of a return to premodern philosophy. The confrontation between modern rationalism as the origin of the present and medieval rationalism raises the serious question as to which one of the two rationalisms is the true one. In Strauss's scholarly *Philosophie und Gesetz*, preclassical rationalism "develops in the course of the study . . . from a mere instrument used to recognize more clearly the peculiarities of modern rationalism to the criterion against which modern rationalism is measured and proven to be a pretense of rationalism." Therefore, Strauss draws the conclusion: "For that very reason the obvious attempt to consider the self-recognition of the present as a necessary and meaningful endeavor gains a

---

54 Ibid., 29.    55 Leo Strauss, *Philosophie und Gesetz* (Berlin, 1935), 22–23.
56 Strauss, *Spinoza's Critique,* 31.    57 Ibid., 6.
58 Leo Strauss, "The Mutual Influence of Theology and Philosophy," *Independent Journal of Philosophy* 3 (1979), 111–18, 111.

surprising justification: The criticism of the present, the criticism of modern rationalism as the critique of modern sophistry is the necessary beginning, the constant escort and the unmistakable characteristic of the search for truth which is possible in our times."[59] But what does the search for truth in terms of the critique of the present involve? At this point the *problem of the true philosopher* arises, the second key element in Strauss's intellectual biography. It is accompanied by a problem that is its twin, the *problem of the scholar*. Once a return to premodern philosophy is contemplated, a new understanding of philosophizing under modern conditions comes into sight: the ascent from the second unnatural cave of modern worldview to the primary natural cave of the City by means of historical learning.

Bearing in mind the classic representation of the natural difficulties involved in philosophizing, in other words, the Platonic allegory of the cave, one can say that today we are in a second, much deeper cave than the fortunate ignorant persons with which Socrates was concerned. We need history first of all to reach the cave from which Socrates can lead us to the light. We need preparatory instruction – something the Greeks didn't need – that is, precisely learning by reading.[60]

In *Philosophie und Gesetz* Strauss once again explains the purpose and the context of his enterprise. The enlightenment critique of tradition was radicalized by Nietzsche to a critique of the very principles of biblical and Greek traditions. Consequently the original understanding of those principles is again possible.

For that reason and for that reason only is it justifiable and necessary to "historicize" philosophy: only the history of philosophy will make it possible for us to climb from the second "unnatural" cave, into which we fell less as a result of tradition itself than due to the tradition of polemics against tradition, to the first natural cave, which is illustrated in Plato's allegory and is the place from where philosophy can pursue its original purpose of reaching the light.[61]

The Platonic simile of the cave – understood differently at different times – was supposed to express Strauss's central philosophical concern:

There were always people who were not merely exponents of the society, or of any society, but who successfully endeavored to leave "the cave." It is those people, and those people only, whom we still call philosophers, lovers of the truth about "the whole," and not merely about "the whole historical process."[62]

59 Strauss, *Philosophie und Gesetz,* 9–10.
60 Leo Strauss, "Review of Julius Ebbinghaus's *Ueber die Fortschritte der Metaphysik,"* *Deutsche Literaturzeitung,* no. 52 (Dec. 27, 1931), col. 2451–53, here 2453.
61 Ibid., 14.
62 Strauss, "Persecution and Writing," 503; Strauss, "On a New Interpretation of Plato's Political Philosophy," *Social Research* 13, no. 3 (Sept. 1946), 326–67 and 354–55; Strauss, *Natural Right and History* (Chicago, 1953), 12; Strauss, *Political Philosophy,* 32 and 92; Strauss, *Classical Political Rationalism,* 68 and 179; Strauss, *The City and Man* (Chicago, 1964), 128.

The reorientation implied in Strauss's turn to premodern rationalism begins with reopening the quarrel between the moderns and the ancients, always against the background of the "Jewish problem." Strauss discovers the potential for philosophy in the true sense of the meaning, that is, Platonic philosophy, in medieval Jewish and Islamic philosophy.[63] Whereas philosophy was recognized in the medieval Christian world, albeit at the price of the imposition of a strict ecclesiastical supervision, the "situation of the Jewish-Islamic world resembles . . . its situation in classical Greece. The precarious situation of philosophy . . . guaranteed, or necessitated, its private character, and therewith a higher degree of inner freedom."[64] Since the problem of the true philosopher, that is, the premodern philosopher, unfolds within the context of the Jewish problem, Strauss's understanding of classical philosophy was intrinsically bound up with the medieval Jewish and Islamic interpretation of classical philosophy. It is hardly surprising that Strauss depicts Fârâbi as the utmost model of a Platonic philosopher. Fârâbi reveals himself as the true Platonist: He is not concerned with the historical (accidental) truth, since he is exclusively interested in the philosophic (essential) truth. "Only because public speech demands a mixture of seriousness and playfulness, can a true Platonist present the serious teaching in a historical, and hence playful, garb." A decisive criterion for qualifying as a Platonist is "his private, and truly original and individual understanding of the necessarily anonymous truth."[65] Many commentators think that this exposition of the true Platonist was meant as a self-description of Strauss. But that does not seem to be the whole truth, because, before we begin the Socratic ascent from the cave to the sun, we need somebody to lead us back to our natural ignorance of the commonsense world, that is, somebody who retrieves us from the lapsed world of modern rationalism, from the "second 'unnatural' cave."[66]

I know that I am only a scholar. But I know also that most people who call themselves philosophers are mostly, at best, scholars. The scholar is radically dependent on the work of the great thinkers, of men who faced the problems without being overpowered by any authority. The scholar is cautious: methodical not bold. He does not become lost to our sight in, to us, inaccessible heights and mists, as the great thinkers do . . . the scholar becomes possible through the fact that the great thinkers disagree. Their disagreement creates the possibility for us to reason about their differences – to wonder which of them is more likely to be right.[67]

63 Strauss, *Philosophie und Gesetz* (Berlin, 1935), 68–86.
64 Strauss, *Classical Political Rationalism,* 222–23.
65 Leo Strauss, "Fârâbi's Plato," in *Louis Ginzberg Jubilee Volume* (New York, 1945), 357–97, 376–77.
66 Strauss, *Philosophie und Gesetz* (Berlin, 1935), 14.
67 Strauss, *Classical Political Rationalism,* 29–30.

Stressing the same argument, Strauss insists that "the good man in the Platonic sense is the philosopher." And he adds: "It goes without saying that the philosopher is not an individual like myself, or like other professors of political philosophy or of philosophy *tout court* or *tout long.*"[68] "We can not be philosophers, but we can love philosophy! We can try to philosophize." Yet, philosophizing in the Platonic sense is beyond our powers. The philosopher's quest for wisdom sets a standard for our love of philosophy, but we fall short of the philosopher's excellence.

> [Our] philosophizing consists at any rate primarily and in a way chiefly in listening to the conversation between the great philosophers or, more generally and more cautiously, between the great minds, and therefore in studying the great books. The greatest minds to whom we ought to listen are by no means exclusively the greatest minds of the West. It is merely an unfortunate necessity which prevents us from listening to the greatest minds of India and of China: we do not understand their languages, and we can not learn all languages.[69]

The implication of this addition is interesting, because it makes philosophizing, dependent on the language requirements for scholarship that had to be met by any qualified practitioner of German *Geisteswissenschaft.* You have to have a reading knowledge of the language used by the great minds in order to be able to listen to them. Paul Oskar Kristaller, who was instrumental in transforming German *Geistesgeschichte* into an American history of ideas, underscores this technical requirement of scholarly philosophizing:

> It should be obvious to every philosopher, but apparently it is not, that the only basis for any responsible treatment of the history of philosophy are the primary sources, that is, the writings of the philosophers, in the original languages in which they were composed. These are the texts and documents that constitute the evidence by which any assertion about the philosopher must be tested. Reliance on secondary sources is completely inadmissible, but it is frequent even in published papers.[70]

Strauss's definition of the scholar was derived from Heidegger's distinction between the scholar and the thinker, but Strauss changed the original connotation of this distinction, indicating that Heidegger was a great thinker but not a philosopher in the true sense of the word. The true scholar, on the other hand, is not just a historian of philosophy but a guide to the world of natural understanding by means of historical scholarship:

> To grasp the natural world as a world that is radically prescientific or prephilosophic, one has to go back behind the first emergence of science or philosophy . . . the information that classical philosophy supplies about its origins suffices, especially, if this

---

68 Ibid., 182.    69 Leo Strauss, *Liberalism Ancient and Modern* (New York, 1968), 7.
70 Paul O. Kristaller, "History of Philosophy and History of Ideas," *Journal of the History of Philosophy* 2 (1964), 1–14, 6–7.

information is supplemented by consideration of the most elementary premises of the Bible, for reconstructing the essential character of the 'natural world.'[71]

Like Nietzsche, Heidegger was a great thinker, and both exemplify the crisis of the West in grand style. Heideggerian "existentialism is the reaction of serious men to their own relativism," it articulates the situation of a "liberal democracy which has become uncertain of itself or of its future. Existentialism belongs to the decline of Europe."[72]

Heidegger carried the self-refutation of modern rationalism to the extreme, that is, to disclosing its self-destructive effects on philosophy, politics, and morality. Moreover, Heidegger proved to Strauss that basing the *Weltanschauungsphilosophie* on the human condition, turning to philosophical anthropology, was no way out. This view separated Strauss from the broad intellectual movement in Germany, which had as its fundaments the quest for philosophical anthropology (Edmund Husserl, Ernst Cassirer, Georg Misch, Helmuth Plessner, Karl Löwith, Karl Jaspers, Max Scheler, Erich Voegelin, and Martin Heidegger). It was the quest for an interpretative self-assertion in light of empirical knowledge about ourselves. The concept of philosophical anthropology was to weld anew the philosophical to the empirical. For Strauss philosophical anthropology lacked the very essence of philosophy: "You do not take the simple sense of philosophy literally enough," Strauss writes to Löwith:

philosophy is the attempt to replace opinions about the whole with genuine knowledge of the whole. For you, philosophy is nothing but the self-understanding or self-interpretation of man, and, that means, naturally of historically conditioned man, if not of the individual. That is, speaking Platonically, you reduce philosophy to description of the interior decoration of the respective cave, of the cave (historical existence), which then can no longer be seen as a cave.[73]

The scholar prepares the way for philosophy: "We agree that today we need historical reflection." Historical reflection, that is, a nonhistoricist approach to understanding the thinkers of the past, is claimed to be "an unavoidable means for the overcoming of modernity. One cannot overcome modernity with modern means," but only by "the way of thought of natural understanding." To the extent that those instruments of natural reason have been lost, we have to learn them from the ancients.[74]

Historical reflection as a means for overcoming modernity evolves from "true historical understanding" and it avoids the fallacies of historicism in

71 Strauss, *Natural Right and History*, 79–80.   72 Strauss, *Classical Political Rationalism*, 36, 39.
73 Leo Strauss to Karl Löwith, Aug. 20, 1946, "Correspondence Concerning Modernity," *Independent Journal of Philosophy* 4 (1983), 111.
74 Ibid., 107.

that it "understands the thought of the past exactly as it understood itself" and does not interpret the past in terms of the present whatever those may be.[75] Strauss's emphasis on "the essentially ministerial element of interpretation proper which is concerned with understanding the thought of someone else as he meant it" involves a methodological postulate that is not completely out of tune with the hermeneutic paradigm of German *Geisteswissenschaft* and its primary subject matter, that is, the art of understanding written manifestations of life.[76] In this regard in particular Strauss remained true to the original intention of hermeneutics since he maintained his commitment to the exegesis of the literary legacy of the past and present.

Strauss, however, asserts that there is only one way of understanding an author as he understood himself. Historical objectivity is ensured solely on account of the possibility of reaching this understanding, since it liberates the past from the arbitrary impositions of modern subjectivism that by definition do not address the question of truth contained in an author's text. Thus, the hermeneutic project serves a philosophical purpose, as mentioned previously, which aims to overcome the destructive force of relativism by restoring the sense for the fundamental problems of human existence.

History, that is, concern with the past as thought of the past, takes on philosophical significance if there are good reasons for believing that we can learn something of utmost importance from the thought of the past which we cannot learn from our contemporaries. History takes on philosophical significance for men living in an age of intellectual decline. Studying the thinkers of the past becomes essential for men living in an age of intellectual decline because it is the only practical way in which they can recover a proper understanding of fundamental problems. Given such conditions, history has the further task of explaining why the proper understanding of the fundamental problems has become lost in such a manner that the loss presents itself at the outset as progress. . . . Historicism sanctions the loss, or the oblivion, of the natural horizon of human thought by denying the permanence of fundamental problems. It is the existence of that natural horizon which makes possible "objectivity" and therefore in particular "historical objectivity."

Beyond the cognitive aspect of the scholarly activity, an existential dimension materializes to the extent that true historical reflection brings about a profound intellectual change in the scholar himself.

He embarks on a journey whose end is hidden from him. He is not likely to return to the shores of his time as exactly the same man who departed from them. His criticism may very well amount to a criticism of present day thought from the point of view of the thought of the past.[77]

---

75  Strauss, *Classical Political Rationalism*, 208–9.
76  Leo Strauss and H. G. Gadamer, April 14, 1961, "Correspondence Concerning *Wahrheit und Methode*," *Independent Journal of Philosophy* 2 (1978), 5–12, 11.
77  Strauss, " 'Collingwood's Philosophy of History," 583–84.

At this point, a brief additional remark seems to be required concerning Strauss's much-maligned suggestion of distinguishing between the esoteric and exoteric teachings of a thinker. It connects the hermeneutical problem with sociological considerations on the one hand and the distinction between the scholar and the philosopher on the other hand. Since Strauss neglected to keep apart the different aspects inherent in his argument, it occasionally lacks consistency. First, there is the sociological contestation that the antagonism between independent thinking and the socially dominant views in all societies at all times affect the writings of important thinkers because they have to minimize the risk of some type of persecution by employing a "peculiar technique of writing." The ensuing "peculiar type of literature in which the truth about all crucial things is presented exclusively between the lines" demands the specific interpretative art of reading between the lines in order to fulfill the requirements of hermeneutical scholarship.[78] Second, the true philosopher is a special and somewhat different case: According to Strauss it follows from "the original meaning of philosophy" that philosophers "distinguish between the true teaching as the esoteric teaching and the socially useful teaching as the exoteric teaching; whereas the exoteric teaching is meant to be easily accessible to every reader, the esoteric teaching discloses itself only to very careful and well-trained readers after long, and concentrated study."[79]

While the relationship between persecution and the art of writing is a universal phenomenon, the dualism of esotericism and exotericism emerges from the true philosopher's role in political society; that is, it pertains exclusively to the world of the natural cave. Interpreting Leo Strauss may require some reading between the lines, but, since he understood himself as the true scholar, there is no reason to assume that he ever claimed the true philosopher's privilege of an esoteric teaching, which would, by the way, be utterly pointless under the conditions of the second cave.

Once the scholar has led us from the second, "unnatural" cave to the cave of natural understanding, the philosopher can take over.

The scholar brings the specifics of the "cave" into focus. The cave encapsulates human existence in society, or to put it more accurately, in *political* society. The scholarly restoration of classical rationalism, which Strauss traces back to a reconstructed historical Socrates (a hermeneutical construct in itself), teaches us that philosophical life, self-knowledge, unaided by divine revelation and knowledge of the eternal order of the whole – presupposes the experience of the political. While pre-Socratic philosophy searched for

78 Strauss, "Persecution and Writing," 491.    79 Strauss, *Political Philosophy*, 227, 222.

the whole in nature, Socrates, "concerned, as every other philosopher with the whole," realized:

that the human things are the key to the whole. . . . The recognition by philosophy of the fact that the human race is worthy of some seriousness is the origin of political philosophy or political science. If this recognition is to be philosophic, however, this must mean that the political things, the merely human things, are of decisive importance for understanding nature as a whole.[80]

For this reason, Strauss argues that:

philosophy, being an attempt to rise from opinion to science, is necessarily related to the sphere of opinion as its essential starting-point, and hence to the political sphere. Therefore the political sphere is bound to advance into the focus of philosophic interest as soon as philosophy starts to reflect on its own doings. To understand fully its own purpose and nature, philosophy has to understand its essential starting-point, and hence the nature of political things.[81]

This introduces the fourth and final key element of Strauss's philosophical project, namely, the "problem of politics." In a discussion of Carl Schmitt's notion of the political, Strauss came to the conclusion that the modern world, which is determined by rationalism and liberalism, negates the political. Strauss radicalizes Schmitt's position, adding his own existential distinction between modern and ancient thought to it. The world without politics (the second, unnatural cave) is a world without seriousness, without morality – a world of divertissement. The quest for the right, the good, and the just would become irrelevant; in other words, man would abdicate his humanity. Strauss agrees with Schmitt by thinking through his arguments. Schmitt's critique of liberalism still stays within the confines of liberalism in that Schmitt's main authority of political thinking is in truth a promoter of liberal apoliticism, namely, Hobbes.[82] Hobbes laid the foundations of liberalism. He rejected the traditional assumption of political philosophy that man is by nature a political or social animal. He accepted the Epicurean view "that man is by nature or originally an apolitical, and even an asocial animal, as well as its premise that the good is fundamentally identical with the pleasant. But he uses this apolitical view for a political purpose. He gives that apolitical view a political meaning." By instilling the spirit of political idealism into the hedonist tradition, Hobbes created political hedonism, "a doctrine which has revolutionized human life everywhere on a scale never yet approached by any other teach-

80 Strauss, *Classical Political Rationalism*, 132, 126.    81 Strauss, *Political Philosophy*, 92.
82 See Leo Strauss, "Anmerkungen zu Carl Schmitt, Der Begriff des Politischen," in Heinrich Meier, *Carl Schmitt, Leo Strauss und 'Der Begriff des Politischen'* (Stuttgart, 1988).

ing."[83] According to Strauss, Hobbes who was replaced in the later writings by Machiavelli, epitomized the apoliticism of the second, unnatural cave.

The return to the natural cave, the City, was Strauss's first step in his efforts to reconstruct classical rationalism. Once the case of the political community is restated, however, the distinction between political life and philosophical life forces itself upon the members of the political community. A precarious balance must be maintained between the few persons who are able to follow a philosophical life and the many people committed to leading the life of a normal citizen. Modeled on the Islamic understanding of philosophy, this balance is understood in terms of a strict separation of philosophical knowledge and social opinion, esoteric and exoteric teaching. True philosophizing requires the restitution of the political. Politics and philosophy, the citizen or statesman and the philosopher are mutually interdependent: At the outset, the philosopher is a person determined "to settle those political controversies which are of a fundamental and typical character in the spirit not of the partisan but of the good citizen, and with a view to such an order as would be most in accordance with the requirements of human excellence." In the course of this activity, the ulterior, more fundamental questions concerning the nature of human excellence and the best political order need to be raised, but this would transcend the domain of common opinion. Finally, the philosopher:

is ultimately compelled to transcend not merely the dimension of . . . political opinion, but the dimension of political life as such; for he is led to realize that the ultimate aim of political life cannot be reached by political life, but only by a life devoted to contemplation, philosophy. This finding is of crucial importance for political philosophy, since it determines the limits set to political life, to all political action and all political planning.[84]

Philosophy delineates the essential limitation of the political by opening the transcendental dimension of the transhistorical and transpolitical. Therefore, philosophy, or the transpolitical, presupposes the political.

Conversely, the political owes its dignity to the transpolitical, to philosophy: "the transpolitical, the supra-political – the life of the mind in contradiction to political life – comes into sight only as the limit of the political."[85] "Man is more than the citizen of the city. Man transcends the city only by what is best in him. . . . Man transcends the city only by pursuing true happiness, not by pursuing happiness however understood."[86] The esoteric teaching of the philosopher is directed at the very few who are capable of philosophical life, exoteric or public teaching educates citizens

83 Strauss, *Natural Right and History,* 169.     84 Strauss, *Political Philosophy,* 90–91.
85 Strauss, *Classical Political Rationalism,* 161–62.     86 Strauss, *City and Man,* 49.

on the fundamental political questions so as to keep the City, the necessary and sufficient condition of philosophy, in good order.

Once modern man becomes aware that he is in the second, unnatural cave – and the crisis brought upon him by the self-destructive power of modern rationalism forces upon him this awareness – the way is paved for restituting the City.

Strauss himself occasionally seems to suggest that the best regime in the classical sense is dependent on the city-state.

In any case, I assert that the polis – as it has been interpreted by Plato and Aristotle, a surveyable, urban, morally serious (*spoudaia*) society, based on an agricultural economy, in which the gentry rule – is *morally-politically* the most reasonable and most pleasing.[87]

Certainly the concept of the City is not compatible with the universal and homogeneous state that would be the end of philosophy and politics, because the resulting perfection of modernity, the universal and finite tyrant, would establish a coercive order that deprives man of his humanity.

But there is a middle course if we study the philosophical concept of the City: restoring the fundament of liberal democracy by returning to the two roots of Western civilization, the biblical and the philosophical. The core of Western civilization rests in the conflict between the biblical and the philosophical notion of the good life. "The very life, of the Western civilization is the life between two codes, a fundamental tension."[88] The West derives its vitality from this fundamental constitution.

The Western tradition does not allow a final solution of the fundamental contradiction, a society without contradiction. As long as there will be a Western world, there will be theologians who distrust philosophers, and there will be philosophers who are annoyed by the theologians. While rallying around the flag of the Western tradition, let us beware of the danger that we be charmed or bullied into a conformism which would be the inglorious end of the Western tradition.[89]

The Straussian philosophical project is to be understood as a restitution of the historical form of Western civilization, that is, the city of man set against the modern project of the universal and tyrannical state, which aims to eliminate the city as well as man.

87 Leo Strauss and Karl Löwith, Aug. 20, 1946, "Correspondence Concerning Modernity," 113.
88 Strauss, *Classical Political Rationalism,* 170.      89 Ibid., 73.

# 6

# Leo Strauss and Martin Heidegger: Greek Antiquity and the Meaning of Modernity

HORST MEWES

At one point in his life, Leo Strauss felt compelled to take an "explicit" stand toward Martin Heidegger.[1] The reasons were a mixture of the personal and the philosophical: As a young university student, Strauss was deeply impressed by Heidegger's "seriousness, profundity, and concentration in the interpretation of philosophic texts."[2] There "had been no such phenomenon in the world since Hegel."[3] Strauss gradually became aware of the "breath of the revolution of thought" prepared by Heidegger.[4] Moreover, he came to sympathize with crucial facets of that revolution. Increasingly, Strauss also thought in terms of a "crisis of the West," rather than subscribing to the pervasive belief in Western progress and enlightenment. Like Heidegger, Strauss recognized the self-destructive nature of modern rationality and the philosophical limits of modern natural science. And like Heidegger, he returned to Greek antiquity to gain the vantage point from which to properly comprehend the essence of modernity.

It is in their respective understandings or interpretations of Greek philosophy, however, that the profound divergence between Strauss and Heidegger most clearly emerges. To put their differences in a nutshell: Strauss's lifework consisted of a "return to classical *political* philosophy" (emphasis added), that was both "necessary and tentative or experimental."[5] Heidegger, however, in Strauss's judgment "never believed in the possibility of an ethics" and "left no room for political philosophy" in his thought.[6] Strauss was furthermore convinced that Heidegger's despicable, never fully retracted sympathies with the Nazi movement had to be understood not as a personal political opinion but viewed in "their intimate connection with

---

1 Leo Strauss, *Studies in Platonic Political Philosophy* (Chicago, 1983), 30.
2 Ibid., 28.    3 Ibid.    4 Ibid.
5 Leo Strauss, *The City and Man* (Chicago, 1964), 11.
6 Leo Strauss, "An Introduction to Heideggerian Existentialism," in Thomas L. Pangle, ed., *The Rebirth of Classical Political Rationalism* (Chicago, 1989), 36. Also, see Leo Strauss, *Studies in Platonic Political Philosophy,* 30.

the core of his philosophic thought."[7] Consequently, Heidegger's lack of a political philosophy also goes to the very core of his thought.

Strauss sees this core in the fact that Heidegger, in order to understand the essence and origins of modern rationalism and science, and thus modern epistemology, found it necessary to return to "Plato's and Aristotle's question, What is Being?"[8] Heidegger felt compelled to return to the most fundamental question, what it is to be, and by virtue of which any being is said to be. Only in terms of the deepest understanding of being in its highest sense can the differences between ancient and modern scientific reason be adequately identified. Up to this point Strauss would fundamentally agree with Heidegger. According to Strauss, Heidegger differs fundamentally, however, from both Plato's and Aristotle's understanding of being in the highest sense. According to them, "to be in the highest sense means to be *always*," while for Heidegger "to be in the highest sense means to *exist*, that is to say, *to be* in the manner in which man *is*."[9] But man, being mortal, exists in time and essentially makes himself through or becomes his history. Heidegger, in Strauss's view, thus returns to Greek antiquity under the sway of the most radical spirit of modernity, the disposition of the historicism of human existence. Strauss's central dictum had always been that one could only escape the "modern prejudice" if one understood ancient Greek philosophers as they had understood themselves. If Strauss is correct, his return to the Greeks is considerably more radically antimodern than is Heidegger's.

Heidegger would deny this emphatically. To rest with Plato and Aristotle as they understood their own philosophic tasks is to remain within the confines of the modern forgetfulness of truth as being. It is precisely the "metaphysical" rendition of being begun by Plato and Aristotle that made possible modernity in its most radical expression. Plato introduced a notion of "truth" which moved away from its original Greek understanding as the unconcealment of being, and which prepared the modern notion of truth as *techne*. One thus does not escape modernity but merely returns to its origins if one simply attempts to revive Plato and Aristotle. The genuine alternative to modernism is not Strauss's, but Heidegger's return to an understanding of being found prior to Plato among the "pre-Socratics." It is here that one discovers being in its most primordial sense, that is, being as its unconcealment of beings. Heidegger's well-known thesis is that being as unconcealment, *aletheia,* and not the metaphysical rendition of being in terms

---

7 Ibid. Strauss thus agrees with Karl Löwith, whose judgment was confirmed by Heidegger himself in Rome in 1936. Cf. Karl Löwith, *Mein Leben in Deutschland vor und nach 1933* (Frankfurt/Main, 1989), 57. Cf. also the recent elaboration of this view by Richard Wolin, *The Politics of Being. The Political Thought of Martin Heidegger* (New York, 1990).
8 Strauss, *Rebirth of Classical Political Rationalism,* 37.     9 Ibid.

of the eidetic characteristics of being, discloses the adequate quest for being as man's highest essence.[10]

Strauss agrees with Heidegger that Plato and Aristotle, following Socrates, offered a new rendition of the truth of being. Their philosophy is essentially the discovery of nature, or *physis*. According to Strauss, only this new rendition of *physis* made possible political philosophy as an independent branch of philosophy. Thus, political philosophy and its central claim that man is by nature political is indeed dependent upon this new post-Socratic view of nature. This is the case because, as I shall show below, especially the Aristotelian view of nature greatly enhances the significance of the political or "commonsense" understanding of man, ignored by the pre-Socratic exclusive preoccupation with the ultimate cause or principles of being. In returning to the pre-Socratic approach to being, Heidegger loses this philosophic interest in the world of commonsense politics, and it is not at all clear what takes its place.[11] What in Heidegger's reading is a moving away from the primordial understanding of being is, for Strauss, a movement toward "wisdom," or the insight that the ultimate truth of being is accessible only through its intimations in commonsense opinions. Strauss's vindication of political philosophy is thus, indirectly, also a vindication of philosophy's discovery of nature as a genuine and lasting accomplishment.

Mainly, though, Strauss albeit in a "tentative and experimental" fashion, defends the Aristotelian view of "human nature." He does so with the express acknowledgment (at least in his early book, *Natural Right and History*) that modern science's understanding of nature has made a simple return to Aristotelian complete philosophy of nature impossible.[12] As I shall show below, in his later work Strauss increasingly tended to rely on the "intimation" of the natural in political experience itself, in a self-evident fashion, as the foundation of political science based on "human nature." In other words, political knowledge of human nature is not based on a theory of

---

10 Cf. Martin Heidegger, "Letter on Humanism," in David Farrell Krell, ed., *Martin Heidegger: Basic Writings* (New York, 1977).

11 The Heidegger of *An Introduction to Metaphysics* (first given as lectures in 1935, then reworked and published in 1953), takes the first chorus from the *Antigone* of Sophocles and understands the essence of man exclusively as the "strange, the uncanny (*das Unheimliche*)," who, through violence, goes beyond "the customary, familiar, secure." This, rather than later "metaphysical" definition of man, is the "authentic" Greek definition of man. Regardless of whether this interpretation is acceptable, Heidegger's interpretation stands in significant opposition to Aristotle's and Strauss's emphasis on "moderation," *sophrosyne,* and prudence as essential practical human traits resulting from philosophical wisdom, i.e., moderation. In the same essay, Heidegger also provides a characteristically "modern" interpretation of the "polis" not as "city-state" (which "does not capture the full meaning"), but as "the historical place" in, out, and for which "history happens." Cf. Martin Heidegger, *An Introduction to Metaphysics* (New Haven, Conn., 1959), 146–53.

12 Cf. Leo Strauss, *Natural Right and History* (Chicago, 1953), 8.

metaphysics of nature. Heidegger, in contrast, insists that precisely this metaphysics established the first form of humanism.

For the late Heidegger, there is no pretheoretical, practical knowledge about man.[13] The thought that determines the essence of man is at the same time the highest and primordial mode of *action,* that is, the act which determines all purposes of practical action. The Aristotelian distinction between theoretical and practical reason is already derivative. It is a distinction within the framework of the metaphysical determination of man as "rational animal" and views theoretical reasons from the vantage point of the primacy of human practical action.[14] For Strauss, the important question about Heidegger's thought is what takes the place of political philosophy in the latter's turn to the pre-Socratic mode of thought? If Strauss is indeed correct to say that Heidegger's central thought is modern historicism transformed into the temporality of being, then it would be the latter notion rather than any view intrinsic to pre-Socratic thought that determines Heidegger's substitute for political philosophy.

### STRAUSS'S INTERPRETATION OF THE "SOCRATIC TURN" IN PHILOSOPHY

Strauss's account of the philosophical origins of political philosophy merits a detailed restatement, if for no other reason than that it is an implicit response to Heidegger's understanding of Plato's place in the "history of being." Strauss clearly identifies with Socratic-Platonic philosophy as a critical rejection of certain antecedent types of natural philosophy and myth. Originally, philosophy understood itself to be the pursuit of truth about the whole of being, or nature, and identified this truth with the depiction of its origins, or *arche,* its reigning first principles. According to Plato, the first natural philosophers were characterized by their inability to distinguish between the phenomena of body and soul, or to recognize the importance of soul as a reigning principle in nature as it most obviously was in man.[15] Their inability was intimately related to their disinterest in human affairs, the realm in which soul or the distinction between body and soul first becomes most clearly evident. It is for this reason, among others, that Socrates' focus on the soul entailed a heightened interest in the study of men and their cities.

---

13  Hubert L. Dreyfus convincingly argues that this was not true for the Heidegger of *Being and Time.* There, according to Dreyfus, Heidegger shows that phenomenology "seeks to show that the everyday world is as self-sufficient and self–intelligible as the objects of theory" and accounts for the possibility of theory. But this position necessarily changes when the later Heidegger substitutes hermeneutic phenomenology with "thinking being historically." Cf. Hubert L. Dreyfus, *Being in the World. A Commentary on Heidegger's Being and Time,* div. 1 (Cambridge, Mass., 1991), 122, 127.

14  Cf. Heidegger, "Letter on Humanism."      15  Cf. the discussion of gods in Plato, *Laws,* Book X.

Socrates' celebrated turn toward the study of human affairs did not mean abandoning the study of nature of its first principles, but involved "a new approach to the study of all things. This approach favored the study of human things as such without reducing them to the divine or natural things."[16] The Socratic quest for knowledge begins with what is "first for us," or commonsense experience, the world of authoritative opinions, because every opinion is "based on some awareness, on some perception with the mind's eye, of something." Philosophy is the ascent from opinions to truth, but the opinions are seen to be "fragments of the truth," to be "solicited by the self-subsisting truth," which "all men always divine."[17] Most important, "Socrates implied that disregarding the opinions about the nature of things would amount to abandoning the most important access to reality which we have, or the most important vestiges of the truth which are within reach." This stance implied that the typically modern "universal doubt" of all opinions would lead us, "not into the heart of the truth, but into a void."[18]

Philosophy as the ascent from opinions to truth entails that philosophy "means no longer primarily to discover the roots out of which the completed whole . . . the cosmos, has grown, or to discover the cause which has transformed the chaos into a cosmos, or to perceive the unity which is hidden behind the variety of things or appearances. . . . "[19] To start with the world of opinions is to realize that the whole has a natural articulation, and that the study of everything is a means to understand "what each of the beings is." For "to be" means to "be something" and hence to be different from things that are "something else"; to be means therefore to "be a part." To understand the whole then means to understand all the parts of the whole or the articulation of the whole. If "to be" is to "be something," the being of a thing, or the nature of a thing, is primarily its substance, its "shape" or "form" or "character," as distinguished in particular from that out of which it has come into being."[20] The question of "what is" points to the "eidos of a thing," the shape or character of "idea" of a thing. Thus, the term "eidos" signifies primarily that which is visible to all without any particular effort or what one might call the surface of the things. "The thing itself, the completed thing, cannot be understood as a product of the hidden process leading up to it."[21] Such reflections issue in the general principles that "the problem inherent in the surface of things, and only in the surface of things, is the heart of things."[22]

This study of what is first by nature by way of ascending from what is first for men, being guided by the "fundamental awareness" or intimations of

16 Strauss, *Natural Right and History*, 122.    17 Ibid., 124.    18 Ibid.
19 Ibid., 123.    20 Ibid., 122.    21 Ibid., 123
22 Leo Strauss, *Thoughts on Machiavelli* (Glencoe, Ill., 1958), 13.

truth contained in the opinions of men, seems to have been regarded by Socrates as "a return to sobriety" and "moderation" from the "mania" of his predecessors preoccupied with the investigation of the ultimate roots or cause of Being. For the study of political action, sobriety meant understanding the principles of politics on the basis of the knowledge intrinsic to the active city itself, rather than on the basis of speculation about the first principles of being.[23] Heidegger, on the contrary, viewed Socrates' return to philosophical sobriety as a definition of humanity contrasting man with beings or objects in his "world" rather than with being itself, thus removing man from his essential relation to being. Thus, for Heidegger, Socrates' definition of man does not aim high enough and underestimates the true human essence. On the other hand, by viewing human beings exclusively from the penultimate vantage point of standing in the unconcealment of Being, Heidegger also obviously lacks the "new awakeness, caution and emphasis" associated with the sober wisdom of Socrates.[24]

Socrates' new approach to the understanding of nature leads not only to the insight that human choice, responsibility, and morality can only exist on the "surface" of nature, but also that the problems inherent in human morality lead to the "heart of things." The more we leave the surface and go to the roots and sources of things, the more men appear to be, in Plato's memorable words, the playthings of the gods. As one of the founders of modern science, Francis Bacon, pointed out, as men delve below the surface of nature, in order to effectively submit it to control, men in order to dominate nature will have to obey its laws. From Strauss's perspective, then, it was Aristotle's discovery of "moral virtue" which most clearly established the limited realm at the surface of nature in which men can attain a limited degree of choice and responsibility.

Greek political philosophy articulates knowledge garnered by commonsense insights in everyday political life. It is for this reason that Strauss can call Aristotle's even more clearly than Plato's political thought "nothing other than the fully conscious form of the common sense understanding of political things."[25] However, we must be clear as to what "common sense" denotes. It is in fact knowledge of politics on part of the morally good man, the "well-bred," the gentleman. Only virtuous men can know the moral virtues. Virtues are known by habituation based on knowledge of human character, or the human soul in action. Thus Aristotle's political philosophy or science can also be said to be a description of an unwritten "law" of human conduct recognized by well-bred people everywhere.[26] This unwritten

23 Cf. Leo Strauss, *Natural Right and History*, 123.    24 Strauss, *The City and Man*, 20.
25 Ibid., 12.    26 Ibid., 26.

law is ultimately based on the indubitable experience that soul rules over body, that a hierarchy exists within the soul. To be recognized as such, and to be choiceworthy for its own sake, this unwritten law of conduct need not be "deduced" from reason or from a theoretical account of either human or the whole of nature. To that extent what is commonsense knowledge for gentlemen is "prescientific," in a manner of speaking self-evident, and independent of a theoretical explanation. But in order to be fully elucidated and explained, this commonsense knowledge is in need of a theoretical account of the virtues, depicting them as being according to man's nature, culminating in a science of all "natures" or essences as parts of a whole "cosmos" or universe. But this does not make the commonsense knowledge of practical life a form of theoretical knowledge, or its practical certainty dependent upon the acquisition of certain knowledge about the (elusive) whole. Only under these conditions can the distinction between practical reason and theoretical reason, practical virtues and theoretical virtues, be valid. Heidegger of course does not recognize this validity and instead reverts to the claim that only thinking about being is genuine action.

Still, the pursuit of "absolute" truth or knowledge is a potential danger to the city's essential requirement for "law and order" precisely because it questions and examines its authoritative opinions without being able to guarantee an adequate substitute for practical life's imperatives and prudence. The most renowned example is the examination of justice in Plato's *Republic*. Strauss summarizes his view about the relation between city and philosophy quite succinctly: "Philosophy is the attempt to replace opinion by knowledge; but opinion is the element of the city, hence philosophy is subversive, hence the philosopher must write in such a way that he will improve rather than subvert the city. In other words, the virtue of the philosopher's thought is a certain kind of 'mania' while the virtue of the philosopher's public speech is 'sophrosyne.' Philosophy is as such transpolitical, transreligious, and transmoral, but the city is and ought to be moral and religious"[27] – a revealing summary indeed but obviously sufficient to dismiss any effort to make Strauss into a Machiavellian or immoral anarchist.[28] Strauss is in sympathy with Heidegger's philosophic mania, but denounces his inability to see the need for philosophic prudence, especially if Heidegger's philosophy leads him directly to mistake the politics of National Socialism as a new stage in the manifestation of being. Strauss's

---

27  Cf. Leo Strauss, "A Giving of Accounts: Jacob Klein and Leo Strauss," *The College* (St. John's College Magazine), April 1970, 4.
28  Like the interpretation found in S. B. Drury, "The Esoteric Philosophy of Leo Strauss," *Political Theory* 13, no. 3 (Aug. 1985).

position does entail, however, that philosophy must remain essentially a "private" enterprise, restricted in its public appearances to schools or small circles of philosophic friends. The unrestricted pursuit of truth, in other words, cannot be turned into a paradigm for the "public life" or public freedom of the city in the manner of the "republic of learning." Public enlightenment is impossible. While philosophy is undeniably favored by the freedom of democracies (and democracy in general is obviously more noble than dictatorship), the truly virtuous city would still be considerably closer to the one found in Plato's "laws" than to modern republics.

But that is not all. A city's break with restraining traditions, its unrestrained pursuit of power and glory, together with the encouragement of constant innovation does effect philosophy. The pursuit of philosophy is stimulated by exposure to doubt, paradoxes, problems, practical dilemmas, bold experimentations with the limits of human capacities. Philosophy, in other words, is elicited more by daring innovation and doubt (Athens) than by perennial tranquility and traditionalism (Sparta). However, this also implies that philosophy is more likely to prosper during the periods of tragic decline of the city rather than earlier periods of moral simplicity. True wisdom about human nature and politics is more likely to be accessible to "thinkers who ride a tiger."[29] The overall relation between philosophy and the city, then, is highly ambiguous at best, because what is best for philosophy is not necessarily best for the city.

Clearly, this view of philosophy and its relation to political life requires an underlying "faith in the natural working of the human mind," or faith in the fact that prescientific human reason has access to certain insights or intimations of truth which are the product of nature rather than human effort or science.[30] It implies that human political opinions (and especially opinions about the soul and the gods) reveal "in a manner" the first things, the truth about the whole. The "understanding which is inherent in the city as such," includes, for instance, understanding that the city "sees itself as subject and subservient to the divine."[31] Faith in the natural working of the human mind entails the view that a natural harmony exists between the whole and the human mind, or that man's soul is "somehow all things." It provides faith that the world is the best possible world, that despite its evils men have no right to complain or rebel.[32] This view of philosophy furthermore entails that elementary experiences of the human soul in political life "point to" certain facts about nature as a whole: Natural inequality between men, for instance, is said to point to the inequality pervading nature as a whole. The natural working of the human mind, if we faithfully follow

29 Strauss, *The City and Man*, 230.    30 Strauss, *Natural Rights and History*, 175.
31 Ibid., 190, 241.    32 Ibid., 41.

its pointers, would influence even cosmology, it seems, despite the fact that it is said to be, in Aristotle, at one level "unqualifiedly separable from the quest for the best political order."[33]

Precisely this faith in the natural working of the human mind and faith in common sense was rejected by early modern thinkers like Bacon, Descartes, Machiavelli, and Hobbes. This break with the primary or natural understanding of the whole was seen by some, like Francis Bacon, as the direct reversal of the Socratic subordination of natural philosophy to natural reason and the teleological morality it fosters.[34] And the early moderns proved the fact, Strauss argues, that radical skepticism about the natural mind or the "natural conscience" is based on a "specific moral attitude" that is "independent of the foundation of modern science." It constitutes the "deepest stratum of the modern mind," and is said by Strauss to be ultimately an "anti-theological passion" which was more important to the early modern thinkers than any merely political questions.[35]

### HEIDEGGER'S HISTORY AND POLITICS OF BEING

For Heidegger, all Western ideas of humanism and the most radical modern anthropomorphism based on human control of a totally objectified world had their roots in Plato.[36] Heidegger's equivalent of the "Socratic question" (Strauss) is Platonic philosophy; namely, the inception of the theory of ideas, while also entailing an accentuation of human being, envisions this novel accent on the human not as a gain in sobriety and wisdom, but instead as a fateful, albeit necessary, turning away from essential being. Plato was for Heidegger a fateful "deviation" from the more original thought of Parmenides, Heraclites, and other pre-Socratics. Pre-Platonic thought essentially consisted of "poetic" utterances expressing man's awe and sense of wonder in the presence of being. Man, standing in the presence of being as it discloses itself as "being that is itself" through human language, constitutes for Heidegger something like a primordial phenomenon or "event" for human existence. Plato's theory of truth as ideas moves thought away from this primordial event attending to the unconcealment of being itself. Not that this is merely the responsibility of Plato the thinker, something that can be remedied through a critical revision of this thought. Heidegger's

---

33 Ibid.
34 Cf. Francis Bacon, "Novum Organum," in *The English Philosophers from Bacon to Mill* (New York, 1939), esp. 70.
35 Leo Strauss, *The Political Philosophy of Hobbes* (Chicago, 1952), xiv, 5. Also, see Strauss, *Thoughts on Machiavelli*, 231; Leo Strauss, *What Is Political Philosophy?* (Glencoe, Ill., 1959), 44; Leo Strauss, *Liberalism, Ancient and Modern* (New York, 1968), 201.
36 Martin Heidegger, *Platons Lehre von der Wahrheit* (Bern, 1947). Cf. also "Durch die ganze Geschichte der Philosophie hindurch bleibt Platons Denken in abgewandelten Gestalten massgebend," 49.

analysis of Plato's theory of ideas, focusing exclusively on an interpretation of the "parable of the cave" in the *Republic,* instead regards that theory as an event in the history of being, as a "turning point in the determination of the essence of truth." Plato is said to "submit" himself to a "coercive" change in the essence of truth, a change issuing from a "decision" about the essence of truth "never made by man himself," but actuated by being itself.[37]

That Platonic turning point in the determination of the essence of truth consisted of the fixing of truth not in the unconcealment of being itself, but in the "ideas" of beings. Originally, truth is the rise of the concealed into unconcealment or disclosure, and the bringing into the open of un-concealment is seen as the basic feature of that which is present, or of pres-ence (*Anwesung*). But for Plato, presence (*ousia*) becomes "idea." That is to say, instead of focusing upon the essence of truth as the essence of "uncon-cealment unfolding by virtue of its own essential plenitude," the es-sence of truth is now seen as that which is unconcealed in its appearance, or idea.[38] But if the truth of what is present is essentially disclosed in its idea or appearance, the "manner of viewing this appearance," in fact, the question as the "right and correct viewing of that idea" becomes the cen-tral concept of truth. Correct awareness or perception of the idea, or cor-rectness of the statements and assertions regarding the representation of the idea from now on becomes the standard criterion for all subsequent West-ern nous, thinking or reason.[39] Thus, according to Heidegger, the "place" or location of truth has shifted from that which discloses (that is, being it-self) to the correct mode of rational representation of the disclosed in its appearance or *eidos*. Philosophical truth from now on meant rational rep-resentation of truth as idea. But since "viewing" the ideas transcends the world of shadowy and deceptive sense-experience, philosophy becomes known as metaphysics. Furthermore, since the "idea of ideas," the idea of the good, is identified by Plato as the divine, metaphysics becomes theol-ogy, and god is equated with the cause of all beings. Finally, in meta-physics, man is always placed in the center of all beings, although by no means as the highest being, and in the context of a metaphysical founda-tion is provided with a "human essence." The essence of man can be "an-imal rationale," or eternal soul, or creature of God, or animal *laborans,* or man the technical controller of nature. Always he is "freed" by being to "fulfill" a differently defined "potential."[40]

Whatever the metaphysical essence of man, it turns him toward himself as a being, and away from attentiveness toward the unconcealment of his

37 Heidegger, *Platons Lehre,* 50.    38 Ibid., 41.    39 Ibid., 34, 41, 44.    40 Ibid., 49.

essence by concealed/unconcealed being. This perception of the truth of humanity is necessitated by being itself, by its partial concealment from which issues its partial unconcealment. Thus being itself induces the eventual forgetfulness of being by man. Hence, the unique "event" of man standing in the presence of unconcealed/concealed being is replaced by quite literally the objectification, dogmatization, and routinization of the partially secured truth garnered during the event of being's self-disclosure. Man settles down in the certainty of the "truth," as it were, the "logos" that now gathers for him a world to live in. Heidegger does once assert that this move toward certainty is caused by man's basic insecurity and his need for security in this "worldgame" of being.[41] But this anthropomorphic explanation of man's forgetfulness of being is dropped for the notion of a self-activating history of being as periodic "revelations" of being. In due time, forgetfulness of being and the "absolute objectification" of his world, the great temporal distance from the primordial event of disclosure drive men into the loss of the provenance and their true, premetaphysical, prehumanistic essence.

Thus not the limits of human understanding and human nature, but being itself accounts for man's errors and ignorance. Can being be understood, is its essence accessible to thinking? It is describable at least in terms of the "ontological difference" between being and beings, as well as a basic dualism pervading being itself. That being manifests itself as the conconcealment of the concealed, as the duality of the presencing of what is present, is the dispensation of what the Greeks called *moira*, or fateful apportionment. But being understood as this fateful dispensation is the provenance of "healing" and "raging," of affirmation and negation, the grounds of all human possibilities of "evaluating." Hence, being is the sole source of authentic human standards. Such standards change, however, with the history of being. Human evil or nihilism is attributable to the fact that "nihilation occurs in being itself."[42] The fateful apportionment of being issues in an assignment to man of the healing and the raging, the affirmative and negative, "grace" and "malignancy." Hence, only being "offers a hold for all conduct."[43] As the original Greek attests, assignment is *nomos*, or law. The source of all human law is therefore originally the law of being, as the fateful apportionment of man's assignments. In its disclosure being conceals itself as well, thus providing the source not only of man's law, but also of his inevitable alienation from being. Man's ineluctable estrangement from being is the "evil fate" of being, not to be regarded as a defect or deficiency (*Mangel*), however, since as the simultaneous initiation of Western history it is the "richest and broad-

---

41  Martin Heidegger, *Nietzsche,* 2 vols. (Pfullingen, 1961), II, 380.
42  Heidegger, "Letter on Humanism," 238.    43  Ibid., 239.

est event." Human history is made possible by this evil fate of being, the fact that it dispenses both law and *Irre,* or errancy and the very possibility of going astray. In effect, the epochs of human history, eventuated by periodic disclosures of being, are essentially epochs of error. History is essentially the history of being as man going astray.[44]

Heidegger's thought is thus visibly imbued with a disturbing ambiguity originating in his vision (not, of course, evidence) of the duality of being and extending all the way into his judgments about mundane politics.[45] The ambiguity pervades every judgment he utters and every descriptive statement about the Western crisis. It has its origins in the very heart of being, in its putative graceful malignancy or evil, derived from Heidegger's often quite esoteric interpretations of texts by Parmenides and Heraclites. For Plato and thus for Strauss, for whom evil is necessary as a contrast to good, evil does not have its source in the very heart of being (or the good) itself. In Socrates' parlance, Heidegger's being or god is unfathomably deceptive. Hence being cannot be thought of as pure good or righteousness. Heidegger's thinking shows the consequences. He is on the one hand critical of the extreme course of Western technology and the "abolition of man," the great danger of extreme reification or "*Seinsvergessenheit,*" while simultaneously denying the significance of human judgment. He condemns phenomena only to deny the validity of such condemnations, and subjects man to the inevitable fate of being.

Since Heidegger's vantage point permits no independent commonsense understanding of politics (for which he has nothing but the contempt he reserves for anything not philosophical or "thoughtful"), nor a separate realm of "natural" political life as one manifestation or one realm or beings within being as a whole, all his "political" observations are aspects of the drama of being itself. The earth, the *Irrstern* or erring star, is engulfed in a global struggle for the domination of technology as one disclosure of being. Nowhere is there a place for the discussion and assignment of even the most limited human responsibility, or for closer scrutiny of either politics or the history of Western political thought. Nowhere are we close enough to the level of human action where individual human beings or nations are discernible in terms of character traits and modes of political virtues. In the late Heidegger's world only lone poet-prophets appear as recognizably human. In the often passionate description of their tranquillity (*Gelassenheit*), their putative courage, their steadfast exposure to utter uncertainty, we discover Heideg-

---

44  Ibid. Cf. also Martin Heidegger, *Early Greek Thinking* (San Francisco, 1975), esp. the essay on *moira* and *aletheia.*

45  For the danger intrinsic to Heidegger's talk about the "darkness" of being and its concealment, see esp. Werner Marx, *Heidegger and the Tradition* (Evanston, Ill., 1971). In the conclusion, Marx assesses the "extremely perilous character of Heidegger's concept of truth."

ger's version of the hero. The hero is the poetic thinker, like Hölderlin, whose language breaks through the destiny of global technical domination, and who by standing in the presence of being receives its "nod" (*Wink*), to be passed along to humanity at large. The poet becomes messenger not of God but of the being from which all gods issue. But even this image of the poetic prophet of being is relinquished by the late Heidegger. Thinking becomes utterly impractical and inconsequential. Neither specially dedicated nations, like the "outstanding metaphysical" Germany of the 1930s nor the poet constitute a link between highest thought and life. At the end, being itself retains within itself all intimations of a new beginning. At best, Heidegger leaves contemporary man with a sense of anticipation of a new dispensation of fate, a state of suspense "with all the strangeness, darkness, insecurity that attend a true beginning."[46] Only the gods can save us.

Strauss suggests that Heidegger's being could be described "superficially," but "not altogether misleadingly" as a "synthesis of Platonic ideas and the biblical God: It is as impersonal as the Platonic ideas and as elusive as the biblical God."[47] Certainly much of Heidegger's concept of being as self-activated unconcealment is reminiscent of revelation. It differs from religious notions of revelation, however, in that it eliminates the distinction between nature and revelation of the spirit or word of God by making nature, or being as *physis,* itself revelatory. With the disappearance of the distinction between nature and revelation, stressed in the work of Strauss, disappears also the traditional distinction between reason and faith, between investigation of nature by natural reason and knowledge of God through faith in his revealed word. The traditional distinction between thinking and faith is blurred by such claims that evidence for the history of being and the necessity of thinking about being is the admission (*Eingeständnis*) of its ultimate dignity. There is no "explanation" (*Erklärung*) for the history of being's unconcealments. Is such admission or *Eingeständnis* beyond explanation or *Erklärung* not a mode of faith?[48] Thinking is identified with "thanking," and the unceasing questioning of being is named "the piety of thought."[49] Thinking as the poetic meditation of the puzzle of being is called thinking about the holy, the noble, and the exalted (*das Edle*).[50] For Heidegger, thinking is intended to bridge the traditionally assumed distinction between natural reason and faith in revelation. Thinking is faith, and faith is thought.

46 Heidegger, *Introduction to Metaphysics,* esp. 39.
47 Strauss, *The Rebirth of Classical Political Rationalism,* 46. Strauss is providing an interpretation that takes seriously the early Heidegger's claim to be "a Christian theologian." Cf. Hans-Georg Gadamer, *Heideggers Wege* (Tübingen, 1983), esp. essays 13 and 14.
48 Heidegger, *Nietzsche,* 485.    49 Heidegger, *Basic Writings,* 317.
50 Martin Heidegger, *Holzwege* (Frankfurt/Main, 1957), 343.

The question remains, however, of how and what we are to think of the claim that the holy and exalted dispenses the "evil fate" or man's forgetfulness of being, and yet at the point of greatest danger to man lets the "ways into the saving power" shine brightly?[51] Being's deceptive power, its secretiveness or elusiveness is simultaneously its saving grace. Strauss calls such statements "fantastic hopes, more to be expected from visionaries than from philosophers."[52] And indeed, Heidegger's very concept of being turns what is traditionally in the aftermath of Aristotle called politics into prophesy of salvation at the moment of highest *Not* or need. But the concealment of being, its unfathomable playful hiding leaves us in utter uncertainty as to the substance of our "new" future fateful dispensation. Yet, modern man, aware of Western history as merely one epoch in the (potentially eternal?) history of being, finds himself in a substantially different position compared to all his predecessors. For only he knows, in part thanks to Heidegger's privileged position in history, that being's next fateful dispensation for man will contain not only a new potential of humanity but also new evil and ultimate estrangement from being. Is Heidegger's vision the ultimate mode of skepticism superimposed upon a pre-Platonic notion of fate? We are the first to know in advance that our next fate will be a deception in disguise. There is only the solace that Heidegger's curious post-Hegelian and post-Nietzschean fusion of the traditional distinctions between temporality and eternity, fate and freedom, thought and action, reason and revelation into the spurious unity of a dual being provides no reason why this amalgamation of thought should be acceptable except through the acknowledgment (*Eingeständnis*) of the "primordial dignity" of this maliciously graceful being.

Strauss, too, is ultimately concerned with the relation between reason and revelation in Western culture. The premodern disposition Strauss explores as antidote to modernity includes two essential elements, namely, knowledge of the presuppositions of classic philosophy, as well as "the most elementary premise of the Bible."[53] Furthermore, Strauss is convinced that "the bible sets forth the demands of morality and religion in their purest and most intransigent form."[54] Thus, a "return to the roots" of Western civilization is a return to the problem posed by the opposition between the highest forms of life demanded by Greek philosophy and the revelation of the Bible.[55]

The dilemma thus posed can be summarized as follows. Greek philosophy and the Bible make fundamentally different claims as to what is high-

---

51  Ibid., 317.       52  Leo Strauss, *Studies in Platonic Political Philosophy*, 334.
53  Strauss, *Natural Right and History*, 80; *Thoughts on Machiavelli*, 12.       54  Ibid., 133.
55  The following account is based primarily on Leo Strauss, "Progress or Return?" in *The Rebirth of Classical Political Rationalism*, 227–70.

est and most necessary for man. Although both call the highest "wisdom," they differ dramatically as to what constitutes such wisdom. For Greek philosophy, it is *theoria,* or contemplation of truth insofar as it is accessible to unassisted human reason. This pursuit of wisdom, since it is an unending endeavor, may never lead to providing practical guidance for human action. It may culminate in the concept of an impersonal god as "thought thinking thought," located beyond all concerns for human justice and interference in human affairs. The Bible's notion of wisdom, on the contrary, is pious and humble love of an omnipotent, personal but unknowable God, who has revealed His truth to man. Whereas the philosopher lives beyond fear, trembling, and hope, beyond tragedy and comedy, the man of God lives in fear, trembling, and hope. And whereas for biblical man the independent and unrestricted pursuit of knowledge constitutes a form of rebellion against God, for the Greek philosopher such pursuit of knowledge is man's highest way of participating in divine reason.

According to Strauss, decisive for the understanding of the roots of Western culture is the fact that neither one of these alternative ways of life can be disproven by its opposite. The Bible cannot on the basis of revelation disprove the possibility of the life of contemplation, nor can philosophical reason by mere reasoning alone disprove the possibility of revelation and thus the life of loving faith. In order to disprove the possibility of revelation, philosophy would have to be in possession of a complete rational account of the whole of being and conclusive proof of the perfect knowability of divinity. But such knowledge is unavailable to man. This fact poses a serious problem for philosophy: The philosopher must conclude that his own opting for the life of reason or philosophy is a choice based on faith rather than a rational account of being. At the root of Western culture lives, then, the choice between two forms of diametrically opposed faiths. Even philosophy appears to be a form of piety. Strauss claims that at its core modern philosophy's attempt to reestablish man on the foundations of the "clear and distinct" ideas of reason and the mastery of nature was a rebellion against both of these underlying forms of faith, biblical faith in revelation as well as the Greek faith in "natural reason" and its "naive objectivism." Inasmuch as modern man's unprecedented skepticism established a radical secularism based, however, on the new Western faith in the historical progression of man's power and self-mastery, that is, the most radical form of anthropomorphism, his diminishing faith in his own progress leaves him utterly without foundations – except, perhaps, for the somewhat foolish pride that to have failed in freedom is more "heroic" than to have remained in "bondage" to either nature of God, or both.

For Strauss, in contradistinction to Heidegger, the contradictory demands of Bible and Greek rational philosophy cannot be harmonized in a philosophical synthesis. Instead, we have to accept the opposition at the heart of Western culture as "our fate." This fate is "the life between two codes, a fundamental tension," which is the ultimate "secret of the vitality of Western civilization."[56] Can the recognition and acceptance of our fate be explained on a level which lies "above" both the standpoint of the Bible and of original philosophy? What are the grounds, the foundations of this fate? For Strauss, no answers are available by means of "transcending" the basic tension between the two. "But everyone of us can be and ought to be either one or the other," a philosopher or a faithful believer.[57] Each, moreover, must constantly reflect upon the possible meanings and significance of the existence of the other alternative wisdom. For the believer in revelation, the existence of the philosopher is a constant reminder, one assumes, to be reasonable. For the philosopher, the existence of the believer is a reminder of the need for piety and humility even to temper his philosophical mania.

From Strauss's vantage point, it appears that Heidegger, rather than having accepted the Western "fate" as an unsolvable dualism providing the West with its fundamental vitality, attempted to find the explanation of that dualism in the very essence of mysterious being itself. It is most characteristic of Strauss's way of thinking that, given his understanding of the "Socratic turn" in philosophy, he refuses to follow Heidegger. Instead, he conjectures only so far as to suggest that the fate of Western civilization is the offspring of a "fundamental dualism in man," rather than being. Human nature, not ultimate (unknowable) being must serve as first, however inadequate, explanation. The dualism of speech and deed, of thought and action, which constitutes human nature, therefore also constitutes our most basic "fate." By transposing this dualism into the very core of being, Heidegger only manages to mystify further rather than to "explain" man's fate or "essence" or human nature. And whereas for Strauss, the original Greek discovery of "human nature" enables us to assert that all human progress is ultimately limited by unchanging human nature, for Heidegger even the greatest need resulting from forgetfulness of fateful being still raises unbounded hope for a "higher" determination of human essence. The blatant unreasonableness of these hopes is perhaps the clearest indication of the price Heidegger paid for his particular endeavor to overcome the fateful dualism of the West.

56 Ibid., 270.     57 Ibid.

# 7

# Leo Strauss: German Origin and American Impact

ALFONS SÖLLNER

Leo Strauss is one of the most influential figures of twentieth-century political philosophy. He has published fifteen books and a great number of articles; his work covers the occidental history of thought from its beginnings to the present and links several other disciplines, such as theology, classical philology, and medievalistics, with its philosophical core. At the same time, Strauss has remained one of the most controversial figures within this discourse. This is, among other things, due to the fact that he advocates a very remote epistemological ideal, that of Greek antiquity, while insisting simultaneously on a direct and practical topicality. The following line of reasoning is founded on the conviction that this scholar's way of thinking is hard to classify and is based on a political attitude that could be called "ultraconservative" – a term that will have to be defined more clearly. His way of thinking can be differentiated from modern philosophy of the early twentieth century by its turn to Jewish tradition and it follows an inner logic that can be reconstructed according to a secularization model of theological origin. Accordingly, the accent in this essay will be put on both the less well-known early writings and the formative writings of the middle period, while the later works will only be touched upon because as yet too little is known of their impact.

Although Strauss objected to contextual explanations of the validity of philosophical argumentation because he considered them "historicist," in his later life he repeatedly afforded his readers an insight into the origins and development of his way of thinking. Thus, in the American preface to his book on Spinoza he describes his intellectual beginnings in the Weimar Republic and places them in the context of contemporaneous Jewish philosophy (Hermann Cohen, Franz Rosenzweig) and its strained relations with the Enlightenment. What has, in sociological terms, been defined as the precarious situation of Jewry in an increasingly secularized Christian environment is, in this rudimentary autobiography, quickly retranslated into en-

121

lightened metaphors of Jewish theology: "Finitive, relative problems can be solved; infinitive absolute problems cannot be solved. . . . From every point of view it looks as if the Jewish people were the chosen people, at least in the sense that the Jewish problem is the most manifest symbol of the human problem insofar as it is a social or political problem."[1]

Leo Strauss will certainly not be wronged by projecting this formulation of 1965 back to the 1920s.[2] In its content, and even more so in its highly abstract form it repeats what already defined the point of departure of his philosophizing: an act of subtle spiritualization through which – not quite without force – a concrete problem is turned into a figure of intellectual history which is suitable as political metaphor. Neither the actual threat to Weimar democracy nor the attempt to find a political solution for the clash between the Jewish minority and the German majority, that is, Zionism, directly motivated Strauss's early writings. Rather, he was motivated by such highly abstract questions as those concerning the relationship between orthodoxy and enlightenment, revelation and reason, law and philosophy. What is remarkable is the accuracy with which so young a scholar was able to pin down the turning points in intellectual history relevant to such questions, the philosophical energy and philological meticulousness with which he kept at them, and the form in which he did not so much solve these problems as take them as points of departure for further research in intellectual history.

Strauss's first independently written work, his book on Spinoza, was the concentrated fruit of research conducted at the Berlin Academy for Jewish Studies (*Akademie für die Wissenschaft des Judentums*). It is a highly ambitious, in method purely immanent study of a philosophy that contributed decisively to the Enlightenment. However, Strauss concluded that it did so at too heavy a price, and with this conclusion he left the field of immanent critique. The emancipation from Jewish orthodoxy appeared to him as the destruction of the traditional context that had found mandatory expression in the belief in the Laws of the Old Testament, and indeed, even as the destruction of tradition as such. In this sense, he tried to prove that Spinoza's *Bibelwissenschaft* (biblical studies), far from being the basis for a critique of religion, rather presupposed the latter and that his critique of orthodoxy was logically based on a *petitio principii*. Mockery, an instrument typical of the Enlightenment, did not suffice to invalidate the orthodox belief in miracles.[3]

1 Leo Strauss, *Liberalism Ancient and Modern* (New York and London, 1968), 230.
2 See also John G. Gunnel, "Strauss before Straussianism: Reason, Revelation, and Nature," *Review of Politics* 53 (1991): 53–74. See other references to this special issue of *The Review of Politics* in subsequent notes of this chapter.
3 Leo Strauss, *Die Religionskritik Spinozas als Grundlage seiner Bibelwissenschaft: Untersuchungen zu Spinozas Theologisch-politischem Traktat* (Berlin, 1930), esp. 126ff.

In its line of reasoning the book on Spinoza follows an epistemological interest that was to remain binding for Leo Strauss. His lifework as a whole aimed at rehabilitating the tradition that had – wrongly in his opinion – been discredited by modernity. With regard to the appraisal of the Enlightenment this meant that its thoroughly approved achievements were, from the outset, dealt with from the angle of the decline of tradition. Thus, Strauss judged Spinoza's theological-political treatise a genuine liberal and democratic foundation of politics, but ultimately he was only interested in the loss it embodied. He argued that Spinoza missed a level of reflection already attained in intellectual history, namely, the reconciliation of philosophy and theology formulated in the teachings of Maimonides;[4] that his *realistische Staatslehre* (realistic theory of the state),[5] originally conceived as a link between theology and ethics, again thwarted the utopian claim of the aspiration for enlightenment due to its Machiavellian image of man favoring passions;[6] and that the unsuccessful mediation was but concealed by the philosophic-historical projection of a future state based on reason, as was made evident by the fact that religion, which had initially been bereft of its function as absolute foundation, was reintroduced on a relative level – as pragmatic means of educating the people.

If one imputes, at the end of the Weimar Republic, a political tendency to Leo Strauss, something that, in view of the high level of abstraction adopted by him, is only possible by extrapolation, one notices an ambivalence. On the one hand, Strauss does not shrink from drawing affirmative conclusions from his critical studies on enlightenment, conclusions that have to be described as conservative, yes, even fundamentalist. On the other hand, Leo Strauss was one of the first to begin the dispute with the author who formulated the most influential fundamentalist theory of the epoch and who, unlike Strauss, did not shrink from translating this theory directly into political practice, namely, Carl Schmitt. As is well known, Schmitt's friend/foe theory was conceived as a secularized political theology that could be transformed quickly and in a manner appropriate to the respective situation. Initially, it was transformed into a plea for an authoritarian solution to the crisis of the Weimar state and later, after 1933, into an idea of order based on racism. In his immanent critique, which reproached the hater of liberalism with his own liberalism and took offense at his "Bewunderung der animalischen Kraft" (admiration at animalist power),[7] Strauss tried to gain "eine Perspektive jenseits des Liberalismus" (a perspective be-

---

4 Ibid., 127ff., esp. 180.     5 Ibid., 219.     6 Ibid., 217ff.
7 Leo Strauss, "Anmerkungen zu Carl Schmitt. Der Begriff des Politischen," *Archiv für Sozialwissenschaft und Sozialpolitik* 67 (1932): 744.

yond liberalism)[8]; however, his alternative remained abstract and, in view of the course of events, politically futile.

This perspective became evident in a booklet published in Germany in 1935, that is, after Strauss's emigration, under the title *Philosophie und Gesetz*. Its analyses of the Jewish classics of the Middle Ages constitute fascinating philological studies.[9] Strauss, following Hermann Cohen, considered Maimonides the "Klassiker des Rationalismus" (classicist of rationalism) because his legal conception of philosophy was balanced with a philosophical foundation of theology and he drew highly interesting parallels to the Arabic approach to Aristotle. Simultaneously, in this booklet, theological traditionalism is not only clearly continued but even reinforced. This is confirmed, for one thing, by the concentration on the crucial doctrine of Jewish orthodoxy, in which the belief in miracles and earthly legislation are meant to form a unity, that is, on prophetology. Furthermore, Strauss offered a fundamentalist interpretation of the crisis of his time which – and in this he parallels Carl Schmitt – showed at least traces of a religiously defined friend/foe constellation:

The Jewish tradition has a more appropriate response to the question of the original ideal of the Enlightenment than does cultural philosophy (*Kulturphilosophie*). . . . Thus the "truth" of the alternative: orthodoxy or enlightenment finally reveals itself as the alternative: orthodoxy or atheism.[10]

But the historical-theological studies of the 1930s proved to be trend setting for yet another reason. For here Strauss came upon the problem of heresy, which in the closed worldview of the Middle Ages had constituted a pronouncedly political conflict, but which he thought had to be positivized and spiritualized in a peculiar simultaneity. The differentiation of "esoteric" and "exoteric" meaning of a doctrine, which appeared for the first time in these studies, was taken up again a little later in his well-known essay *Persecution and the Art of Writing*, published in 1941.[11] It now became binding for his self-understanding, or at least so it seems in retrospect. This actualization of a pre-Enlightenment figure of thought was not without its peculiarities not only because it underestimated the potential for persecution of modern totalitarianism, but also because in deliberate secrecy it evaded the alternative contemporary situation of intellectual emigration.

8 Ibid., 749
9 Hillel Fradkin, "Philosophy and Law: Leo Strauss as a Student of Medieval Jewish Thought," *Review of Politics* 53 (1991): 40–52.
10 Leo Strauss, *Philosophie und Gesetz: Beiträge zum Verständnis Maimunis und seiner Vorläufer* (Berlin, 1935), 25 and 28.
11 Leo Strauss, *Persecution and the Art of Writing* (Glencoe, Ill., 1952).

However, it seems that this was exactly why it could serve as a model for Strauss's own philosophizing: It allowed him to hold on to a political theology that, in the age of the Holocaust, seemed rather dated to many thinkers, among these the most representative of the Jewish refugees from Hitler. Conceived as a methodological introduction to the reading of classical texts, it escaped this objection, yet still allowed a secularized continuation of the theological problem. By introducing in addition to the (exoteric) reading of "normal science," which could proceed either philologically or sociohistorically, a second (esoteric) reading, which would discover the actual meaning of a text "between the lines," he was able to adhere to his project of pursuing intellectual history as reestablishment of tradition. Consequently, it was not the absolute *Zivilisationsbruch* (breakup of civilization), symbolized by Auschwitz, which came to the fore in his American phase, but rather the study of the Greek classics, which evaded (and leveled?) this break through abstraction.[12]

"The theological-political problem has (since the book on Spinoza) remained the theme of my research."[13] What is stressed in this reminiscence of 1965 as the essence of his philosophizing in fact manifests itself most clearly when Strauss concentrates on the methodological continuity that is apparent in both his early and his later work. The method applied was and remained one of theological exegesis and it was its avowed intention to bring authoritatively to mind binding traditions. A late work, such as *Jerusalem and Athens,* cannot be understood as long as the fact that its author was equally interested in both confession and cognition is not taken into consideration.[14] In this essay Strauss was finally able to give a conciliatory perspective to the alternative of either Greek humanist or Christian tradition by pointing at the convergence of the Platonic and the biblical myth of the creation of the world. This was only possible by means of a preestablished unity of exegetic method and authoritative self-interpretation of classical texts which Strauss presupposes throughout his work and which is the unmistakable mark of every hermeneutical substantialism.

Certain parallels can be drawn, by the way, to the cryptotheological tendencies of Martin Heidegger, manifest in his later writings in particular.[15] These need to be researched urgently since Leo Strauss, too – although it is hardly apparent in his published work, it has been credibly testified by his students – seems to have been fascinated by "the hidden king . . . in the

---

12 Dan Diner, ed., *Zivilisationsbruch. Denken nach Auschwitz* (Frankfurt/Main, 1988).
13 Leo Strauss, *Hobbes politische Wissenschaft* (Neuwied and Berlin, 1983), 147ff.
14 Leo Strauss, *Studies in Platonic Philosophy* (Chicago and London, 1983), 147ff.
15 Georg Steiner, *Martin Heidegger* (Munich, 1988).

realm of thinking," as Heidegger was called by Hannah Arendt in 1971.[16] This fascination outlasted the shock caused by Heidegger's commitment to National Socialism. Although it would be overdrawn to equate the concept of *Seinsgeschichte* with that of the history of thought in Leo Strauss's work, some lesser parallels clearly manifest themselves, all of which seem to be related to that ontological turn in hermeneutic sciences which Hans-Georg Gadamer has described so penetratingly.[17] On the one hand, there are similarities between the areas of discretion offered for interpretation, aimed at by favoring the esoteric above the exoteric reading, and Heidegger's private etymology, which has been praised just as often as it has been criticized. On the other hand, they are both searching for the origins of human thought as such in classic Greek philosophy, although this shared orientation toward *prima philosophia* produced quite different results, as indicated by their concentration on the archaic and/or the classic phase. Furthermore, they parallel one another in the manner in which these results were reached: Just as the author of *Being and Time,* whose training had been that of a Catholic theologian, arrived at the "fundamental-ontological question" and, later on, at the "seinsgeschichtliche Kehre" (turn in the history of being) only through studying the scholastic approach to Aristotle, so Leo Strauss discovered in the other representative strand of the reading of the ancients that decisive link which led him to his "very own" issue.

This connecting link is to be found in an essay written in 1945, which was – not without reason – taken up again in the introduction to *Persecution and the Art of Writing,* where it achieved almost programmatic rank. In this essay, Strauss concentrates on the comparatively purest conveyance of Platonic idealism, which the Arabic "falsafa" Fârâbi had undertaken in an apocryphal book, and here he established the connection that was to become the model for his own philosophizing: the conception of philosophy as "natural religion" and the accompanying (political/nonpolitical) concept of the philosopher as king, presented in a strictly exegetic reading of the *Nomoi* in particular. As we will see, it was exactly this dialogue that for Strauss was to become the most authoritative of all texts, the quintessence of the classical as such. In the beginning, however, he did not use a Platonic text but rather Xenophon's dialogue *Hieron, or On Tyranny* to demonstrate this unity of subject and method, which resulted in a strictly antihistoricist reading:

The goal of the intellectual historian is to understand the thought of the past "as it really has been," that is, to understand it as exactly as possible as it was actually understood by its authors.[18]

16  Hannah Arendt, "Martin Heidegger at Eighty," *New York Review of Books,* Oct. 21, 1971, 51.
17  Hans-Georg Gadamer, *Wahrheit und Methode,* 2nd ed. (Tübingen, 1965).
18  Leo Strauss, *On Tyranny. An Interpretation of Xenophon's Hiero* (New York, 1948), 4.

This meant pure textual interpretation without considering any of the historic and social references and – in the present case – a rigid observance of the dialogue form.

While the latter directive resulted in rather interesting insights, a drawback became evident in the claim that one may arrive at topical diagnostic statements through purely immanent textual interpretation. For Strauss established in the introduction to his interpretation of *Hiero* a direct connection between the practical failure of the scientific public to identify and practically counter (fascist and Stalinist) totalitarianism and the ignorance of the "classical" analysis of tyranny. This constellation, which could be considered an intentional break through the hermeneutic circle or even a methodological decisionism, has since remained binding for Leo Strauss; it became the promotive force behind both his positive and his negative impact. Thus, to give an example, the dispute Strauss had with Alexandre Kojève in the 1950s appeared to be about philological differences. In truth, however, they argued about the rank a classical text was to be assigned in the diagnosis of the present world. That Strauss thought he could respond to topical political analysis with footnotes to Platonic dialogues showed most clearly, and for the first time, how far removed from the analysis of the present his model of the application of the ancients remained.[19]

Just as Leo Strauss avoided a clear option for either theology or philosophy in his Weimar publications, he again showed an analogous indecision in the formative writings of the middle period. There, Strauss's typical, yet productive rejection manifests itself in the highly tense relation between philosophy and history, or, with regard to the disciplines, between political philosophy and the history of political thought. "Political philosophy is not a historical discipline. . . . In particular, political philosophy is different from the history of political philosophy itself."[20] He stated this in a programmatic essay published in 1949. And yet, this was exactly the year in which Strauss gave his Chicago Walgreen Lectures on the history of political thinking, which, more than anything else, established his reputation as a political philosopher. The theoretical but still intentionally practical ambivalence expressed in this statement represents a possible key to the obscure center of those writings that could perhaps be categorized as political philosophy in the sense of a subdiscipline of modern political science. They begin in the 1930s with a study on Hobbes.

Strauss's book on Hobbes coincides with the momentous break in his life that was caused by the emigration from Hitler's Germany. Yet the book

19 The controversy with Kojève is documented in Leo Strauss, *Über Tyrannis* (Neuwied and Berlin, 1963), 145ff.
20 Leo Strauss, *What Is Political Philosophy?* (Glencoe, Ill., 1959), 56.

conceals this fact in a manner already anticipated by the distinction between esoteric and exoteric styles of writing. Begun during his research sojourn in Oxford, the Hobbes book was published in English in 1936. The original German version, however, did not appear until 1965. Strauss focused not so much on the *mos geometricus,* that is, on Hobbes's new method as such, but rather on its prerequisites, which he described as explicitly moral and characterized as a selective reinterpretation of Aristotelian ethics. Vanity and fear of violent death are pronounced the anthropological constants,[21] and from this pessimistic concept of man he merely infers the construction of a sovereign state that has to be simultaneously omnipotent and worldly, egalitarian and mechanical, in order to meet the crucial task of securing the peace.[22] Of decisive importance is the discovery of the realm of history, which replaces the ethics of obedience to an ideal natural order with a technically oriented morality of reasoning. "Bourgeois" ideals such as thrift, work ethics, legal rationality, and domination over nature supersede the Platonic ethical hierarchy of wisdom, justice, prudence, and bravery.[23]

Strauss summarized these and other moral-typological differentiations in several theses concerning the functional change in political philosophy:

And for this reason political philosophy no longer has the function, as it had in the classical antiquity, of reminding political life of the eternally immutable prototype of the perfect State, but the peculiarly modern task of delineating for the first time the program of the essentially future perfect State. The repression of history in favor of philosophy from now on means in reality the repression of the past – of the ancient, which is an image of the eternal – in favor of the future.[24]

Or

The break with rationalism is thus the decisive presupposition for the concept of sovereignty as well as for the supplanting of "law" by "right," that is, the supplanting of the primacy of obligation by the primacy of claim.[25]

It is worthwhile to pay close attention to such formulations, not only because they represent brilliant results of research in intellectual history, but also because they suggest a differentiation that serves to prepare for critical conclusions about Leo Strauss's own philosophizing. His book on Hobbes was still dominated by an attitude that aimed at the critical comparison of cultural values – an attitude that was not value-free, but which pursued evaluation in the sense of a typological definition and not yet primarily in the sense of devaluation. The latter exactly describes the direction in which Strauss started moving after his study of Hobbes.

---

21 Leo Strauss, *The Political Philosophy of Hobbes* (Chicago, 1959 [originally 1936]), 6ff.
22 Ibid., 59ff.        23 Ibid., 108ff. and 132ff.        24 Ibid., 106.        25 Ibid., 159, 160.

This presupposed that Strauss again broadened his horizons with regard to intellectual history by more than a millennium by moving from Spinoza back to Maimonides and Fârâbi. Now he was concerned with the exhaustion of the sources themselves, which in the medieval worldview had still manifested themselves in distinct directness, namely, with the philosophy of the Greeks. By thus relaxing the productive tension of his interpretation of Hobbes, he reached the level of the earliest history of occidental philosophizing, which from then on characterized his style of argumentation, a *prima philosophia,* in which he skips over entire epochs. He once more touched off the "querelle entre anciens et modernes," which had stirred the eighteenth century not only in France, and he resolved it in a manner that diametrically reversed the perspective of the Enlightenment, something which had already been inaugurated by the retraction of Spinoza's critique of orthodoxy. His detailed answer to this was the collection of his Walgreen Lectures into a book called *Natural Right and History* (1953), which also achieved unity of content and form insofar as it became a modern-day classic of political philosophy, soon translated into the most important European languages.

The thematic structuring of the book alone shows what mattered to Strauss. It begins with an immanent critique of historicism which, being a lot more than a mere strand in the epistemological and disciplinal pluralism of twentieth-century scholarship, rather dominates the latter by being both a sweeping and uncomprehended weltanschauung.[26] According to Strauss, the core of this weltanschauung is formed by the assertion of the historical relativity not only of ideas and values, but of the human cognitive competence as such. Exactly on this most general level, however – the historical implementation of truth cannot be taken as a truth beyond history – the fake radicalism, even the inconsistency of historicism itself, already becomes evident. Yet, it was not this epistemological problem which interested Strauss the most, but rather its correspondence on the moral level: the loss of binding value orientations or, positively put, modern nihilism. Accordingly it was not merely the methodological distinction between values and facts in the contemporary social science initiated by Max Weber that irritated him but even more so its precondition, namely, irrationalism.[27]

One has to have grasped this negativism and its moral quality, that is, a radical diagnosis of crisis, in order to understand why Strauss strove for a counterposition and what he expected of it, namely, an absolute point of reference in which both human knowledge and human will found a safe ba-

26 Leo Strauss, *Natural Right and History* (Chicago, 1953), 9ff.    27 Ibid., 35ff.

sis, were beyond all doubt. It was essential to radicalize Descartes and, at the same time, to surmount him through turning backward. Accordingly, he found in the Platonic dialogues, which served the purpose better than the works of Aristotle, not only the historically earliest style of thinking that deserves to be called "philosophy" but also the original form of knowledge – original because it inquires into the origins as such:

> Philosophy is the quest for the "principle" of all things, and this means primarily the quest for the "beginnings" of all things or for "the first things."[28]

It is true that this inquiry into the origins is anticonventional, even antireligious and therefore critical of authority – the ironic expression for this would be the Socratic "I know that I know nothing" – however, in its progress it merely establishes a new authority, which is now thought to be created by and appropriate to human thinking itself. The term for this authority is "nature":

> Nature is older than any tradition; hence it is more venerable than any tradition. . . . By uprooting the authority of the ancestral, philosophy recognizes that nature is the authority.[29]

Within this *prima philosophia,* Strauss focuses on one specific point in particular, which he refers to by the term "natural law" and at which the contemplative ideal of the Greek weltanschauung achieved practical obligation. In his opinion, this also is the only point from which political philosophizing could possibly start, not least because what had fallen apart in the modern worldview still seemed combined, namely, ethics and institutional knowledge, moral justice and state authority, subjective right and objective law, society and politics. With the Greek concept of *politeia* – a term that he translated as "constitution" or "regime" – Strauss aimed at the unity of all these elements; in this he initially followed the constitutional doctrine of Aristotle. Now, as is well known, this doctrine – in following the Aristotelian principle of induction – derives from a comparative approach. Strauss, however, was much more interested in its implied normative aspect, namely, the unique model of the Athenian polis:

> The best regime will then be a republic in which landed gentry, which is at the same time the urban patriciate, well-bred and public spirited, obeying laws and completing them, ruling and being ruled in turn, predominates and gives society its character.[30]

Accordingly, it was not the pragmatism of the Aristotelian conception of politics that came to the fore but rather Plato's conception of the "ideal

28 Ibid., 82.    29 Ibid., 92.    30 Ibid., 142.

state." This principle of a moral hierarchy, founded on natural law, is trans-posed into a model of political elites and culminates in the idea of the philosopher as king. Consequently, the thesis "that some men are by nature superior to others and therefore, according to natural right, the rulers of others" established not only a social hierarchy but also the identity of philo-sophical knowledge and political order, which had to demand the greater theoretical obligation for, in practice, it seemed to be precarious, and that not only in the classical texts, but also in Leo Strauss's interpretation of the latter.[31] While, in this case, he had achieved an extremely compact and orig-inal reconstruction of classical political philosophy, which comprised the history of its impact from the Stoics and Cicero up to Thomas Aquinas, the last representative of "classical natural right," the transfer to "modern nat-ural right" represented not just an analytical step but, rather, one of moral evaluation. Here a basic hiatus yawned, in view of which the venture that had begun as an involuntary history of the conceptions of natural right, metahistorical as such, was quickly turned into a history of the decline of political philosophy.

This is already apparent in the chapters in *Natural Right and History* on early modern political philosophy. What was of particular interest to Strauss in the works of Hobbes and all subsequent thinkers was the ques-tion "how modern he is or how much he deviates from the natural right tradition."[32] Consequently, a method of analysis was applied that was nothing but the reversal of the modern progressional pathos itself: It judged a thinker according to the degree to which he deviated from clas-sical natural right. We have already seen that this does not preclude as-tounding insights into the ambivalences of the evolving modernity. Thus, Strauss did not hesitate to consider Hobbes the actual initiator of liberal-ism – a result that not only ran diametrically counter to the ideological neoliberalism of postwar America but also contributed to a permanent deepening of the philosophical fundamentals of modern democracy in its progressive as well as in its conservative versions. Accordingly, he could, with regard to Locke's seeming return to a more moderate conception of human nature ("pursuit of happiness"), state conversely and without con-tradiction that

Locke's teaching on property, and therewith his whole political philosophy, are revolutionary. . . . Through the shift of emphasis from natural duties or obligations to natural rights, the individual, the ego, had become the center and origin of the moral world . . . man owes almost everything valuable to this own effort.[33]

---

31 Ibid., 135.     32 Ibid., 165.     33 Ibid., 248.

The problematic side of his method, to which attention has to be called, became more evident the nearer Strauss came to the era of the bourgeois philosophy of freedom and the rule of law. It not only amounted to a highly selective perception to restrict the analysis – under the title of "The Crisis of Modern Natural Right"[34] – to Rousseau and Burke, thus leaving out those thinkers who, like Kant, Hegel, and Marx, had tried to embed modern individualism into an objective conception of justice, be it labeled constitutional state, objective spirit, or revolution. Already in his study of Rousseau, Strauss has furthermore renounced the possibility to explore the question whether, for instance, the category of compassion (instead of egotism) or the idea of self-governed democracy (instead of governmental absolutism) suggested models that had postulated a balance of freedom and order, of the individual and society, thus showing the way to an immanent (instead of a transcendent) critique of modernity. Differentiations such as these had to disappear in a history of the decline of political thinking in which the relation between classical and modern times was no longer regarded as an open relation of reflection but, rather, came under a verdict that was hardly inferior to Heidegger's verdict of *Seinsvergessenheit*. However, we cannot be sure that the picture will remain unchanged if, one day, the as yet unpublished part of Leo Strauss's work, especially his encyclopedic university lectures, becomes available.

A high point in Leo Strauss's condemnatory (instead of historical-critical) method of interpretation was reached in his *Thoughts on Machiavelli*.[35] This book focused on new lines insofar as it no longer located the decisive change in intellectual history in English rationalism but in the powerful realism of the great Florentine political writer; yet, it gains even more in relevance when placed in the context of American contemporary history. Notwithstanding careful textual interpretation, long passages from *Thoughts on Machiavelli* read almost like an exercise in intellectual exorcism, in which the dichotomous worldview of McCarthyism, that is, of the Cold War and an idiosyncratic apocalyptic gesture, at no time unfamiliar to Strauss, overlap and even reinforce each other momentously. While Strauss did not lack a demonstrative, even aggressive anticommunism, especially in the 1950s, he did not in turn allow the slightest doubt about the fact that his attack on the moralism and atheism of modern political concepts was equally aimed at both Western liberalism and, especially, the American present. This is documented in several of his pedagogical works of that time.[36] This double op-

---

34 Ibid., 252ff.
35 Leo Strauss, *Thoughts on Machiavelli* (Glencoe, Ill., 1958), esp. 9ff.
36 Leo Strauss, *Liberalism Ancient and Modern* (New York and London, 1968).

position suggests that – although it was not wrong to read Leo Strauss's impact as a plea for an American conservatism – his position was finally "ultra-conservative" insofar as it took offense at *all* modern regimes. As we have seen, this ultraposition was from the very beginning inherent in his apocalyptic fundamentalism and it designates the core of a political theology that cannot, however, be pinned down to a conservative tendency just because of its final farewell to modernity.

Strauss's late works, in which this farewell proves to be a definitive arrival, defy a concise discourse and therefore cannot be described here. Consisting of four monographs and two collections of essays, this body of late works is not only very extensive, but it also constitutes a separate genre of extreme inner unity, of which the purposeful esotericism alone is apt to provoke differences of opinion. But at least there seems to be no dispute about either the direction Strauss's work took in the 1960s and early 1970s or his objectives. He no longer played the role of the involuntary historian, which he had addressed for the last time when co-editing a history of political thinking,[37] but left the business of historical reflection behind and virtually immersed himself completely in those sources that had always supplied his moralizing gesture, half theology and half philosophy. At the center of this definitive *prima philosophia* is now one single figure who, being much more than a mere monument of Occidental history of philosophy, figures as a sort of archetype: Socrates. To Strauss, Socrates is the incarnation of a life-style, a way of being that is synonymous with philosophizing as such (we have to insist on the verbal phrasing), which is of classical simplicity and, hence, of direct actuality.

Strauss approached his philosophical archetype in an iterative manner: He set Socrates off from the rather pragmatic style of Aristotelian politics[38]; he defended him against the ridicule in Aristophanes' comedies[39]; he characterized him from the point of view of one of his prominent disciples, Xenophon[40]; and he tried to disclose Socrates' inner core through a very close reading of another even more prominent disciple of his, namely, Plato. It was certainly not by accident that the last work Strauss managed to finish is a line-by-line interpretation of Plato's *Nomoi,* that is, of that dialogue in which Socrates remains absent but is still present in the figure of the "Athenian friend."[41] But there is yet another reason this interpretation is considered an eloquent symbolization of the final point Strauss aimed at and

37  Leo Strauss and J. Cropsey, *History of Political Philosophy* (Chicago, 1963).
38  Leo Strauss, *The City and the Man* (Chicago, 1964).
39  Leo Strauss, *Socrates and Aristophanes* (New York, 1966).
40  Leo Strauss, *Xenophon's Socrates* (Ithaca, N.Y., 1972).
41  Leo Strauss, *The Argument and the Action of Plato's Laws* (Chicago, 1975).

probably reached in his late work. If Plato's late dialogues are to be regarded, on the one hand, not only as the completion of his theory of ideas but also as the disclosure of the latter's theological basis, then this step into transcendence could appear to be the crowning of a lifelong effort to bring together theology and politics. On the other hand, it is remarkable how simple, true to life, humorous, and, in this sense, anti-idealistic Strauss's description of Socrates' nature sometimes reads. Even the "pious Socrates" is finally left hanging in the balance by sticking to the dialogical style of thinking and seems to remain resistant to theological mystification.

In peculiar contrast to "final questions" such as these, the history of Strauss's impact has always been linked with the cycle of contemporary intellectual history. It reflects the sorrowful course of emigration of a Hitler refugee as well as the changing contexts into which this migration led him. The distribution of Leo Strauss's early writings was initially blocked with bitter efficiency by Hitler's takeover. This story has been told by Heinrich Meier in his documentation of the relation between the young scholar Strauss and Carl Schmitt. After 1933 the initially very lively intellectual exchange between the two men turned abruptly into a "dialogue between absentees," a change that had little to do with the quality of Leo Strauss's further theoretical development but a lot with the anti-Semitism of the Prussian *Staatsrat* (councilor of state). The writings completed during his time in England and the works of the early American years did not extend beyond the limited discussion among colleagues. Just as his essays on the philosophy of religion were hardly noticed outside Jewish Studies, so too did Strauss's writings on the history of philosophy, which were increasingly published in the house organ of the New School of Social Research, remain marginal at first. In fact, they were as marginal as the discipline of political philosophy at this newly established, yet itself marginal "university in exile," where research and teaching activities focused on economy and politics.[42] Nonetheless, from the beginning of his appointment Strauss was not only a highly esteemed colleague within the New School, but soon he also became known on the outside as the guardian of select cultural traditions, no doubt due in large measure to his command of classical languages.

Strauss's decisive and soon also interdisciplinary impact began to be felt in the 1950s and is as closely as negatively connected with a trend toward dogmatism in American social science. While political science, as academic discipline, was increasingly characterized by the triumphant advance of behavioralism – it is not without good reason that one speaks of the "be-

42 C.-D. Krohn, *Wissenschaft im Exil* (Frankfurt/Main, 1987).

havioral revolution" – Leo Strauss played an important role as the incarnation of opposition to this development. This was not only furthered by the antipositivistic way of thinking he adopted in his introduction to *Natural Right and History* but also by the fact that, from 1949 onward, he taught at the University of Chicago. With scholars such as Charles Merriam and Harold Lasswell, Chicago represented at that time a bastion of the "science of politics." Strauss often wrote apodictic sentences such as: " 'Scientific' political science is in fact incompatible with political science."[43] He also expressed a biting irony concerning the methodological naiveté and the irrelevance of empirical political research and asserted that through it were eliminated all the great and, above all, the practical questions of politics.[44] These statements constituted a kind of program that could almost be considered the proclamation of a theoretical counterrevolution.

While this program agreed with the organic consensus on the "science of democracy" (*Demokratiewissenschaft*) of the generation that had initiated political science in the Federal Republic of Germany,[45] the discipline in general, and especially in its highly institutionalized and professionalized form, which had existed for a long time in the United States, was at first hardly affected by such attacks. This holds true in spite of the fact that during the 1950s an antipositivistic milieu developed in Chicago's academic community that was promoted not only by other German emigrants, such as Hans Morgenthau and Hannah Arendt, but also by the neo-Thomists who gathered at neighboring Notre Dame. However, Leo Strauss did not hesitate to establish a direct connection between his conception of "political philosophy proper" and political teaching, or even contemporary political practice. He propagated the equivalence of the reading of the classics and "liberal education." By this he did not only mean "studying with the proper care the great books which the greatest minds have left behind."[46] Rather, he combined this with the assertion that, realistically – and as a countermove to its decline in modern mass democracy – democracy could be nothing but the moral aristocracy of the ancient Greeks: "Democracy, in a word, is meant to be an aristocracy which has broadened into a universal aristocracy."[47] By integrating the model of the philosopher-king into the American tradition of democratic common sense, Strauss suggested the reverse inference that liberalism and democracy had actually nothing to do with one another. He thus laid foundations for the neoconservative read-

---

43 Leo Strauss, *What is Political Philosophy?* 14.
44 Leo Strauss, *Liberalism Ancient and Modern* (New York and London, 1968) esp. at 103ff.
45 W. Hennis, *Politik und praktische Philosophie* (Neuwied and Berlin, 1963).
46 Leo Strauss, *Liberalism Ancient and Modern* (New York and London, 1968), 3.    47 Ibid., 4.

ing of his works, wherein the esoteric Strauss still looms as a clearly exoteric factor in the immediate present.

Strauss's long-term influence has probably been greatest for the development of political philosophy in the narrower sense. His late work, which has already been regarded as a both monumental and mysterious proof of the end of the behavioralist era, furthermore sparked an extensive controversy about the appropriate place of political philosophy in the discipline as a whole. While several authors who are Strauss's direct disciples associated a renaissance of political philosophizing in the classical style with the figure of their master,[48] they were opposed by a group who rejected this "mythologization of the tradition" and considered it not only the results of an antidemocratic elitism but even feared the renaissance of a new political irrationalism.[49] Though the implicit factual problem may well be important, the constellation that manifests itself here refers to the peculiar dialectic of esoteric form and exoteric impact, which is probably the secret of Leo Strauss's success. It consists in the simple sociological fact that as a charismatic representative of Teutonic learnedness in the very different American academic milieu he knew how to gather around himself a more or less sworn community of "Straussians."

The Platonic idealism apparent in the later works of Leo Strauss are indicative of the fact that the theologian had finally gotten the better of the philosopher.[50] While emphasizing pure textual interpretation, Strauss omits all reference to historical knowledge about the Greek polis.[51] In accordance with this antihistorical method it is then logical that the Platonic dialogues are stylized into "holy texts," which are to be read reverently and which – according to the axiom: Classics apply themselves! – virtually expound themselves. And it is furthermore logical that the classicism of Strauss's students sometimes develops into a caricature of their "master's" classicism.

Still, we cannot be sure that he would have rejected a book critical of contemporary civilization, such as Allan Bloom's bestseller, on account of its success.[52] However, the formation of a conservative school of American constitutional thinking, which can be traced back to the Founding Fathers, certainly represents an authentic actualization of the "Straussian

---

48  Dante Germino, *Beyond Ideology. The Rivival of Political Theory* (Chicago and London, 1967).
49  John G. Gunnel, *Between Philosophy and Politics. The Alienation of Political Philosophy* (Amherst, Mass., 1986), esp. 91ff; and S. B. Drury, "The Esoteric Philosophy of Leo Strauss," *Political Theory* 13 (1985), 315ff.
50  Thomas L. Pangle, *Introduction to Strauss. Studies in Platonic Philosophy* (Chicago, 1983).
51  Carl A. Meier, *Die Entstehung des Politischen bei den Griechen* (Frankfurt/Main, 1983).
52  Allan Bloom, *The Closing of the American Mind* (New York, 1987).

Mind."[53] Both are part of the as yet unwritten chapter on the conservative branch of the German academic emigration to the United States, which will have to cope with the paradox that a scholar who did not at all deny his origin in the tradition of the "German Mandarin" (using Fritz Ringer's term) had such lasting influence on the most modern country in the Western world.[54] However, by intensifying the antimodern habitus to the extreme, Strauss both elucidated and exposed the most problematic aspect of this tradition, a tradition that – to prove its worth – culminated in the relation to the self-proclaimed field of contemporary political practice.

Yet, even if one considers the gap between this idea and democratic politics as unbridgeable, the way Strauss paved for himself – from Spinoza to the Jewish classical authors of the Middle Ages and from there to the Platonic Socrates – points at least to a doctrine of salvation no longer centered on the severe God of Jewish legal orthodoxy but rather on the milder, polytheistic Greek humanism. Behind this impressive intellectual achievement, *From Jerusalem to Athens,* to modify one of Strauss's most telling titles, is perhaps the hidden and therefore all the more powerful inner conflict of a Jewish heretic whose charismatic temperament one may reject but whose courage is beyond doubt. Strauss embodies that imperturbable spirit of saying "no," which is not restricted to a single line of affirmative impact. He hardly differs in this legacy from Herbert Marcuse, who is otherwise often referred to as his political antipode. In a society that experiences the "revenge of nature" every single day it is highly ambivalent to speak of the "right of nature." Detached from the antidemocratic elite model a political theology could become – just because its basic concept, like the name of Jahweh, may not be mentioned – a vehicle for a fundamental change: the utopia of redemption in a graceless world.[55]

53 Gordon S. Wood, "The Fundamentalist and the Constitution," *New York Review of Books* (Feb. 18, 1988); Karl L. Deutsch and W. Soffer, ed., *The Crisis of Liberal Democracy. A Straussian Perspective* (Albany, N.Y., 1987); and recently, Thomas G. West, "Leo Strauss and the American Founding," and Christopher Bruell, "A Return to Classical Political Philosophy and the Understanding of the American Founding," in *Review of Politics* 53 (1991): 157–72 and 173–86, respectively.
54 Fritz K. Ringer, *The Decline of the German Mandarins* (Cambridge, Mass., 1969).
55 A more general and fascinating interpretation is now given by Steven B. Smith, "Leo Strauss: Between Athens and Jerusalem," *Review of Politics* 53 (1991): 75–99.

# 8

# The Modern World of Leo Strauss

ROBERT B. PIPPIN

I

There are a number of very well-known controversies associated with Leo Strauss.[1] However, while arguable, it seems fair enough to claim that it is his complex and multifront attack on the insufficiencies of modernity that stands as his most influential legacy in America, both inside and outside the academy. This probably has something to do with the unique importance of the ideas of Enlightenment, religious tolerance, and scientific optimism in American political life, when compared to the more homogeneous societies of Western Europe. The very possibility and fate of an American nation-state is tied deeply to the possibility and fate of Enlightenment modernity, and so Strauss's reflections were bound to find a distinct (and distinctly contentious) audience in the United States.

Moreover, the problem of Strauss's reception has become even more fascinating and confusing in the contemporary American academy. His attacks on the self-satisfaction of post-Enlightenment culture, his doubts about the benefits of technological mastery, about the attempted avoidance of any public reliance on religion, and about the modern confidence in the power of enlightened self-interest in the formation of a polity, all often delivered in a rhetoric sometimes bordering on biblical prophecy, have now suddenly reappeared, more quietly but insistently, on the agendas of neo-Aristotelians, critical theorists, communitarians, and postmodernists. The literature on the newly rediscovered "problem of modernity," Strauss's central and, until recently, quite neglected problem, could now fill several shelves a year and shows no signs of abating. It has also created a different,

---

1 I mean such things as: his theory of esoteric writing, his passionate attack on the political science community, with its "fact–value" distinctions and "historicism," his partisan support for what appears to be an antiegalitarian political agenda, his unusual, "classical" defense of liberal democracy, and his apparent ability to inspire a sectarian consciousness among followers.

139

and in many ways more receptive context for Strauss's claims. However, in the following I am mostly interested in the philosophical nature of Strauss's basic dissatisfactions with modernity and with the adequacy of his criticisms.

I shall focus attention on his noted "wave hypothesis," his claim that the modern experiment should be understood as occurring in three waves – a great instauration attributed mainly to Hobbes (though built on ground well prepared by Machiavelli),[2] a first "crisis" correctly diagnosed but not solved by Rousseau, and a second crisis, the continuing "crisis of our times," correctly diagnosed and ruthlessly explored by the thinker arguably more influential for Strauss than anyone other than Plato, namely, Nietzsche. In particular, I want to argue that Strauss's interpretation of the second wave (or first crisis) misinterprets and undervalues the alternatives presented by the German thinkers so influenced by Rousseau, the German Idealists: especially Kant, Fichte, and Hegel. Strauss had a number of reasons for the belief that this tradition must eventually result in a self-undermining historicism, one that intensifies rather than resolves the "modern crisis." I disagree with those reasons, and thereby disagree that there is some fatal *aporia* within modernity finally and decisively revealed by Nietzsche.[3]

However, before addressing that specific controversy, I should admit that Strauss's theory of modernity is very difficult to discuss as an isolated theme in his work, and that something first needs to be said about both the Straussian project as a whole, and its complex reception in America.

This problem of reception and, because of it, what one might consciously or implicitly bring to any discussion of Leo Strauss is quite complicated. For opponents, Strauss is everything from a rebarbative crank to a dangerous cult figure, and for many such critics he raises "the problem of modernity"

2 Strauss's works will be cited as follows, using the abbreviations indicated: "A Giving of Accounts," (*Acc*), *The College* 22 (1970): 1–5; *The City and Man* (*CM*) (Chicago, 1964); "Correspondence Concerning Modernity," (*CCM*), trans. Susanne Klein and George E. Tucker, *Independent Journal of Philosophy* 4 (1983): 105–19; *Liberalism Ancient and Modern* (*LAM*) (New York, 1968); "On Classical Political Philosophy," (*OCPP*) in *WIPP*: 78–94; "On Collingwood's Philosophy of History" (*C*), *Review of Metaphysics*, 5, (1952): 559–86; *On Tyranny* (*OT*), ed. Victor Gourevitch and Michael S. Roth (New York, 1991); *Natural Right and History* (*NRH*) (Chicago, 1968); *Persecution and the Art of Writing* (*PAW*) (Chicago, 1980); *The Rebirth of Classical Political Rationalism: An Introduction to the Thought of Leo Strauss* (*RCR*), (Chicago, 1989); *Spinoza's Critique of Religion* (*S*), trans. E. M. Sinclair (New York, 1965); *Studies in Platonic Political Philosophy* (*SPP*) (Chicago, 1983); *Thoughts on Machiavelli* (*TM*) (Chicago, 1978); "The Three Waves of Modernity," (*TW*) in Hilail Gildin, ed., *An Introduction to Political Philosophy: Ten Essays by Leo Strauss* (Detroit, 1989): 81–98; "An Unspoken Prologue to a Public Lecture at St. John's," (*UP*) *The College* 30 (1979): 30–31; *What Is Political Philosophy?* (*WIPP*) (Chicago, 1959). Here, *TW*, 84.

3 For one thing, such rational-will theories, in the work of Rawls, Habermas, Gewirth, prominent Kantian theorists like Onora O'Neill, and in attacks on Strauss like that by Luc Ferry, occupy a far larger area of the political theory stage than during Strauss's lifetime, and that fact alone suggests a modernist strategy in political thought that at least appears far more resilient, both culturally and philosophically, than Strauss seems to have anticipated.

only because he is an anti- or at least premodern thinker, wedded to a premodern view of natural hierarchy and a kind of religious sense of human
finitude, and so believes in the permanence of insoluble political problems.[4]
Even his followers present him as both a pious natural law absolutist and,
on the other extreme, a closet Nietzschean; a sincere enemy of modern relativism, or an opponent merely of the openness of the modern discussion
of the deeply conventional nature of moral and political life; a moral cru-
sader against modernity, or a sophisticated, dissembling zetetic.[5]

In the light of these controversies and this recent reemergence of the
modernity problem, I need to begin with a few very general remarks about
what Strauss understands by the modernity problem, the question to which
his three-wave analysis is the response.

The least controversial claim one could make is that his modernity critique is everywhere motivated by one great opposition, or *gigantomachia,* the
*quarrel between the ancients and the moderns.* The best-known implication of
Strauss's understanding of such a fundamental clash, and the origin of by far
the greatest scholarly controversy, is his claim about ancient and much of
early modern writing. It is esoteric. Great thinkers do not say what they
mean when they write publicly; they dissemble or write in a way that will
not be easily and clearly understood by the many, the hoi polloi, and they
indicate, deftly and most carefully, their true intentions "for those with ears

---

4  This view of Strauss as an antimodern proponent of ancient thought has persisted, despite Strauss's
   many warnings against expecting classical "recipes for today's use," his clear admission that modern
   political thought has produced a kind of society "wholly unknown to the classics," for which "classical principles . . . are not immediately applicable" and his frequent defense of modern liberal democracy. Cf. *LAM,* 4–5, 10, 23; 207–08; *WIPP,* 27–28, 78–87; and *CM,* 11. There is of course still the
   ambiguity of that "immediately." Perhaps, it would be more accurate to see Strauss as a tentative supporter of Nietzsche's interpretation of those dissatisfied with modernity: "The main thing about them
   is *not* that they wish to go "back," but that they wish to get–*away.* A little *more* strength, flight, courage,
   and artistic power, and they would want to *rise,* not return!." *Beyond Good and Evil,* trans. W. Kauf-
   mann (New York, 1966), sec. 10: 17.
5  Cf. Thomas Pangle, "Introduction" to *Leo Strauss: Studies in Platonic Political Philosophy* (Chicago,
   1983); the review by Harry Jaffa, "The Legacy of Leo Strauss," *Claremont Review* 3 (1984): 409–13;
   and their subsequent exchange in vol. 4: 18–24. Some support for a "Nietzschean" view of Strauss
   can be found in ch. 2 of *NRH.* While Strauss sometimes slips into the voice of the position discussed,
   the remarks on p. 107 about the "fictitious" nature of the city are striking.
       Shadia Drury has presented the most extreme Machiavellian/Nietzschean/esoteric reading of
   Strauss in *The Political Ideas of Leo Strauss* (London, 1988), 29, 36, 170–81. The idea of Strauss's
   "philosopher" as Nietzschean "superman," "*creating* values, is an absurd overstatement and misses a
   very central issue in Strauss's account, the problem of nature, nowhere explored with any sensitivity
   in Drury's book. The crude characterization of Strauss as a "consequentialist" does not much help
   matters either. A much more subtle discussion of Strauss's "exotericism" and his relation to Nietzsche
   can be found in Stanley Rosen, *Hermeneutics as Politics* (Oxford, 1987), 107–23. See especially his remarks on why the Straussian "hypothesis" is "*an act of will,* and hence a moral matter," 111, 118, 119,
   122, 125 ("my thesis is that Strauss is himself almost a Nietzschean . . . "), 127, and the top of 133,
   where Rosen suggests his own position, a more dialectical relation between pretheoretical intuition
   and discursive account giving.

to hear," for the few capable of following the hints and clues. This strategy is, first of all, prudential. If Straussianism were a religion, its central icon, rivaling the crucified Christ, would be Socrates drinking the hemlock. According to Strauss, it is by no means a mere contingency that the emergence of the first great philosopher coincided with his condemnation and execution by the city, and virtually everything Strauss (himself a political and "ideological" émigré)[6] wrote is in one way or another informed by that event. There is a necessary hostility between "the city" – any political unit that must rely on opinion, convention, and religion (that is, any political unit) – and "philosophy" – an enterprise devoted to inquiry about the universal and eternal and so inimical to the locally sacred and ancestral. However, this also means for Strauss that the philosopher writes secretly not only to protect himself but also as a way of discharging his debt to the city; he knows his own danger, and knows how much his leisure accrues a debt to the city, and so acts beneficently by writing carefully.[7]

This hermeneutical issue already evinces Strauss's fundamental claim, a tragic view of the human predicament: political life, its sacrifices, compromises, and effort, is worthwhile to the extent that it allows and helps promote human perfection, the distinctive, extremely rare excellence of the species, the philosophical life.[8] But no political community could be based on such an ideal, no call for sacrifice or effort for the sake of the "few" could ever hope to enlist the support of the "many," who love "their own," especially their own families, and can live together politically only by coming to regard the city as also "their own," itself an extremely difficult task. Although we tend to think of justice as a paradigmatic human good, Strauss often contrasts justice (even if only understood as "doing good to friends as harm to enemies") with "the good," whose possession, if possible, is essentially private. If such claims are coupled with the assertion that such an excellent, or even a second- or third-best regime, is wholly a matter of chance, then we should conclude, as he does, that the chief political virtue is moderation; the chief vice, idealism; the central modern folly: the promise that philosophy can play a public role, that by understanding ourselves as we truly are (and by relaying some of these truths to the Prince, or, ultimately, by publishing our results, speaking *als Gelehrte*), we will also be able to establish peace, conquer *fortuna*, rationally coordinate the pursuit of private

---

6 Cf. Nathan Tarcov's discussion of how the "crisis of the West, of modernity," "was, for Strauss most clearly exemplified by the Jewish problem, which he [Strauss] regarded as 'the most manifest symbol of the human problem insofar as it is a social or political problem.' " *Epilogue* to *History of Political Philosophy,* 3rd ed. (Chicago, 1987), 909. The quotation is from *S,* 6.
7 Cf. *CM,* 52.
8 Cf., however, the remark in *CM* that "Socratic conversation" and "Platonic dialogue" are "slightly more akin to comedy than to tragedy," 61.

ends in a public realm, achieve a social order and rule of law held together, defended, and reproduced by appeal to reason; or that we shall become, finally, the subjects of history.

Said a different way that will be relevant later, the modern promise could be put in Hegelian terms: it is the promise of *Versöhnung* or a full reconciliation among fellow citizens. The modern demands for legal equality, politically secured self-determination, a fair distribution of collective resources, all involve, when understood as ethical demands, the hope for a full reconciliation among fellow citizens. This will mean that the "realization" of each, whether as rational egoist or as free, self-determining agent, requires, and is understood to require, the realization or at least the possible realization, of all. There will then, thereby, be a full reconciliation between all citizens and their social, political, legal, and indeed religious institutions, all regarded as the products of, or at least rationally protected by, their collective, and so mutually reconciled will, and not merely required by chance, necessity, tradition, class power, or circumstance. Essentially, this is also the Christian promise: that there need not be masters and slaves, that, exactly like Christ, each is both master and slave, ruler and ruled, father and son, at once. I think it is fair to say that Strauss's attitude toward such claims is exactly the same as Nietzsche's, even if he hides his contempt a bit better.

The "ancient" position by contrast (at least if we adopt Strauss's usual *façon de parler,* and abstract from the vast differences among Plato, Aristotle, the Stoics, etc.) is easy to state: no reconciliation.[9] The city or the public world of human affairs is a permanent cave. Even if the philosopher in the *Republic* can be persuaded (perhaps by the force of the argument that he owes the city a debt) or, paradoxically, can persuade the many to compel him to return, it is clear that he must rule in the dark. He cannot bring the outside light in, and it never seems to enter his mind to attempt to bring those inside out (apart from the select few).[10] By remembering the complex, censored education, and the control of images presented in the early

---

9  Cf. Victor Gourevitch, "Philosophy and Politics II," *Review of Metaphysics* 22 (1968): 296.

10  I am alluding here to recent controversy created by M. F. Burnyeat's review, "Sphinx without a Secret," *New York Review of Books,* 32, no. 9 (May 30, 1985): 30–36. See the exchange in 32, no. 15 (Oct. 10, 1985), "The Studies of Leo Strauss: An Exchange." The problem of the philosopher's return to the cave in Book VII of the *Republic* is the single philosophic issue at stake between Burnyeat and the respondents in Strauss's name. On the general issue of Strauss's reluctance to engage in the more "technical" aspects of Platonic philosophy, cf. the apposite remarks by Stanley Rosen, *Hermeneutics as Politics,* 121. But whether Burnyeat or Strauss is right about the interpretation of that passage seems to me to miss the larger point. The "unrealizability" of the city described in the *Republic* is a central, explicit theme *in* it. Not only does Socrates make very clear how unlikely its realization is, he goes on to claim that in the unlikely, chance event it were realized, it is *impossible* that it could survive beyond the first generation. (There is no knowledge of the "marriage number.") So, it is highly unlikely that such a city could be realized and even if realized, *impossible* that it could survive. So in what sense could the *Republic* be an "ideal" to be *imitated*? That is the only question important to Strauss's larger purposes.

books, we can even surmise that Socrates as ruler assumes the role of chief puppeteer, at least projecting salutary and philosophically informed shadows.[11]

Both positions, when thought through, involve dialectical twists that are important but cannot be explored in this context. That is, the promise of reconciliation in someone like Hegel famously requires and never overcomes (even while it "sublates") the modern experience of "alienation," a great diversity and opposition within civil society, and especially the loss of the natural world and even the family as "home," and the promise of a final reconciliation only within institutions produced by human will. For Strauss (and Hannah Arendt, incidentally, both decisively influenced by Heidegger), such a promise of a genuinely modern, "artificial" reconciliation of self with self, others, and world is a disastrous promotion of a self-defining subjectivity, connected with the thoughtless attempt to establish human dominion over the planet, and with the apotheosis, not the overcoming, of alienation or loss. It inaugurates what will become apparent in Nietzsche: a complete "measurelessness" for human deeds and a dangerous, vain, and finally apolitical (either moralistic or aesthetic) self-absorption. By contrast, Strauss (and again Arendt) regards a genuine recognition of the finitude of "the human things" (or the "human condition"), or an acceptance of the permanently unreconciled "natural" condition of human life as itself the realization of reconciliation, and so the beginning of a truly humane politics not based on hybris or resentment. As we shall see, many such issues in Strauss devolve from his understanding of Rousseau. Consequently, how he understands what is everywhere for him the central issue: the problem of nature in modernity.

These sorts of considerations introduce Strauss's sweeping claim that any form of this modern promise can be fulfilled only in one of two unacceptable and ultimately incoherent ways. A fully mutual, common reconciliation among all citizens might be possible if we drastically "lower" our conception of the ends to be served by political life, if we actually find a lowest common denominator, minimally common to all persons and so a possible goal of rationally coordinated action, and if we treat such a goal as

---

11 This is all not because the philosopher "knows things" of great danger to the city. His only knowledge is knowledge of ignorance, and *that* is why he is so dangerous, or far more dangerous than if he represented a determinate set of claims. The radically skeptical, incomplete, or zetetic character of Strauss's version of Socraticism is what promotes a kind of homelessness potentially subversive in contexts where steadfast loyalty, faith, and dedication are the required virtues. See the very helpful discussion in Victor Gourevitch, "Philosophy and Politics II," 304–11.

Paradoxically this characterization also undermines somewhat Strauss's claims about "tension" since it suggests what is at least as manifest in Platonic dialogues as is the political problem of Socrates – the political irrelevance of Socrates, his being ignored, mocked, his not having a *techne*, and so being an *idiotas*, his lack of success in influence as well as in arguments.

the whole of the political problem. Strauss associates this strategy first with Machiavelli, who rejected the ancient orientation from how men ought to be, and took his bearings from how men are, and then, decisively, with Hobbes's "political hedonism,"[12] his beginning with what are in fact the most powerful passions. And he regularly asserts that such a reconciliation based on enlightened self-interest founders on the gang-of-robbers problem, or that the position must recommend noncooperation and active defection when the risk of detection is low, and faces insurmountable problems in situations like war or risk of life.[13]

Second, and more elusive, Strauss is aware that a principled form of reconciliation, a model for self-ruling rather than ruler and ruled, would be possible if the basis of that reconciliation were the mutual recognition of a common capacity worthy of such universal respect and clearly capable of generating and sustaining such respect; if our mutual claims on and debts to each other were not based on a strategy of self-interest or self-preservation but on the realization that any act of mine (insofar as I am an agent) presupposes a like capacity in all such agents, and so I may not act as if it did not, as if I were a unique exception. Starting with Rousseau, of course, this capacity is "freedom" and a central hope in the modern tradition is that some nonegoistic principle of freedom could be the basis of a universally self-ruling, socially integrated, self-reproducing, or what I am calling a reconciled, political community.

Strauss strongly disagrees. In the first place, he often alludes to many familiar dissatisfactions with this option. Why is freedom only one among many competing goods, not at all a "supreme condition" of any other good being a good? How could such a morally rigorous, even absolutist requirement ever serve as a guide to political life? How could a formal criterion of permissible action, a principle that rules out the forbidden and requires the strictly obligatory, ever substantively guide human life, provide a measure for what sort of life is worthwhile, the highest? More generally he is clearly most worried that any position that links right with what the will legislates for itself or produces quickly heads down the slippery slope toward legal positivism, historicism, relativism, and finally nihilism.[14]

12  *NRH*, 169. Machiavelli had been "ancient" enough to recognize the importance of glory in any account of a stable, thriving regime. This drops out in Hobbes and, for Strauss, decisively distinguishes him from Machiavelli.

13  Clearly of course, from the modern point of view sights are raised, not lowered, particularly when the point of comparison is scholasticism and papal or feudal politics. In a phrase: *sapere aude*! See Stanley Rosen, "A Modest Proposal To Rethink Enlightenment," in *The Ancients and the Moderns* (New Haven, Conn., 1989), 1–21.

14  *NRH*, 17. I should note here that Strauss only asserts that "The historical school had obscured the fact that particular or historical standards can become authoritative only on the basis of a *universal*

He realizes of course that there is a difference between the beginning of a slope and the end-point (that Rousseau and Kant intend to be universalists and rationalists), but his general position clearly assumes some sort of strict disjunction: either there is a natural (nonconventional and nonposited) standard for right, or there is (ultimately if not initially) positivism, historicism, nihilism. Early modernity (pre-Rousseau) still preserved such an appeal to nature but at far too low and accommodating a level, one insufficient to sustain any genuine political community. Later modernity is too vulnerable to Nietzsche's challenges and Heidegger finally represents the "culmination," the "highest self-consciousness" of "modern thought."[15] These latter claims, about the "second wave" and its consequences, are what I want to explore.

## II

Several ambiguities, often remarked upon, arise in what Strauss claims.[16] And these ambiguities are compounded by a more fundamental ambiguity: Strauss's hesitancy to say very much as a "political philosopher" in the modern, conventional sense. That is, his own account of political philosophy (apart from his historical studies of others' attempts to philosophize about

principle which imposes an *obligation* on the individual to accept . . . " Depending on what Strauss means by "authoritative," such a claim is either a tautology, or begs the question at issue. Some principle can be authoritative for me if, in some situation it counts as a reason *for me* to act; to claim otherwise would require a much more serious confrontation with a figure Strauss (and, as far as I can see, most of his students) neglect: David Hume.

15  *WIPP,* 57. Heidegger is not here mentioned by name, but there is little doubt whom Strauss means. For Strauss's comments on his own debts to Heidegger, see *WIPP,* 248; *Acc,* 2–3; *UP,* 31. See also Pangle's somewhat Heideggerian characterization (or so it seems to me) of the role of "need" (or "care") in "shaping" awareness, "Introduction," 5.

   Luc Ferry, in *Political Philosophy I: Rights – The New Quarrel Between the Ancients and the Moderns,* trans. Franklin Philip (Chicago, 1990), makes a *very* great deal out of the relation between Strauss's modernity critique and Heidegger's. See esp. pp. 19 and 37, where he criticizes the results of this affinity for Strauss's political thought. Strauss subscribes to "the neoconservative [sic] tendency to sacralize natural inequalities . . . ," 21. Ferry nowhere addresses the enormous differences between Strauss and Heidegger over the nature of the "pretheoretical orientation" so crucial for Strauss and so underplays Strauss's vigorous attacks on Heidegger's historicism.

   Moreover, Ferry's criticism, which also takes up the post-Rousseauian or German Idealist themes introduced here, is limited by relying on a traditional and, I think, deeply flawed reading of Hegel (as a metaphysical "identity theorist," with a historicist theodicy) and by a reading of Fichte (essentially Philonenko's) which presents an elaborate, idiosyncratic interpretation of the *Wissenschaftslehre,* only to end up attributing to Fichte a Kantian position still vulnerable to many of Hegel's original worries. See my *Hegel's Idealism: The Satisfactions of Self-Consciousness* (Cambridge, 1989), ch. 1 and ch. 3, and *Modernism as a Philosophical Problem: On the Dissatisfactions of Self-Consciousness* (Oxford, 1991), ch. 3.

16  Many of the most puzzling have to do with a central theme in his multifaceted worries about modern secularism and enlightenment, what he calls the Athens–Jerusalem theme, or the competing claims of reason and revelation. Cf. *NRH,* 74, 75, 86; *S,* 30, and Richard Kennington, "Strauss's *Natural Right and History,*" *Review of Metaphysics* 25 (1974): 69.

the political things) seems mostly concerned with the political problem of philosophy, or the political issue of a philosophic life, rather than a philosophy of politics.[17]

Moreover, Strauss's account sometimes slips into an indictment of the hubris or folly of the modern founders and so neglects the larger issue of the *motivations* for the modern revolt against antiquity. Any further consideration of that theme would introduce issues rarely mentioned by Strauss: the role of Scholastic controversies (especially nominalism, and the continuing problem of the Gnostic heresy[18]); the Reformation, and the transformation of political notions of right directly linked to Reformation ambiguities about church–state relations.[19] Moreover, while Strauss is clearly out to defend the classical notion of natural right, he never does so in his own voice, preferring to write historical studies. These studies sometimes seem to propose logical connections among ideas, or "necessary deteriorations" of positions, which commit Strauss to a complicated historiography only rarely discussed as such, and which leave the details of his own views, or his strategy for defending natural right, hidden in asides, allusions, remarks, marginal comments, and so forth.[20]

But there is a deeper issue involved in the way Strauss presents the ancient–modern contrast, one that will lead us directly to problems with his second wave. That problem has to do with his motivation for presenting the issue as a *quarrel* between the ancients and moderns. Given the obvious deep continuities between the traditions, and the difficulties it raises in understanding the connections between Christianity and modernity, what do we gain by viewing the issue this way?

Partly, Strauss thinks, this gain stems from our own historical situation. He writes that only "men living in an age of intellectual decline" have a suf-

---

17 In *OCPP*, he contrasts a "provisional" definition of political philosophy, in which philosophy is the manner of treatment, and the political is the subject matter, with a "deeper" meaning, in which, "the adjective 'political' in the expression 'political philosophy' designates not so much a subject matter as a manner of treatment; from this point of view, I say 'political philosophy' means primarily not the philosophic treatment of politics, but the political, or popular, treatment of philosophy, or the political introduction to philosophy – the attempt to lead the qualified citizens, or rather their qualified sons, from the political life to the philosophical life," 93–94.

18 As in, e.g., Amos Funkenstein, *Theology and the Scientific Imagination from the Middle Ages to the Seventeenth Century* (Princeton, N.J., 1986), and Hans Blumenberg, *The Legitimacy of the Modern Age*, trans. Robert Wallace (Cambridge, Mass., 1983). See my "Blumenberg and the Modernity Problem," *Review of Metaphysics* 40 (1987): 535–57.

19 Cf., e.g., Quentin Skinner, *The Foundations of Modern Political Thought* (Cambridge, 1978).

20 Interestingly enough, as Nathan Tarcov has pointed out, many of these standard criticisms of Strauss were first raised by Strauss himself in a 1946 review of John Wild. This introduces a new level of ambiguity, an ambiguity about how Strauss himself understood these ambiguities in his work. Cf. Nathan Tarcov, "On a Certain Critique of 'Straussianism'," *Review of Politics*, 53, no. 1 (Winter 1991), 7.

ficiently powerful and ultimately fruitful motive for a devoted reading of old books. In such a situation alone does history "take on philosophical significance." It is a profound dissatisfaction with our own situation that provides us with "good reasons for believing that we can learn something of utmost importance from the thought of the past which we cannot learn from our contemporaries."[21]

What is that "thought?" In "Political Philosophy and History," Strauss claims that modern historicism "creates an entirely new situation for political philosophy," one that raises "the most urgent question for political philosophy."[22] In a remarkable discussion of the "natural obstacles to philosophy" in *Persecution and the Art of Writing,* Strauss describes this situation with an image and tries to explain why it is novel. Using the classic Platonic image of the cave, Strauss suggests that it is as if people had "dug a deep pit beneath the cave in which they were born" and had withdrawn into that pit.

If one of the descendants desired to ascend to the light of the sun, he would first have to try to reach the level of the natural cave, and he would have to invent new and most artificial tools unknown and unnecessary to those who dwelt in the natural cave. He would be a fool, he would never see the light of the sun, he would lose the last vestige of the memory of the sun, if he perversely thought that by inventing his new tools he had progressed beyond the ancestral cave dwellers.[23]

That is, our situation is "beneath" the natural obstacles (passion and superstition) described by Spinoza; "it is obvious that that situation does not exist in our time"[24] – where "that situation" is some "natural" experience of the nature of political life and its relation to philosophy. Instead, the "twin sisters," Science and History, have conspired to render impossible anyone's taking seriously the possibility of a genuine account of "the whole" (and this especially has shaped, forever altered our direct experience of the "things around us"). Our "natural" experience has been thoroughly distorted by an unphilosophic science, and a weak competitor, unscientific, ever more "poetic" philosophy. Science still needs some sort of historical narrative to establish its authority, its progressive character, but this history now incoherently replaces rather than introduces philosophy. Thus, in a remarkably sweeping conclusion, Strauss asserts, . . . *there no longer exists a direct access to the original meaning of philosophy,* as quest for the true and final account of the whole. Once this state has been reached, the original meaning of philosophy is accessible only through recollection of what philoso-

---

21 *C,* 576, 585 (my emphasis). See also Nathan Tarcov, "Philosophy and History: Tradition and Interpretation in the Work of Leo Strauss," *Polity* 16, (1983), 24.
22 *WIPP,* 57.      23 *PAW,* 155–56.      24 *PAW,* 156.

phy meant in the past, that is, for all practical purposes, only through the reading of old books.[25]

Our artificial tools are hermeneutical, linguistic, and, ironically, historical; our reward is at least to climb out of our artificial "subcave," and to confront the natural obstacles to (and, presumably, natural opportunities for) philosophy, as these were "originally" understood in classical philosophy. In such old books, we are said to experience what Strauss calls the "natural" understanding of political things,[26] or "the understanding of political things which belongs to political life."[27]

So, if we could recover this "natural" experience of the human things, we could at least understand and, presumably, perhaps, begin to defend the classic "natural right" doctrine, the claim that there is by nature a best life. And with such a promise we are introduced again to that most important and least developed of Strauss's themes, nature.[28] He does not deny that "natural right in its classic form is connected with a teleological view of the universe" at the same time that he freely admits that "the teleological view of the universe, of which the teleological view of man forms a part, would seem to have been destroyed by modern natural science."[29] He admits honestly that "an adequate solution to the problem of natural right cannot be found before this basic problem has been solved."[30] But there is no indication whatsoever that he thinks he solves it.

The problems are manifest already in Strauss's use of Plato's very image. In the *Republic,* Plato's depiction of the prephilosophical situation makes it very clear that the obstacles to philosophy are both natural and artificial. The cave itself is natural image, representative of our initial, natural ignorance, but that situation is made extraordinarily worse by very ambiguously presented artifices. Someone has chained the prisoners to the ground, pre-

---

25  *PAW,* 157 (my emphasis). See also *CCM,* 106–7, 109, 114, esp. the claims about our being "still natural beings with natural understanding" even though "the way of natural understanding has been lost to us."

26  *NRH,* 79.      27  *CM,* 11–12.

28  "Strauss was dedicated to the restoration of a rich and concrete natural consciousness of the political phenomenon." Allan Bloom, "Leo Strauss: September 20, 1899–October 18, 1973," *Political Theory* 2, no. 4 (1974): 376. See also 379 and the reference to Kant. Cf. also, on the general problem of nature in Strauss, Kennington's "Strauss's *Natural Right and History,*" cited previously, is indispensable.

29  *NRH,* 7–8.

30  *NRH,* 8. See also *TW.* 85. Strauss's own reliance on teleology is quite limited. His concern is not with teleological *explanation,* and he certainly does not write as if final causes are also efficient. Moreover he has little to say about a complex natural hierarchy, or chain of being. It is only important to him that in some sense the human kind is not the highest, and that the nature of the human kind provides a "standard" for life, something Strauss most often interprets as a limit, as in *TW,* 86. This raises interesting questions about his view of philosophy, the most immoderate of activities. Cf. *WIPP,* "For moderation is not a virtue of thought. . . . " even though "moderation is a virtue controlling the philosopher's speech," 32. Cf. also Gourevitch, "Philosophy and Politics II," 290–93.

venting them from turning their heads; the light within the cave is wholly
artificial, and the images they see on the wall are themselves many removes
from reality, "shadows of artificial things" (515c). These are all presented as
such powerful obstacles that it is hard to see why Strauss thinks he needs to
add a new, artificial subcave to describe "our situation." The original
prephilosophical situation seems designed to show how effectively the possibility of philosophy in any sense, let alone some knowledge of "the
whole," has been completely suppressed, and suppressed by opinions of various sorts, not necessarily ones derived mainly from "passion or superstition." In fact, interestingly enough, the suppression seems politically
motivated, as if to preserve the power of the puppeteers.

The situation is so bad, in fact, that it could be argued that the image presents a serious *aporia.* There is no explanation of how anyone might free
himself from such chains (nor even why he would want to, given that he
does not know that he is seeing images), and plenty of evidence that even
after being freed by others, an ascent to the light would be too frightening
and uncertain. Indeed, when considered in terms of the three great images
that dominate the middle books of the *Republic,* the cave appears to be in a
"metaphysical space" itself underneath the possible ascent captured by the
divided line. There is no evidence of *eikasia,* the lowest and most important
faculty described in the line image, the ability to see images as images. Thus,
if we "work our way back" to the ancient experience of political life and
its relation to philosophy, what we would seem to discover is a powerful image of the impossibility of any natural experience of each other, or
our own political situation, obscured and mediated as such experience is
by natural ignorance, political power, nearly insuperable barriers to our
even coming to know that we don't know, and by the ever present chains
of *doxa.*

Of course it is possible that Strauss may be quite wrong about some historically privileged and natural (rather than merely different, otherwise oriented) experience of "what belongs to political life" and still be right that the
classical alternative itself, even if indebted to unique and long lost conven-
tions, is superior. But it is essential to the classical alternative itself, or at least
to the critical force of Strauss's position, that we be able in some way to identify the "natural order of things," the situation of the human qua human.[31]

---

31  Rosen, in *Hermeneutics as Politics,* has rightly suggested that the better Straussean strategy (sometimes
    followed by Strauss) would be to try to show that the fundamental political problems emerge as the
    same *in all times.* "Then the Greeks as Greeks become irrelevant," 128. This would still, however,
    run afoul of the Kantian and post-Kantian objections to the *possibility* of such an identification of our
    "natural situation."
      Rosen himself, in his own work, is not concerned with that problem, since he believes that such

And this, above all, is what is so incompatible theoretically with post-Kantian critical philosophy and its political implications. Modern historicism, after all (assuming for the sake of argument that there is such a unified phenomenon) did not originate in the conservative reaction of the German historical school and it does not primarily develop as a consequence of the modern emphasis on the "individual (eventually the individual national character), so visible in Hobbes and Rousseau. The decisive modern book in philosophy, especially for *that* problem, is not Machiavelli's *Prince* or *Discourses,* or Hobbes's *Leviathan,* or Locke's *Essay* or Rousseau's *Second Discourse,* or even, I would argue, Descartes's *Meditations.*[32] It is Kant's *Critique of Pure Reason* (again, particularly given Strauss's concerns with Weber, Nietzsche, and Heidegger, that is, with positivism and historicism), and none of Strauss's allusions to the recovery of a "natural" orientation, or of *the* human things, will be of much philosophic interest unless the Kantian attack on the entire rationalist and empiricist tradition, on the dogmatism of the classical notion of nature, is taken into account in philosophic terms.[33] After all, Strauss himself would point out that it is only after Kant that the discussions of "natural" right end. Machiavelli, Hobbes, Locke, and, though the decisive transitional figure, Rousseau still appeal to nature as a standard, even if a mechanistic, purposeless, or subhuman nature. That all becomes in a certain sense "impossible" after Kant. And, at least originally, one must take seriously the claim that the Kantian attack on nature is based on a theoretical attack on the very possibility of such appeals and on a complex, "transcendental," nonskeptical alternative.[34]

The Kant problem is especially important because Strauss himself sometimes suggests or at least alludes to a kind of neo-Kantian solution to his own great problem of teleology. That solution involves denying that a teleological understanding of ourselves and of nature is a direct competitor with nonteleological accounts, that they are not answers to the same question,

---

Kantian objections stem from a project that is in itself essentially practical, based on a kind of Nietzschean recommendation to "will" a different world, and so that it is not in a better theoretical position in its critical stance. Once there is no "natural standard" . . . "all theory is construction." See 126, inter alia. I've the same problems with this "slippery slope" argument (here, in Rosen, from Kant to Nietzsche) as I do with Strauss's Rousseau-to-historicism slide. The ride is so fast that many potential safe stops on the way down are too hastily ignored.

32 See my *Modernism as a Philosophical Problem,* and "Hegel, Modernity, and Habermas," *Monist* 74 (June 1991).

33 See the very brief reference in *NRH,* 19–20.

34 I put it this way because it is open to someone sympathetic to Strauss to argue that Kant's own critical attack is motivated by a practical project not finally defensible discursively, but only intuitively. See Stanley Rosen's chapter on "Transcendental Ambiguity" in *Hermeneutics as Politics,* 19–49, and my discussion of Kant in ch. 3 of *Modernism.* For a discussion of the "moral foundations of Kant's critical philosophy," see Richard Velkley, *Freedom and the End of Reason* (Chicago, 1989).

and that each question, understood properly within its own domain, is a legitimate one. Strauss himself suggests this solution in language that seems to reflect his debt to Husserl and Heidegger, more than to the systematic reflections of Kant or Hegel. He invokes, often incidentally and without elaboration, the indispensability of a teleological perspective in any attempt to understand the "human experience of the human," the natural or lived world, as it is lived, for us, and as it forms the subject, say, of novels, drama, poems; the sine qua non of any adequate political reflection on human life, rather than an "object" of study artificially created by a methodology.[35]

However, unless we are willing to accept something like Husserl's methodology, with its suspensions, bracketings, and reductions, such a strategy will still not uncover, and would make much more dubious, any notion of a distinctive "natural" point of view, only later overlaid with scientific and historicist prejudices. The whole notion of a practical point of view, a life-world, or lived perspective is a descendant of the idealist denial that an unmediated appeal to nature or any sort of immediate experience is possible. There may be structural characteristics common to the possibility of such an agent-centered framework, but these are clearly logically formal and compatible with all sorts of content, and there is no way, without begging the question, to claim that the content of the classical experience of an ordered, natural hierarchy, even if not understood as a theory about objects, but as an articulation of an experience and a pretheoretical orientation, is original or decisive.[36]

## III

In his essay, *Belief and Knowledge,* Hegel emphasizes a common theme in his account of modernity: The modern age is the realization of human freedom, indeed of "absolute freedom." But he also stresses that what makes this freedom possible is the experience of a great and terrifying loss; indeed

---

35 Perhaps the most well known of such passages: the reference to the "simple experiences regarding right and wrong which are at the bottom of the philosophic contention that there is a natural right," and the surrounding discussion in *NRH,* 31–32. For passages that resonate with Husserl's influence on Strauss's view of the natural attitude, see pp. 78–79. Of the many tensions in *NRH,* none seems to me more puzzling than the contrast between Strauss's claims about such a natural experience on p. 24, where the experience of "fundamental problems" is introduced, but immediately qualified by the claim, "To leave it at this would amount to regarding the case of natural right as hopeless," and qualified by the argument that a philosophic *solution* of these problems must be possible, must be in view, if there is to be a philosophic issue of natural right; and, by contrast, p. 32, where *"no more is needed to legitimate philosophy* in its original, Socratic sense" than a grasp of these problems *just as problems* (my emphasis). Cf. Rosen's remarks on Strauss and Husserl, *Hermeneutics as Politics,* 131.

36 An experience can be pretheoretical; but it can be preconceptual or wholly "unmediated" only if one is willing to buy into, say, more of Heidegger's program than Strauss, for other reasons, ought to.

the experience that "God himself is dead, upon which the religion of recent times rests."[37] However much this loss creates an "infinite grief, . . .
dogmatic philosophies" and "natural religions . . . must vanish," there must
be a "speculative Good Friday . . . in the whole truth and harshness of its
Godforsakenness" before the modern "resurrection" can occur.

As we have seen, Strauss doubts that the loss Hegel speaks of – essentially,
in his terms, the loss of nature as standard – will be followed by any resurrection; modernity is better described as a Good Friday with no Easter
Sunday. Again, Strauss fundamentally agrees with this aspect of the Nietzschean critique of modernity. Once the human subject is understood as a
self-legislating, even self-defining spontaneity, the German Idealist's hopes
that such spontaneity would realize itself as "law" or "reason" were
doomed. For Strauss, such an unmasking of a self-legislating reason as will
to power is reason enough to return to the ancients; for Nietzsche, it is an
unmasking of the ancients as well, and a situation that demands courage
rather than moderation.

However, since Strauss realizes that the sort of "freedom" Hegel appeals
to is not at all a species of the "early modern" liberation of the passions or
restriction of the self to self-interest and of reason to calculation, the reasons
for his doubts emerge only in his account of the "second" modern wave,
that is, the first crisis of modernity. The most self-contained expression of
his interpretation of this issue is his account of Rousseau in *Natural Right
and History*.

Naturally enough, Strauss concentrates a good deal of his discussion on
Rousseauian themes central to Strauss's own project. No writer, after all,
has had more to say about the "tensions" between individual and society
than Rousseau, and no one wrote in more "glowing terms of the charms
and raptures of solitary contemplation."[38] Of course, such contemplation is
not philosophy, but the general issues replay the Straussian theme, with civil
society "good" only for certain individuals, a type of man who "justifies
civil society by transcending it," by "living at its fringes,"[39] even if in
Rousseau "his claim to privileged treatment is based on his sensitivity rather
than on his wisdom,"[40] and even if, for Strauss, such a criterion finally "lacks
any definite human content."[41]

Nevertheless, Rousseau sees for the first time how much had been lost
in the first modern wave, especially sees the Faustian bargain, how modern

---

37 G. W. F. Hegel, *Glauben und Wissen*, in *Gesammelte Werke*, ed. Rheinisch-Westfälischen Akademie
der Wissenschaften (Hamburg, 1968ff.), vol. 4: 414; *Belief and Knowledge*, trans. W. Cerf and H. S.
Harris (New York, 1977), 191.
38 *NRH*, 291.    39 *NRH*, 292–93.    40 Ibid.    41 Ibid.

man had sacrificed virtue for ease, and had acquired freedom only freely to traffic in goods and money, to trade, to acquire, to lose himself in idleness. And Rousseau sees the potential hostility, not just the potential practical benefits, in the relation between the requirements of the small, Spartan, virtuous city and science, with its universalism and cosmopolitanism and skepticism. But nevertheless, however much Rousseau was drawn to the "classical view," he always "succumbs to the powers from which he sought to liberate himself,"[42] and remains a sort of conscientious objector within modernity, and not a genuine opponent.

The reason for this goes back to the theme we have been exploring in Strauss – the problem of nature. Rousseau is justly well known for his doubts about the attempt by Hobbes and other moderns to argue from the natural human condition. They have not, he claimed, identified the truly natural and appeal instead to contingent features of already socialized man (like pride, suspicion of others, vanity, even rationality itself). For this reason, their attempts to argue from the inherently unstable or self-contradictory situation in the natural state, justifying or requiring the sort of civil society that would resolve this problem, do not succeed. This at once opens up a great ambiguity in Rousseau, since it allows him both to appeal to a truly original state of nature as a critical weapon against all society, even as the sheer contingency of civil life makes possible a claim for such a great naturally unrestricted malleability that a far more perfected political situation becomes possible and desirable (i.e., more perfect than what Hobbes or Locke settle for, falsely constrained as they were by their illusions about nature). So Rousseau appeals both "from the modern state to the classical city" and "almost in the same breath . . . from the classical city to the 'man of nature,' the prepolitical savage."[43] "He presents to his readers the confusing spectacle of a man who perpetually shifts back and forth between two diametrically opposed positions."[44]

As he develops his picture of this tension, however, Strauss begins to stress only one, more romantic direction in his overall portrait of Rousseau. On the one hand, Strauss admits the strain in Rousseau in which, put paradoxically, nature still serves as a criterion for right only by being unavailable. "By thinking through" the appeal to nature "Rousseau was brought face to face with the necessity of abandoning it completely,"[45] and so "showed that man's beginnings lack all human traits," that it was "absurd to go back to the state of nature in order to find in it the norm for man."[46]

But this is hardly a mere negative point; it has historic positive results. It means that "what is characteristically human is not the gift of nature but is the outcome of what man did . . . in order to change or overcome nature."

42 *NRH*, 262.    43 *NRH*, 254.    44 *NRH*, 254.    45 *NRH*, 274.    46 Ibid.

And this very fact itself implies a new wholly modern notion of virtue, one according to which man is good or virtuous only as self-determining, free; that we owe ourselves and others respect only for what we have done or made. While Strauss hints at his own objections to this doctrine (by implying that it confuses freedom as a condition of virtue with virtue itself[47]) he clearly recognizes that Rousseau is attempting to preserve the notion of public or civil right on a wholly new basis, by appeal, again, to the absence of a usable natural standard, and so by appeal to the only conditions under which the human will can exercise its distinctive function. This alternate account of the will is a " 'realistic' substitute for the traditional natural law," according to which "the limitation of human desires is affected, not by the ineffectual requirements of man's perfection, but by the recognition in all others of the same right which one claims for one's self."[48]

Such a "substitute" for classical and early modern natural right should also be understood as grounded in the wider implications of Rousseau's still influential suspicions that any appeal to nature often disguises an already socialized, artificial situation. Such doubts wholly transform our notions of ends, desire, reasons, the whole structure of practical, intentional activity. One could say that Rousseau was one of the first to realize how deeply even what we feel, what feels immediately and most closely our own, might not be genuinely our own, might itself be the product of the desires of others, or the derivative result of our own desire to be desired by others. Or one might say that he lived in the sort of society for the first time powerful and influential enough to generate these worries. It doesn't matter here how one puts the issue; the result is the same. No matter how powerfully I feel drawn to an end or goal, how intimately important it seems to me, nothing about such an immediate orientation ensures that such a goal is indeed mine, truly expresses "me." Only some assurance that *I* have freely determined to pursue such a goal (an assurance, in the tradition Rousseau founded, provided by some sort of reliance on practical reason) will allow me to count the goal as mine. (This is the original meaning of the Hegelian doctrine of negation: Only by losing or "negating" my natural self can I become a genuine self, or self-conscious subject. Put another way, in its full Hegelian flourish: The true human "home" is a fully realized "homelessness," although when fully realized, no longer experienced as such.) Given such a worry, the "natural" in all the senses invoked by Strauss is "lost"; that "god" is dead.

This is not the first time in the history of philosophy that the subject would be portrayed as strange to, or ignorant of, itself, that I could "do the

---

47 *NRH*, 278.    48 *NRH*, 276.

very thing I hate." But for the first time, this dissatisfaction cannot be solved by knowledge of some substantial self, knowledge of what the human soul really is, or what it by nature needs. The subject is now an agent, a self-determining will, and so a nonalienated form of self-realization will involve securing the conditions under which I can genuinely exercise such agency, wherein my deeds reflect what *I* determine. The politics of perfection has become the politics of self-determination.

But having made all these points, and having suggested the direction of this tradition, Strauss chooses to present Rousseau as one still requiring an account of nature. He denies that Rousseau finally conceived of the "law of reason" as independent of the "law of nature," and that he was afraid of a "doctrinairism" were he to do so.[49] While Strauss admits that Rousseau himself "distinguishes true freedom or moral freedom" from "the natural freedom which belongs to the state of nature, that is, to a state character-ized by the rule of blind appetite and hence by slavery in the moral sense of the term," Strauss nevertheless insists that Rousseau "blurs these distinc-tions." He notes that Rousseau still maintains that in civil society "one obeys only himself and remains as free as before." However, Strauss inter-prets him to mean not that the citizen or moral agent simply does not lose his freedom, does not become "dependent" in imposing a law on himself. According to Strauss, Rousseau means to claim that man must be free in the same sense, "as he was in the state of nature." And for Strauss, "this means that natural freedom remains the model for civil freedom." (I note that Strauss does not say a postcivil or postsocial freedom.) After having himself reminded us unequivocally that for Rousseau it was "absurd" to find a norm for man in nature, Strauss concludes his discussion of Rousseau by insisting that nevertheless "the state of nature tended to become for Rousseau a pos-itive standard," and "hence Rousseau's answer to the question of a good life takes on this form: the good life consists in the closest approximation to the state of nature which is possible on the level of humanity."[50]

There is of course a great deal of truth to this characterization, but it seems to apply much more to *le promeneur solitaire,* a self-conscious and hardly natural refugee from civil society, and not to Rousseau's conception of a self-created political life. Or, it may be true as a statement about the good life; but it does not define the virtuous life, the only worthy or praise-worthy life possible for us. That is, Rousseau's great worry about civilized life already reflects a moral concern that makes it unlikely that Strauss's fi-nal characterization of Rousseau's position, or at least his final emphasis on one of the many aspects of Rousseau's position, could be accurate.

49 *NRH*, 277.    50 All quotations are from *NRH*, 282.

I suspect that Strauss wants to reemphasize Rousseau's romantic senti-ments, his clear pessimism about the possibility of a modern, virtuous com-monwealth, because Strauss has his own grave reservations that "moral and political ideals" can be established "without reference to man's nature."[51]

These reservations include a number of very familiar charges. First, Strauss clearly thinks that by relying simply on "reason," Rousseau's sweep-ing reservations about political life invite the famous emptiness and rigorism charges leveled against Kant by Hegel will have some bite.

> To have a reservation against society in the name of the state of nature means to have a reservation against society without either being compelled or able to indi-cate the way of life or the cause, or the pursuit for the sake of which that reserva-tion is made.[52]

Second, Strauss believed that the central modern question about the re-alization of a regime based on such principles will now require not an ap-peal to men's interests and passions but an ultimately mysterious "historical process" or fate, independent of human will, something which leads neces-sarily to Heideggerian fatalism or some form of relativism.

Third, as already indicated, Strauss believes that assigning to politics the task of the protection of "the one natural right," liberty, confuses a neces-sary condition for the realization of virtue with its sufficient condition. This is something particularly clear in his debate with Kojève in *On Tyranny*. The achievement of "universal recognition" is an empty historical achievement unless we know for what, for what great deed or achievement, individuals are being recognized. To recognize and value them for a capacity, without some natural measure for evaluating their use of that capacity, is pointless.[53]

Finally, at other places, as in his discussion of Weber in *Natural Right and History,* Strauss also implies that, without a substantial, natural theory of the human good, the appeal to reason will be unmotivated and arbitrary, suggesting some Aristotelian worries about Kantianism again very much in the news.[54]

However, while it is typical of Strauss to show that a certain position or tradition ends in a kind of *aporia* as a way of at least motivating an alterna-

51  *TW,* 92.
52  *NRH,* 294. Strauss realizes that Rousseau intends to preserve a distinction between "liberty and li-cense," but he implies throughout these concluding remarks that his theory does not have the re-sources to sustain that distinction. See also *WIPP* and his remarks there about "horizontal" as opposed to "vertical" limits on liberty, 53.
53  *OT,* 177–212. See also *TM* on modern philosophy in general, 298, and the discussion by Michael S. Roth, *Knowing and History: Appropriations of Hegel in Twentieth-Century France* (Ithaca, N.Y., 1988), 125–46.
54  See Alasdair MacIntyre, *After Virtue* (Notre Dame, Ind., 1984).

tive position, he hardly gives this "replacement" notion of autonomy a run for its money, he nowhere establishes such an *aporia* as such, and, especially, he does not discuss the many reasons in Rousseau for resisting a natural standard for civil freedom.

In the *Second Discourse,* for example, where Rousseau introduces us to the calamity of modern civilized life, his chief concern is the problem of independence.

The savage lives in himself; sociable man, always outside himself, is capable of living only in the opinions of others; and, so to speak, derives the sentiment of his own existence solely from their judgment.[55]

Given such a dependence, we are always

forever asking of others what we are, without ever daring to ask it of ourselves, in the midst of so much Philosophy, humanity, politeness, and Sublime maxims, we have nothing more than a deceiving and frivolous exterior, honor without virtue, reason without wisdom, and pleasure without happiness.[56]

Thus resurfaces Rousseau's famous problem, a problem that cannot be resolved by "making the state of nature a positive standard." On the one hand, Rousseau is very clear that savage or primitive independence is actually only chance isolation from, and ignorance of, others; not true independence from them. Further, and most important, no such savage is truly self-determining because he is so ignorant of himself. (Each savage may have "considered himself master of everything," but only because of his "weakness and ignorance." In reality, by having no understanding of others outside their family, "*they did not know themselves.* They had the concept of a father, a son, a brother, but not of a man." They are not dependent, without being truly independent.[57]) On the other hand, what we eventually establish as marks of independence in society – property, prestige, all the other consequences of *amour-propre* – and the self we end up caring so much about, everywhere involve a slavish dependence on the "opinions of others." In society, independence is always fragile and suspicious, and, ironically, establishing such independence seems to require acknowledgment by or dependence on others.

What then will count as the achievement of freedom? As Strauss shows, Rousseau believes that we must completely achieve civic virtue for this problem to be resolved.[58] Most famously this means subjecting ourselves to

55 Jean Jacques Rousseau, *The First and Second Discourses Together with the Replies to Critics and Essay on the Origin of Languages,* trans. and ed. Victor Gourevitch (New York, 1986), 199.
56 Ibid.     57 Jean-Jacques Rousseau, 261 and 262 (my emphasis).
58 I pass over the tension between the solution proposed in such works as the *Second Discourse* and the *Social Contract* and that suggested by *Reveries of a Solitary Walker.* The latter intimate that the former

the "general will"; but more complexly it also means coming to understand ourselves, our individual egos, in a wholly new way, as intimately bound up with the will of all other citizens. The *moi individu* is both the source of the self-serving egoism that generates the anomie, fragmentation, and chaos Rousseau sees as typical of modern political life, and is itself illusory, and that is the key to its overcoming. Once we are socialized, the very sentiment of our own existence, so thoughtlessly esteemed by us, in which we take so much pride, is not ours, but depends upon others. However, to be dependent on the civic unit or state, on the whole as general will, is not to be dependent on others but, finally and truly, on ourselves.[59] Acting "for ourselves" in the usual sense (egoism) is acting in the service of what others (or brute circumstances) have taught us to want. Only by freely subjecting ourselves to the general will, by identifying ourselves with the general, wholly objective good, not the preserve of any one or group, can we be self-determining agents. Or at least, only in this way can we ensure that we are not other- or nature-determined.[60]

To be sure, this is only the beginning of the issue. Rousseau is clearly interested in such autonomy because he is also still interested in happiness, in the fullest or sweetest satisfaction of our passions. This all greatly complicates the Kantian direction of the foregoing remarks, and would take us far afield in the present context. Here I only mean to suggest that the concern with autonomy so prominent in Rousseau, and the necessarily accompanying "unavailability" of any politically relevant appeal to nature, is more thoroughly and consistently motivated in Rousseau than Strauss allows for, and generates a far more powerful and influential legacy in later philosophy than the romantic, "natural" sentiments (or classicist nostalgia) pointed out by Strauss.

Let me conclude by pointing to the line of reasoning inaugurated by Rousseau and, I am claiming, seriously underrepresented in the modernity

would be, but cannot be, a solution. On the character of Rousseau's utopianism, see Judith Shklar, *Men and Citizens: A Study of Rousseau's Social Theory* (London, 1969). See also David Gauthier's remarks about the "post-social" self in his "*Le Promeneur Solitaire:* Rousseau and the Emergence of the Post-Social Self," *Social Philosophy and Policy* 8 (1990), 35–58, esp. 55.

59 This is the infamous, paradoxical claim of the *Social Contract*, book I, ch. 7, that such a "giving of each citizen to the country," or the ominous "forcing him to be free," "ensures him against all personal dependence." *The Political Writings of Jean-Jacques Rousseau*, ed. C. E. Vaughan (New York, 1962), vol. 2: 36.

60 There is obviously much more to this story, especially with regard to the infamous general will and legislator problems. Strauss clearly shares, say, Hegel's worries that Rousseau cannot effectively distinguish such a general will from the will of all, that the "general will," is "for all practical purposes, the will of the legal majority." *NRH*, 286. But Strauss seems also to reject, without much consideration, the attempt by Kant and Fichte to extend what Strauss calls Rousseau's "horizontal" limitation of liberty (*WIPP*, 53) by insisting that this very appeal (the constraint of the will of others) itself represents a "vertical" *ideal*, a genuine "kingdom of ends."

narrative told by Strauss. The central foundational issue is entwined in complex epistemological and metaphysical issues and is difficult to state simply. Obviously, the sweeping Kantian and post-Kantian attack on the possibility of a rational or a priori account of "nature" (or "substance"), as well as its attack on the efficiency of any attempt at a radically empirical account, set the stage for a drastically altered context for ethical and political thought. Most prominently, such theoretical accounts of the role of an "active" subject in "forming" and "legislating" what could count as an appeal to nature or any fact of the matter, ended up greatly influencing the way in which the "bindingness" or obligatory character of normative principles was understood. I can be so bound or obliged only if I bind myself, freely impose on myself a principle or norm. What I am by nature inclined to do, or what might be naturally satisfying or naturally flourishing and so forth, will henceforth count as reasons for action, only if they can be reasons for me, if I can count them as principles of action, under conditions that ensure that I am freely so counting them or self-imposing them.

Such an idealist attack on the possibility of givenness or immediacy or the "natural" as such thus creates the modern post-Rousseauian problem of freedom. Or: in what sense can I be said to impose a "law" on myself, such that I can be assured that I am freely legislating in such a way? Already in Rousseau, as we have seen, the problem of freedom is largely the problem of independence, and already such a good is what Kant would call a *supremum bonum,* a condition for any other good. Nothing could be said to be good for me unless I can recognize it as a good for me and pursue it as such. And already with him, such independence is crucially linked with rationality. In any case where I count as a reason to act some contingently produced or socially powerful desire or interest, I am acting in the service of others or the vagaries of nature, not as a self-determining agent. I can act as a self-determining agent only as a rational agent, only under principles equally applicable to all such agents.

And all of this introduced a rich and complicated set of problems, most of which have to do with (i) the sense in which such a notion of freedom can itself be said to be a substantive good (rather than a mere condition for the pursuit of any substantive good) and (ii) how the requirement of universality in any possible, genuine, self-legislation (how the necessity of "taking others into account" in such self-legislation) is to be understood. These are controversial, much disputed claims, but I hope to have said enough to indicate that such a tradition remains an unexplored option in Strauss's account, or a modern "wave" that has not yet peaked or crested, much less crashed and dissipated.

PART III

*Roundtable Discussion*

# Discussion

A roundtable discussion on the last day of the Boulder conference summarized the main issues examined in the essays of this volume. It also served to hone the questions raised during the conference and thus offers spontaneous insights into the interpretation of Arendt's and Strauss's work on both sides of the Atlantic. The discussion touched upon three basic themes: (1) the influence of German philosophy on these two philosophers, (2) their American experience, and (3) their respective views on democracy. What follows is an abridged and edited version of the discussion transcript, wherein redundancies have been omitted.

PETER GRAF KIELMANSEGG: I propose to begin with questions concerning the intellectual and cultural background, that is, the origins, roots, and connections between Hannah Arendt's and Leo Strauss's thinking. Next, we could revisit the question of what could be called the Americanization of Arendt and Strauss, that is, the question of the extent to which the books they wrote in this country reflect the fact that these authors have become Americans. And third, I suggest that we take up a topic of more general relevance, namely, the relationship of Arendt and Strauss to democracy. They experienced the failure of democracy in Germany, had an existential encounter with a totalitarian dictatorship, and eventually became citizens of a successful republic. Many of our questions could be brought into this context, by which I do not mean that their biographies are necessarily the most important factors in explaining their attitudes toward democracy; but it is perhaps one way of looking at the problem.

First, I would like to invite contributions related to what I have called the intellectual and cultural background, the questions of intellectual origins, roots.

## THE INFLUENCE OF GERMAN PHILOSOPHY

HARVEY MANSFIELD: I'd like to raise a question about Heidegger, whom Strauss regarded at least as the most powerful figure of this century, and who

163

I think also deeply influenced Arendt. I ask those of you, especially from Germany who are closer to this than we are, what you think the relationship was, and how he may have influenced Arendt and Strauss and how, then, Heidegger's influence may have been brought to America.

ERNST VOLLRATH: Well, it is obvious that Hannah Arendt was educated by Martin Heidegger, and some of her concepts, like loneliness, certainly stem from Heideggerian philosophy. But, I think, she transformed all those concepts, which in Heidegger are nonpolitical and apolitical, into a political framework. As a result, you are left with Arendt's personally ambivalent attitude toward Heidegger. In any case, she remained fond of him, in fact, very fond of him.

JÜRGEN GEBHARDT: I think that one important feature of Hannah Arendt's thinking that is Heideggerian is her understanding of philosophy. There is a strange tension between her return to the polis and, in fact, her use of an Aristotelian concept, on the one hand, and her dissociation from Aristotle as a philosopher, on the other.

I would like to comment on the general problem of Heidegger. Until 1926 Heidegger had not published much, but he must have had an incredible impact upon people who came to him and listened to him. All these bright young women and men went to hear him and they were enthusiastic about him, but he had not written anything besides *Being and Time*. Heidegger was a powerful personality, and it is difficult to reconstruct the impact of this powerful personality. A good deal of his influence, even of his writings, in my opinion, stems from the very fact that people heard him, listened to him. Maybe if he had not been such a powerful personality fewer people would have read and discussed his ideas.

ALFONS SÖLLNER: I would like to point out a major feature of the German style of philosophizing in the 1920s that is incorporated in Heidegger. This feature can be described using Fritz Ringer's term, the "German Mandarin."[1] But what are the characteristics of this intellectual type? I think that one of the major characteristics, which is also apparent in the work of Hannah Arendt and Leo Strauss, is a certain way of criticizing society through a very abstract *Kulturkritik* (critique of contemporary civilization or culture). I think the approach of *Kulturkritik* is one of the most important ways of seeing how they perceived an extremely political crisis as something apolitical at one and the same time. It renders concrete analysis of the crisis in

1  Fritz K. Ringer, *The Decline of the German Mandarins. The German Academic Community, 1890–1933.* (Cambridge, Mass., 1969).

highly abstract philosophical and cultural terms. Both Hannah Arendt and Leo Strauss were deeply affected by this approach.

TIMOTHY FULLER: Yes, each of the people who have spoken so far has referred in one way or another to the idea that Arendt and Strauss took Heidegger's ideas and translated them into concepts useful for political analysis. I think that is true, and it seemed to me for a long time that the most obvious example of this in Strauss is that he took inspiration from *Being and Time* in titling his most well-known book, *Natural Right and History*. The idea that the fundamental problem is encountered between natural right and history is Strauss's translation into political terms of the philosophical crisis identified by Heidegger and by Nietzsche. This translation had great merit, not only by making that problem identifiable to an American audience. Thus, to me for a long time it seemed that the very phrase "Natural Right and History," which has become one of the essential terms in the discussion among all political philosophers in the last forty years, is exactly the way in which Strauss quite ingeniously introduced that question and yet at the same time tried to protect its introduction into the American scene from what he would have considered the wrong use of it.

ERNST VOLLRATH: I would like to comment on Söllner's and Fuller's remarks and I will start with the reference to Fritz Stern's book, *The Politics of Cultural Despair*.[2] There, Stern comments on versions of cultural critique, as exemplified by Paul de Lagarde and Arthur Möller van den Bruck, among others. You see, you have a very vulgar version of cultural critique in Germany – and Fritz Stern's book is about that – but you have also a very high-standing cultural critique of modernity, and the name that has to be mentioned here is of course Friedrich Nietzsche. Nietzsche's impact on German awareness, consciousness, is not that of a philosopher but that of a cultural critic. Strauss's as well as Arendt's thinking can be regarded as some kind of answer to the awareness of cultural critique on a very high level.

HORST MEWES: I think we should also remember that there are very profound differences between Arendt and Heidegger, Strauss and Heidegger, and Strauss and Arendt on the central question of the relation of philosophy to politics. Those differences in fact show, without going into all the details at this point, that Arendt certainly no longer shares Heidegger's concept of philosophy and its relation to politics. She makes a clear-cut distinction between thinking, and therefore philosophy, and acting, one that

---

2 Fritz R. Stern, *The Politics of Cultural Despair. A Study in the Rise of German Ideology* (Berkeley, Calif., 1961 [1974]).

Heidegger himself is unable to make. We all know that the precise relationship between philosophy and politics in Heidegger is very much an
open question and subject to wide-ranging debate, but there are the well-
known instances where he talks about poets and philosophers as the voice
of being, or the transmitter of being. In fact there are plenty of places in
Heidegger where the philosopher, or something like the philosopher, does
play a genuine political role.

   In contrast, Arendt makes this clear distinction, and that is why she can,
at least up to her *Merkur* essay, literally excuse Heidegger from many of his
actions. Of course, she did not know many of the revelations that were
made later on. And, whereas of course Strauss – again putting it in short
form – objected to Heidegger's fatalism and thereby really objected to the
fact that Heidegger had – to use Tim Fuller's words – totally separated
moderation from wisdom, or had totally separated philosophizing from the
restrictions of human nature, which, according to Strauss and Strauss's version of Socrates, can and should never be done in the process of philosophizing. And so that one should not look from being to man but from man
to being. If one works this out in greater detail, I think that, although these
people were clearly under the influence of Heidegger, somehow they both
fundamentally rejected his very diffuse notions of the relation of philosophy
to politics.

GEORGE KATEB: When I think of the relationship of both Arendt and
Strauss to Heidegger and the nature of his influence on them, I would distinguish the level of cultural criticism, the cultural pessimism Alfons Söllner
referred to, from what I hesitate to call a deeper level. But it may just be
that, namely, the relationship of the thinker to existence, or to being, if you
allow me to use that charged word. On that level, it seems to me that Arendt
is the more faithful and tenacious student of Heidegger than Strauss is. I see
Arendt's life's work as an effort, in spite of everything, to adopt a philosophical love of the world, of existence, of being. She spoke recurrently of
wonder and admiration and gratitude for being, or for existence. I do not
think her political thought is understandable without reference, continuous
reference, to her anxiety that the world may not be lovable after all because
of the element of human cruelty in it. But she persisted in the effort to be
a lover, and she would be fortified by certain passages in *Being and Time,* in
which the world is made new once you die, and by Heidegger's *Einführung
in die Metaphysik* (1929), an essay on wonder and admiration.[3] If you take

---

3 Martin Heidegger, *An Introduction to Metaphysics* (Garden City, N.Y., 1960 [1959]).

Heidegger seriously, the effort to love the world after the death of God, the effort to love the world in spite of the cruelty in it, to be smitten by *Schein,* the beauty of appearance, all these are profoundly embedded in Arendt's thinking and are meant eventually to have a political effect as well.

When you come to Strauss, leaving aside for the moment the level of cultural criticism and focusing instead on the existential level, what is his relationship to the world? Or to being? I know of no expression in Strauss of wonder, or admiration, or gratitude. Is Strauss a hater of the world? Or is he still persuaded that the only way to love the world is to be religious, and because he cannot be religious, no matter, how hard he tries, he cannot love the world? It is, I think, on the existential level that Heidegger's influence may be at its most benign, which shows itself in his influence on Arendt and his failure to influence Strauss.

ROBERT PIPPIN: I think Strauss writes often about the classical sense of awe and wonder as the beginning of philosophy. The most fundamental way of expressing the point would be that he is in wonder and awe of cosmos (yes, of a design) perhaps of the world as Arendt meant it, although I think he certainly tried to articulate the sense of awe and wonder as the beginning of philosophy, instead of curiosity or control or mastery in the modern sense. But, on this larger point of the relation of Strauss to Heidegger and Nietzsche, which is a mind-boggling point that is very hard to discuss, I would first support the comment made about their relations to cultural critique. The distinctness of their positions certainly falls within all cultural critique, that they connect all four of these figures, let's say, a distaste for the socialeconomic effects of rapid modernization, anomie, mass culture, consumer culture, materialism, a growing vulgarity in the culture. It is not simply a distaste for the socioeconomic effects upon a specific organization but for the entire modern project, for the secularism and materialism they regard as inherent in modernity. Yet, how they regard these socioeconomic problems, deracinated cultures, and alienated labor is quite distinctive in the philosophical projects of Nietzsche and Heidegger and in the contemporary critiques of Strauss and Arendt. However, the great difference, of course, simply to set the facts out, is that Heidegger and Nietzsche both connect the origin of this subjectivity, willed truth, rationalism, in Plato and Socrates. For them, that is the beginning, both Heidegger and Nietzsche are quite clear about this; Nietzsche more with respect to Socrates, for Heidegger, Plato is quite clearly the beginning of the advent of nihilism. Strauss and Arendt, in contrast, both vigorously disagree with this association of the beginning of modernity with the Greeks. So, I think that marks quite a radical break with both Nietzsche and Heidegger and has other implications for their theoretical relationship with Heidegger. But there are, just to state it briefly, two important points about continuity in their adoption of the Heideggerian or Nietzschean way of thinking about the problems of modernity. One is that neither Arendt or Strauss – unlike Heidegger or Nietzsche – is led to think concretely about what one could call the provocation of modernity, about the specific early modern project, about what made the secularism and rationalism, let us not say inevitable, so as to beg the question, but necessary and perhaps historically rational. Compare their approach, for example, with that of another German scholar, Hans Blumenberg, which is much more historically specific, sensitive to nuances, to what made – given a crisis of late Christian theology and to some extent the crises of early modern science – the project of modernity, post-Copernican invention and post-Cartesian project, unavoidable. It can be said for Strauss and Arendt that, when it comes to the question of their own account of the origin of modernity, they think of it as a kind of fall, or sin, a mistake, an act of human pride, a false act of will. And that, I think, is a terribly vulnerable position, and one of the most vulnerable in their entire project.

Second, the consequence of this association with Heidegger is that their own attempt to restore what is lost in modernity, that is, to correct the problem, makes much more reference to a kind of worldliness or love of good or sense of the natural or naturally right, and ignores what is the great modern hysteria, which generally is to say epistemology; that is, the problem of reason, how we demonstrate or know or reason that what we claim to be, what we need can be had; that is, their style of reasoning is often very much like Heidegger and Nietzsche, given the fix we're in, and we got in this fix because we gave this up. Let us get it back. But the modernist position is that it would be nice to be able to believe in natural rights or in the possibility of an autonomous politics. And both schools of thought, again, influenced by Heidegger and Nietzsche, think more in terms of the end-point they want to arrive at than in terms of the problem of getting there.

TIMOTHY FULLER:  I want to make a comment that is partly generated by what Robert Pippin just said. One of the issues that lurks in the background of all these discussions is the question of whether America is an exception in the midst of modernity or not. There is a way in which both Arendt and Strauss in my opinion treat America as if some of what they think has been lost still exists here, and that it can actually be experienced here, not just that you can philosophize about it here, it is not just that people are free to think, it is that they can see something going on here that is the catalyst of the thinking experience so that there might be more continuity than in more dramatic philosophical expression of the problem than sometimes apparent. So the question for me is, "Did they think that it was an exception?" That is, did they take up the question that many Americans have also repeatedly taken up: "Is America an exceptional case in modern history or isn't it?" And sometimes, I think, they speak as if it is certainly not an exception, and it is the place where all of the problems of modernity are going to work themselves out for better or worse, and sometimes I think they treat it as somehow it is the place where you could actually retrieve, protect, or preserve certain things that need to be preserved. So, what I see in it is an ambivalence precisely of that point which is an ambivalence characteristic of Americans when they think about their own experience themselves. Therefore, I do not mean that Strauss is not loving the world, I think he loved this part of the world quite a lot. In fact, that there was a lot in it to be protected and that, maybe, some Americans did not fully understand how well off they were and that his job was to help them to see that, for all their faults as a consumer society and all the rest of that which certainly is true, there is something else about it, namely, its founding documents, certain historical experiences, successful experiments in constitutional government, which ought to be impressive to any philosopher when he starts to philosophize.

BONNIE HONIG: I want to respond to a point that Robert Pippin made, with reference to your association of Arendt and Strauss versus Nietzsche and Heidegger. I think that Arendt agrees with Nietzsche about Plato, actually, not with reference to his having been the founder of modernity – that would be silly – but with reference to his being responsible in a kind of linear sense for our predicament with modernity, which is the distinctly antipolitical tradition of thinking about politics. And in this I think the best way to think about this is in terms of the possibility of thinking about her having turned to Nietzsche as a cure for Heidegger because we talked briefly about Heidegger's effort to love the world after the death of God. But that for Arendt the problem of Heidegger's politics is produced by his failure to be really the worldly philosopher and by his embrace of a kind of introspection that she might have identified as Platonism that was responsible for a kind of incapacity to act in the best Arendtian sense. So, in some ways I think that the question of Heidegger's influence on Arendt is always interesting, but equally interesting is the source to which she turned for antidotes to that influence, which she thought was much more vital and worldly than Heidegger's philosophy was.

HARVEY MANSFIELD: Yes, I want to comment on some of the remarks of others. I agree with Robert Pippin that Strauss often did speak of the wonder that is attached to philosophy and has also expressed admiration and gratitude. One cannot wonder at something or admire something without looking up to it, perhaps literally, perhaps metaphorically. And if you look up to it, then it is no longer strictly in this world. It is not quite an argument, but it is an explanation, for I would say, according to Strauss, that it is impossible to love this world, when the world is understood, strictly speaking. If you try to love this world, you idealize it in some way or another, and then it is no longer simply the world. You could illustrate this, I think, even from Heidegger, who speaks of *Alltäglichkeiten,* or everydaynesses, impersonal in the boring sense of the world, as we so often experience, but that this has to be relieved, it has to be challenged by a resoluteness in the face of such despair. That, I think, is no longer worldly, strictly speaking.

On another point, Strauss also attended Heidegger's courses. And the one he used to speak of especially was the one on Aristotle's physics, which he said was the first serious reading of Aristotle in two or three centuries, since the Enlightenment. He said that Heidegger was the one – he blamed it on him – who taught him how to read a text and showed him just how much could be got from reading the text of a great book. Arendt was there in the same course, along with Gadamer and others.

Arendt, I think, was influenced by Heidegger not only apolitically but also politically. Her famous thesis about Eichmann seems to be related to Heidegger, the banality of evil. Eichmann was just a small cog in a gigantic bureaucratic machine, a reflection of the evil of modern technology, essentially, and not anything greater. I know Strauss always disagreed with this and he thought that this evil was enormous. It is true he did not often write about the Holocaust, but he personally lost all his family except for those who fled.

Another angle, coming back to Arendt and Heidegger's perhaps more political influence, would be her understanding of republican virtue. Let me discuss that first, the agonistic resistance. It has to do with the Americanization of Hannah Arendt. I would say it is because of her that the Left in America no longer attacks the American Revolution. That was the rueful address of Charles Beard in 1913 that the American Revolution was made by rich, bourgeois property owners who put across this constitution that was intended to defend the interest of property owners against debtors who were led by Shays, the Massachusetts Rebellion. But now I think we find a good deal of praise for the Revolution as an expression of this republican virtue.

JÜRGEN GEBHARDT: In the present situation, we have not only the breakdown of Marxism but also a change in the assessment of the Revolutionary Age, of the French and American revolutions. Slowly the American Revolution becomes the more important one, more important in some ways than the French Revolution because it was a political revolution, and I think Arendt was right in this. If you go back to the famous speech of Ernst Troeltsch where he tells the German mandarins the difference between the romantic historicism of Germany and the West.[4] Now Arendt and Strauss took this seriously, and one could understand through the rise of National Socialism, the breakdown of the Weimar Republic, that this was the outcome of what Troeltsch had described as the pure substance, the quintessence of German political, social, and cultural thought. So one could say that the cultural pessimism of the mandarins led them to take seriously the other side of the Troeltsch argument, namely, that the West had a common tradition, that is, the tradition of natural right. And they turn – and I think this is the most interesting thing – to Greek and Roman politics. And I think those were the sources of the antidote, to go back to the tradition of the West, as Troeltsch had described it. And then they came up, finally with America, American self-understanding that was also expressed in the self-understanding of the Americans, namely, that they were the true heirs to the Western tradition and that, indeed, the Declaration of Independence and the Constitution set a standard for the rest of the world, and this was a standard of natural right. Strauss and Arendt turned to the United States, and this was philosophically linked with their rediscovery of Roman-Greek antiquity. And I think that Voegelin, Strauss, and Arendt are different in this respect from any other émigré scholars.

ERNST VOLLRATH: Yes, particularly from a German point of view, Arendt offers to Germans interested in politics a different interpretation of their own culture. Regarding modernity, we can show a bit of difference between Strauss on the one hand and Arendt on the other, by pointing to two terms they use. Strauss always pointed to the self-alienation of modernity, whereas Arendt pointed to its world alienation. These are two very different concepts, I think.

## THE AMERICAN EXPERIENCE

HARTMUT LEHMANN: Carrying some of the arguments one step further throws light on a different aspect. I think we should be aware of the crucial role of the émigré political scientists, people like Arendt and Strauss, in achieving a seeming return of the German critical thinking to the fold of

---

4 Ernst Troeltsch, *Deutscher Geist und Westeuropa. Gesammelte kulturphilosophische Aufsätze und Reden,* ed. Hans Baron (Tübingen, 1925).

Western tradition, that is, linking it back up again. That, I think, is a two-step process. Step 1, adjustment to America after exile, and then step 2, transferring the message back to Germany again. There can be no doubt that Strauss and Arendt made major contributions to the process of democratization in Germany after 1945.

ALFONS SÖLLNER: We are apparently discussing the problem of continuity, which sort of bridges German origin and American impact. At this point, I would like to remind you of Bernard Crick's wonderful formulation when he wrote his review of Hannah Arendt's *On Revolution*.[5] He begins by saying that apparently every émigré has, once in his or her life, given a present as a sign of gratitude to his or her host country. This book, *On Revolution,* is Hannah Arendt's present and sign of gratitude to her host country. So, the continuity in terms of life, of time, is apparently also a psychological need to bridge origins and later work. This is probably true for all émigrés, but I agree with some of you that in the cases of Hannah Arendt, Leo Strauss, and Eric Voegelin, they found the antidote – the bridge – both in Greek and Roman antiquity and in the American present.

I'm not sure, Professor Lehmann, if and how the way back worked. Arendt's book on totalitarianism, along with all of the others, and Leo Strauss's *Natural Right and History* were among the first books translated into German after the war. Especially if you, for example, compare them to the major achievements of other émigrés, like Franz Neumann's *Behemoth,* which was first translated only twenty years later, while many other books were not translated at all.[6]

ROBERT PIPPIN: It might be interesting to compare Strauss's and Arendt's reactions to critical theory on this question of merit. There was a difference in their reaction to the uniqueness of the American experience. Clearly, to Strauss and Arendt the stability and success of American constitutionalism was quite impressive. Given what they had experienced, it is quite obvious why they were so impressed by the continuity of American constitutional government as well as its social order and stability, and wondered so much about what produced and allowed such stability to flourish. But, of course, for other émigrés, it would be fair to say that the conformity and hegemony of American culture was precisely the problem. For people like Marcuse, it

5 Hannah Arendt, *On Revolution* (New York, 1963).
6 Franz L. Neumann, *Behemoth. The Structure and Practice of National Socialism, 1933–1944* (Toronto and New York, 1944), the German translation was published as *Behemoth. Struktur und Praxis des Nationalsozialismus 1933–1944* (Cologne and Frankfurt/Main, 1977).

was precisely the spirit of resistance or negation or the potential cultural an-
archy of American mass culture that he liked and thought most distinctive
aspect of America, not what he would regard its social rigidity or conformism, rather that the possibility of cultural politics in America was much
freer. It was thus possible to have cultural politics – not traditional constitutional or democratic politics – but politics of a new kind, a form of cultural discussion or cultural, self-formative politics around issues that were
not traditionally political. This was possible in America, while it was not
possible in Western European democracies. I do not know how far we can
go with this, but there is, it seems to me, clearly some kind of contrast between reactions to the question of stability and cohesiveness, precisely that
which other German émigrés found troublesome. Marcuse liked a lot of
things about American culture; Adorno liked almost nothing.

GEORGE KATEB:  On this last point, I think Professor Pippin is perhaps attributing to Marcuse too much love of the wildness of American culture. I
can think of only one book by Marcuse that seems to take some pleasure or
even joy in American culture and that is his *Essay on Liberation* (1969).[7] That
book, I think, is as much about Paris as it is about Columbia, Berkeley, and
the United States more generally. In contrast, his *One-Dimensional Man* is
one of the most sustained and total critiques of American culture in this century.[8] I think it is as ferocious in its way as the chapter on the movie industry that Horkheimer and Adorno included in *Dialectic of Enlightenment*.[9] So,
I would not exaggerate Marcuse's affection for American culture. That he
chose to stay here, that when Habermas visited him in San Diego toward
the end of his life Marcuse would not speak in German to Habermas, that
is, I think, a detail of some importance. But that he loved American wildness, I would not say. Arendt also hated it. And Strauss hated it but did not
see it as wildness but, curiously enough, as drabness. One has to be careful
in saying how these three figures responded to American culture as a whole.
I do not think they ever really felt an affection for it, comparable to the affection they felt for Germany before Hitler.

BONNIE HONIG:  I want to intervene again on Robert Pippin's identification of Arendt and Strauss on this point. You said that Arendt and Strauss
were both very impressed with the stability and the order of the American

7 Herbert Marcuse, *Essay on Liberation* (Boston, 1969).
8 Herbert Marcuse, *One-Dimensional Man. Studies in the Ideology of Advanced Industrial Society* (Boston, 1964).
9 Max Horkheimer and Theodor W. Adorno, *Dialectic of Enlightenment* [original German title:
*Philosophische Fragmente*], trans. John Cumming (New York, 1972).

regime. At the same time, Arendt, I think, was also very worried about this stability. If you rely on Strauss too much on this point, I think you miss an important distinction. What she worried about is that the incredible stability and order that she thought she saw – things were a little more turbulent than she saw them to be – might be coming from the wrong place, from what she called the rise of the social and the normalization of the mass culture, instead of where she would have wanted it to be coming from, that is, an activist reverence for constitutional order that would have been a kind of stability, but a disordered stability, with a little more of an activist component in it. So, I think that the stability and order she saw in the American regime were a source of great concern to her. And the moments that disrupted it were moments that she celebrated, particularly in the student movement of the 1960s. I do not think that they were the same moments Strauss would have celebrated.

ROBERT PIPPIN: No, no, I just meant to raise the general question of the way in which both Strauss and Arendt were acting in contrast to other immigrants. They focused a great deal on the American founding, constitutionalism, the philosophical principles of the American perception of justice and so forth, in ways that were quite impressive and interesting to them about this American exceptionalism, in ways that were quite differently experienced by émigrés coming in a way from the same kind of mandarin tradition, and with many of the same worries about mass culture and vulgarity, in different ways, from different points of view, but they came out in a way on the other side regarding American conceptionalism, let us say, not in terms of constitutionalism or the American founding.

HELMUT DUBIEL: I would like to come back to the point made about the different reception profiles of critical theorists, comparing their experience of America in the beginning with Arendt's. It was indeed the fact that for them, especially for Horkheimer and Adorno, the American experience was nothing completely new. They interpreted it as a kind of transition without interruptions. For instance, they interpreted "advertisement" as a simple extension of, or even the equivalent to, totalitarian propaganda. The authoritarian elements in liberal democracies were seen as omens of the possibility of totalitarian overturn in the United States – and that was completely different for Arendt. Horkheimer and Adorno began to hold Western democracy in a certain esteem only after their return to Germany; and their self-understanding, their secret self-understanding, which they never would express in public, was somehow to help establish domestic democracy in West Germany, just to introduce, for instance, empirical methods. Letters at the Institute demonstrate that they were well aware of the split between their self-understanding as Marxist critical theorists, on the one hand, and their being deeply involved in the reconstruction, or in the construction for the first time of a stable democracy, on the other.

JÜRGEN GEBHARDT: Whoever looked at the world in terms of the split between capitalism right now, socialism in the future, just around the corner, certainly would consider the United States to be part of the capitalistic world to be destroyed. But Marcuse, indeed, in *Liberation* thought that the revolution was going to be based in the United States. And in that, I think, he really differed from other Marxist scholars, who viewed America in the context of a critique of political economy. A second point: Those people who turned to Rome and Greece and identified the Roman-Greek tradition with the American political tradition certainly could interpret the United States in terms of an American experiment that went quite well for 200 years and was kind of a beacon to be adhered to. Your argument is based on a cultural interpretation of politics and society, certainly neither Strauss nor Arendt had this cultural interpretation. Your interpretation may be more German than Arendt's and Strauss's. Now, you need not love McDonald's in order to be impressed by the American Constitution and by the political operation of the public. You need not love the wilderness in order to look at the political substance in the Constitution, of constitutional government, and I think Arendt would say . . . [that] she certainly did not love the wilderness; rather, that she loved New York City.

Strauss was a bookish man who loved to sit in his study, but he interpreted and understood and assessed and even may have loved the United States as an intellectual and/or political enterprise of some success.

HORST MEWES: Let me just sharpen one point. As Gebhardt was saying just now, I think the difference between Arendt and Strauss and the German Left and their reaction to the United States is obviously that the Left in its theory of capitalism saw a degree of affinity between the United States and Europe that Arendt and Strauss did not see. That is because they had discovered what the Marxists had not, and simply denied, and that is the central significance of politics. Arendt and Strauss, curiously enough, found their concepts of politics in their relation between thought and politics, in the founding of a concept of government by way of reflection and choice rather than by accident and force. Strauss saw reflected in this founding act his relation between philosophy and politics. It was precisely the constant references to human nature, not to mention natural rights, but just the commonsense references to human nature in terms of the significance of checks and balances that one finds in the Federalist Papers and in all the correspondence surrounding the founding act. Arendt, of course, found the uniqueness of action reflected in the founding of the Novus Ordo Saeculorum. What strikes me is that they could both see reflections of their own disposition. The genuine nature of the American founding really must be recomposed by at least putting both of their perspectives together.

ALFONS SÖLLNER: I would like to raise another issue, one wherein the integration of Arendt, Voegelin, and Strauss into American society clearly differed from that of other émigrés. This issue is their relationship to American political science as a discipline, as an organized discipline. As we all know, Hannah Arendt and Leo Strauss did not have much respect, especially for contemporary developments within this discipline, as incorporated in behavioralism, in empirical research, in institutional research, and so on. But there is the entire other group of people who not only became highly integrated but who also became influential through this very development of the discipline. I would like to mention a few examples: Arnold Brecht, who became vice president of the American Political Science Association in 1949; Karl Deutsch, who was president of the same organization in 1969–70; as well as Franz Neumann, Sigmund Neumann, and Hans Morgenthau, who were all highly visible in the discipline. They were not necessarily proponents of behavioralism, but they had a high esteem for empirical and institutional research. Even Horkheimer and Adorno tried, when they returned to Germany (that is, to the Federal Republic), to introduce empirical research in the study of politics, instead of relying exclusively on philosophical and cultural criticism. So, there is a whole group of people whose way of integrating into American society was through identification with the goals of the discipline. And if and when they returned to Germany, they were something like the founding fathers of a new political science that completely contradicted the German tradition. Thus, we did not have any political science in the modern sense (the Weimar experiment of the *Deutsche Hochschule für Politik* in a certain way failed) until 1949 or 1955. There was no place for a political science as a modern discipline within Weimar universities. I could mention many more people for whom political science as a modern project of – no so much philosophical but – empirical research was their way of integrating German and American traditions, then connecting this hybrid to West German culture.

PETER GRAF KIELMANSEGG: But with regard to politics present or not present at German universities, of course, you would have to add that, up to the end of the nineteenth century, every historian taught a systematic course on politics. Otto Hintze was the last one in this tradition, and we should not forget that when saying that political science was something completely new to Germany.

ALFONS SÖLLNER: But what I mean is this kind of political science was neither a . . .

PETER GRAF KIELMANSEGG: . . . not in the modern sense, empirical, but neither was it in the United States in the nineteenth century.

ALFONS SÖLLNER: But it was also not oriented to democracy, and what we see in the 1950s, via the influence of the immigrants, is something like what you could criticize as "science of democracy" (*Demokratiewissenschaft*), rather uncritical towards Western democracy as an empirical fact.

ROBERT PIPPIN: Connected with this point, I would like to know more about the American constitutional tradition and the reception of Arendt's and Strauss's interpretation of American constitutionalism, and about the influence of their interpretation. My impression, from before and from our discussions, is that, however interesting, both of them still regarded it, in different ways, as somewhat eccentric of Pickwickian. Their ability to integrate themselves into America, contrary to the other people you mentioned, involving inventing an America that they could love rather than accepting the one they actually found.

HARTMUT LEHMANN: It may be important in this context to point out that the view of America being discussed here is very eclectic, in that much of the nineteenth-century America escaped their attention. Rather, they returned to the Constitution, and then they went back to Greece and Rome. Thus, they seemed to construct an ideal genealogy that helped them, by going back to antiquity, to understand what America is all about. As is well known, nineteenth-century America rediscovered the European Middle Ages. The Christian America of the nineteenth century was a Protestant nation, a nation on the forefront of civilization's progress toward a Christian Protestant world. Between 1850 and 1890 this view was much influenced by Teutonism, that is, by belief in the superiority of the white race. We should see that the America of Strauss and Arendt was one America, but there are other Americas that were also influential, not only in the nineteenth but well into the twentieth century.

BONNIE HONIG: I was thinking that America is like the poor Narcissus. There is a story that Oscar Wilde tells about Narcissus, who used to walk in the woods every day and pause near a pond and look into it in order to gaze at his reflection. And one day, when he did not appear, the flowers asked the pond whether it missed Narcissus, and the pond water said yes, because every day when he used to pause to look into it, the pond could discern its own reflection in his eyes. I think that Strauss's and Arendt's America is a reflecting pool for them to look into. These émigrés look into America and what they see are visions of longing and yearning that they project into it and it reflected back. For Arendt – and I do not mean it pejoratively – this is how you make yourself at home in a new place, you judge America's greatness in the Arendtian sense: You tell a story of it, you give it a narrative structure, it is somewhat fabulist, and you see it as a projection. For her, that is not only an expression of gratitude but also a way of bridging the most important gap that marked her thinking at that point.

TIMOTHY FULLER: I see these last few comments in a somewhat different way. I continue to believe that what people like Strauss and Arendt were up to was not inventing an America they could live with. I think what they were trying to do was to figure out philosophical assumptions underlying the American regime. And it would be perfectly characteristic and consistent for Strauss, being interested in that, to go back to the founding documents and try to understand what kind of arguments they presented. Now, it may very well be that in doing that, any of us will come up with a particular interpretation of what we find there. But it is not because we are trying to invent the story, though people may see it that way, but because we are trying to figure out what is the guiding spirit of this regime, what is the thing that gives it its life, its vitality, its stability. In finding out those things we would inevitably attempt to do interpretations of it, and you discover also reasons why there are things about it that are not so good. And since all earthly regimes are not so good in some respect, I would think that would be one of the first principles for any good scientist from beginning to end. No early regime would ever be perfectly livable, but there might be differences among them which can be given an actual account. And I think they both try to do that. And I think that, when Horst Mewes referred to the opening paragraph of the first Federalist Papers – Hamilton's most famous remark – that this is the moment at which we have to find out whether we can reflect and choose a form of government, as opposed to simply suffering the imposition of a form of government upon us. That, while he was undoubtedly speaking in part rhetorically, in defense of the ratification process, he also meant what he said, that when Strauss read things like that, he took it seriously – that would be a practical, not a philosophical realization of the fundamental problem he identified when he talked about the conflict between natural right and history. From this point of view, Hamilton would have, in that sense, expressed most of what is important to know about the conflict between natural right and history. So, I cannot quite agree with these ideas that these people simply invent something to make themselves feel at home in a foreign place. I am sure we all do that to some degree, but I think that when you read what they actually wrote about the American view – I speak here as an American – I find that they were full of insights about it, that they understood the documents, . . . [that] the documents can also be understood by an attentive reader who is not an American.

JÜRGEN GEBHARDT: I would like to comment, to argue the same point there. If Arendt's understanding of the Revolution and the Constitution is so dead wrong that you really do not bother to read it, then I still do not understand why American historians and political scientists tell their students to read the Federalist Papers. They may be outdated, they may be antidemocratic, they may be all this, but then just stop reading them, then do not assign them any more to Government 101.

ERNST VOLLRATH: I think Arendt's interpretation of the American experience is deeply colored by her reading of the Federalist Papers. In the Federalist Papers, she met a kind of thinking that she was not aware existed because she had learned Heideggerian philosophy. And she really was surprised to find a kind of reason that did not exist – at least not to any degree of importance – in Germany. The Germans do not have them, the Federalist Papers. Carl Schmitt has written that American constitutionalism or *Staatsrecht* has no importance at all. This is a reflection of the German incapability of understanding what the American experience is all about. The Federalist Papers are not only read by political scientists or people like me who are not political scientists, but by politicians as well.

HORST MEWES: I wanted to first respond to Bonnie Honig. Of course that dimension is definitely there, the personal dimension, the personal concern, and the attempt to build a new home. But I think we must admit that it goes far beyond that. I think that is where we return to the theme of having experienced the decline of democracy, or the crisis of democracy, in the attempt to build it in Central Europe, and in its total rejection with the rise of totalitarianism. Therefore, it was more than a personal experience; it was

an attempt to go back to the roots of the nature of democracy, in their different ways. I think that they did not go back to the experiences of the postwar years and the tumultuous nature of America in the 1940s and 1950s,
primarily they did not go back to the variety of experiences in the nineteenth century because they felt that what made all this variety possible was
the order that constitutes the framework within which it could take place
or be possible. And therefore the real nature of understanding the variety,
and the possibility of the variety, lay in the retracing of the roots. I think
they were also, therefore, trying in a sense to see what it was in the nature
of the crisis of democracy that could perhaps be traced back to its roots. That
was the next stage because from their perspective in the 1950s and 1960s
they saw that a kind of a crisis of democracy was developing in the United
States as well. They were turning back to the roots for these two different
reasons. And they were quite worried, quite concerned, about the parallels,
as many people have pointed out since then, between Weimar and the
United States. Actually, *Social Research* published a special issue on the
Weimar Republic to which, among others, people like Hans Morgenthau
contributed.[10] This conjoined with Arendt's packing her bags during the
Vietnam War – and on the way toward Watergate. She was literally worried that she witnessed a repetition of Weimar, and she had to leave. And
so, there was a kind of an interaction between their experiences in Weimar,
their looking for the roots, their seeing perhaps a repetition of Weimar, and
their concern with the crisis phenomenon of democracy, which they were
trying to understand in terms of the intrinsic dynamics of democracy itself
rather than referring to the older tradition of *Kulturkritik* or *Geisteswissenschaft*. To them this tradition had not worked to explain anything that
was going on precisely because it lacked this crucial understanding of politics and perhaps the philosophical dimensions of politics.

On another point, there is no major influence in the sense that they are
sort of pervasive in the entire discipline of political science. We already
mentioned J. G. Pocock and the entire new way of interpreting republicanism. But there is also something that has not been mentioned, namely,
Harvey Mansfield's book on the soul of the Constitution.[11] In that book
Mansfield refers to the considerable number of people whose interpretation of the Constitution was influenced by scholars at the University of
Chicago. I am thinking of Herbert Storing, for instance, and his very innovative work on the anti-Federalists and the need to integrate the anti-

---

10 *Social Research* 39 (Summer 1972). The essays in this issue came from a "Conference on Weimar
   Germany, 1919–1932: Intellectuals, Culture, and Politics" that took place at the New School for
   Social Research on Oct. 29–30, 1971.
11 Harvey C. Mansfield, *America's Constitutional Soul* (Baltimore, 1991).

Federalists into the entire interpretation of the position . . . not only the
position of the Federalists but the entire founding period.[12] One really
ought to count them as part of the founding period. So, there was considerable influence, although it may not compare with Karl Deutsch and
Arnold Brecht within the discipline.


GEORGE KATEB: In response to Jürgen Gebhardt, I repeat the point: No
one here has anything but great respect for *On Revolution* and Arendt's other
writings in America. The fact remains that her interpretation is *an interpretation*. I would say there are two main elements involved in her interpretation
of the American founding. One of them has had tremendous influence, with
which I am not happy. The second has had much less influence, but perhaps
that is the way things must be. The first element is her insistence that in the
founding period many involved in the Revolution and in the framing of the
Constitution experienced a self-fulfillment, a self-conceptualization, a self-
understanding that showed that they truly knew that there was nothing better in the world than political participation. I think this is a romanticization
of the mentality of some of the great figures of the founding period. This
romanticization has then fed the whole resurgence of republicanism in
American political thought. I find American republicanism with a small "r"
a basically undesirable tendency because of its insistence on virtue.

  There is, however, a second element in Arendt's selective, albeit broad,
reading of the founding period, and that is her rather quiet and almost un-
dramatic sense that the greatest thing about the American political system is
that you cannot have a *Staatslehre* because there is no *Staat*. There is a government, and what she meant by that was not so much representation – and
here Ernst Vollrath and I agree she is deficient – as constitutionalism, that
is, of the limits on power, on the American reluctance to use the word
"state" except in that department of government which deals with other
states, and of the greatness of separating and dividing and thereby subduing
and chastening power and making it limited and somewhat apprehensive in
its exercise. This second theme in Arendt is for me the most important. I
can tell you that, as an American, my eyes were opened by, if you will, her
revelation of the absence of the state in the American Constitution, and I
wished that this had proven more influential than the cant about virtue.


ALFONS SÖLLNER: I'd like to compare this philosophical approach to
the American tradition to the influential works of other émigrés who have

---

12 *The Complete Anti-Federalist,* ed. by Herbert J. Storing with Murray Dry (Chicago, 1981).

a less – much less – idealized and certainly less romanticized picture of the American form of government. I will mention only Karl Löwenstein's book on the American constitutional system, called *Verfassungsrecht und Verfassungspraxis der Vereinigten Staaten* (1959), Ernst Fränkel's *Das amerikanische Regierungssystem,* published in German after he returned, Ferdinand Hermen's book, Arnold Brecht's book, which is political theory but in certain ways incorporates the whole tradition of European political theory and compares it with the American, empirical tradition, and Karl Deutsch's *The Nerves of Governments.*[13] All these works integrate a picture of America into a comparative approach to democratic governments, yet they do not require an idealization of the American project. There are different reactions to America, and I think we should also look and compare the Arendtian and Straussian approaches with those of other émigrés who helped to reintegrate American democracy and tendencies within European democracies and arrived at a comparative approach of democracy, which, from my view, is of ongoing and important interest to political science as an academic discipline.

PETER GRAF KIELMANSEGG: The distinction between government and state, if I may say this in passing, played a role in the founding of the Federal Republic in 1948–49. Whereas the Americans talked in terms of setting up a government in western Germany, the Germans talked in terms of founding a state, which was much, much more difficult for them than setting up a government because it meant a definite division of the country. The Americans could never understand that having two German states was a very different question from just setting up governments in different parts of the country. This misunderstanding has very deep roots.

### VIEWS ON DEMOCRACY

PETER GRAF KIELMANSEGG: We have already touched upon the subject of Arendt and democracy. Perhaps we could now explicitly take up this subject once more. I remember that to a certain extent there were divergent views on this question, I remember Helmut Dubiel in a way being quite enthusiastic about Arendt as a philosopher of the new German democracy, and, if I understood George Kateb correctly, he was perhaps a little bit more skeptical about her qualities as a guide toward democracy.

13 Karl Löwenstein, *Vom Wesen der amerikanischen Verfassung* (Frankfurt/Main, 1950); Ernst Fränkel, *Das amerikanische Regierungtssystem* (Cologne, 1960); Arnold Brecht, *Politische Theorie* [*Political Theory*] (Tübingen, 1961 [1959]); Karl W. Deutsch, *The Nerves of Government. Models of Political Communication and Control* (London, 1963).

HELMUT DUBIEL: Not just since the reaction to my essay but for some time now I have had a simple question. No, indeed, I have been guided by an interest to develop somehow or to use Arendt's work among others, to lay the foundation for a, to put it weakly, less state-oriented understanding of politics in the given historical context of the Federal Republic of Germany, and then, undoubtedly, lay new roots of what we now refer to as civil society. The reality of West Germany cannot be understood within the concepts identified with the state, or with politics in general. But I am not an Arendtian, I am just a political sociologist interested in the instrumental habit of dealing with currents of the history of ideas. I am often confronted with doubts and accusations that there is a latent Heideggerian heritage in Arendt that is responsible for the elitist and aristocratic implications of her theory. I know, of course, of this connection, but I never found out on the level of an argument or systematically what kind of restrictions are imposed on her because of that heritage. Is there anybody who could explain it to me?

ERNST VOLLRATH: There is a strain, or a moment, in Arendt's thinking that might be called existentialist, stressing the authenticity, or the authentic moments of the political. In this sense she is not very favorable to democracy, pure and simple, that is, to normal democracy. But I believe one can distinguish between these moments and more conceptual moments where she tries to develop a concept of the political; she never succeeded in developing that concept of republican constitutionalism clearly, which would have led her to a concept of the political which is not state-centered. She never was a systematic political thinker, she was always concerned with very momentous phenomena; she was a dilettante to a certain degree, but there are certain elements in her thinking which could be used, at least in the German context, to get rid of that state-centered conception of the political, and more civil polity-oriented notion of the political.

ALFONS SÖLLNER: Earlier in our discussion I think we already had approached methodologically the problem of how she views democracy as a political theorist. To me, it depends on what you take as a starting point. In the case where you take as a starting point, let us say, the underlying concepts of "vita activa," of the human condition, here you see clearly antidemocratic branches of thinking. In this sense, she is very close to Strauss's formulation when he says, in one of his essays on education, that democracy is nothing . . . can be realistically nothing else than a universal aristocracy. In contrast, if you take as your starting point, let us say, her essay on civil disobedience, it looks different. To me, it boils down to the question of how it is possible to read together these two major works in political theory, *The Human Condition* and *On Revolution*. It is not clear to me how they fit together. One way could be her conceptualization of the institutional preconditions of a functioning democracy, and I have the feeling she is not very clear about that, and perhaps not even very interested in it.

ERNST VOLLRATH: The healing power of institutions . . .

ALFONS SÖLLNER: . . . but she does not elaborate on this, she does not have a theory of the institutions that make a representative government work, so I have my doubts and am not clear how these two tendencies fit together.

GEORGE KATEB: Professor Söllner has mostly said it, but I would like to respond specifically to Helmut Dubiel's point, namely, that she is antistate. Indeed, she does not produce a state-centered political theory but rather an antistate political theory. She is antistate first and most important of all because she is a theorist of participation. And the notion of political participation or politics as participation seems, in at least her judgment, to go in the opposite direction from belief in the validity of the state. A second reason is that she believes strongly in constitutional limits on modern political power in general. But, as Professor Söllner just said, Arendt has no theory of the normality of governments in the modern age; she never worked one out. In my judgment you cannot combine theories of participation and constitutionalism and confine yourself to these two elements to produce any kind of theory of modern government. If you do not want the state, you must have a theory of government, or what government shall be . . . the answer would seem to be constitutional representative democracy. And to say it for the thousandth time, Arendt did not work out a theory of representative democracy in the modern age, which represents a tremendous gap in her political theory.

PETER GRAF KIELMANSEGG: "Not worked out," does that mean there are elements which could be worked out following her own lines of thinking?

GEORGE KATEB: No, I do not think so. I think that, by and large, she is contemptuous toward representation as such. I do not know what resources are present in her own theory that we could reassemble to create a theory of modern constitutional representative democracy. I do not find them. I like the formulation that all normal politics is estranged politics, that is, the normal that is alien to her. As Harvey Mansfield just said, that is Heideggerian.

ERNST VOLLRATH: Thus, it is German?

GEORGE KATEB: Yes.

TIMOTHY FULLER: I would like to respond to Dubiel's question in a slightly different way. To try to respond exactly as you formulated the question: Is there something in the Heideggerian background that puts a limit on her thinking about these things? I think that one place to look is in her discussion of authority – an essay called "What Is Authority?" – in which she argued that authority had disappeared from the modern world. This is a very dramatic thing to say, of course, because she coupled with it the question whether that did not mean that freedom had also disappeared from the modern world. That strikes me as reflecting that background, to think of it in that way and then to give this long historical exegesis about what authority was, which leads to the conclusion that because it was that, it now could not be. It seems to me that this is perhaps the source of the problems that George Kateb and others have been talking about, namely, why she could not deal with representation or why she could not construct a theory of government. Because in order to do so in the modern situation you have to have a theory of authority, which is different from the conception of authority, which she outlined in her historical exegesis of the original concept.

Now, where do you look in modern political thought for the theory of authority which comports with the requirements of the modern regime? You look to Hobbes, Locke, John Stuart Mill, and in contemporary situations I would say most important to Oakeshott. In other words, she looked at this British tradition which, as Robert Pippin and others have said over and over again in these discussions, she misunderstood in certain important ways. Her conception of Hobbes, for example, as a kind of protototalitarian power theorist completely neglects what is the really central feature of Hobbes's political theory. And that is the problem of establishing a new theory of authority that is compatible with a regime resting on the foundation of a set of people who understand themselves to be free individuals. That is the fundamental modern starting point for any reflection on an adequate theory of political authority in a modern democratic state. And – this is just my hypothesis – because she started with this other way of thinking about authority and committed herself to this dramatic proposition that it could not exist in the modern world, it seems to me she completely missed the fact that there is a very important and very well worked out conception of political authority in the modern world, which is essential to working out these problems of representation that she did not work out. That is what I think is the Heideggerian limitation of her way of thinking about politics, not because she is opposed to representation so much as because she did not understand it. She did not understand it in terms of what the requirements of the idea of authority would be under our circumstances as opposed to what they were.

ROBERT PIPPIN: I am not quite sure that she did not understand. If she did, she did project a self-regulation of civil society, not for politics. Now I think she is wrong about that, but it is not that she just missed something.

BONNIE HONIG: I want to respond to what George Kateb said about Arendt being contemptuous of representation as such. I do not think that she was contemptuous, maybe impatient and dismissive of representation – I think contempt is a little bit strong for what the mood was – but I want to know if we could not read this contempt rather than just react to it. And to pick up on a favorite Katebian theme, maybe we should think about what the dangers of representative democracy are, dangers to which she might have been alert and therefore her dismissal of it might have been a response to them. And they would be things, I think, like worries about the alienation of the citizenry, sedimentation of interests into group identities that are better represented that way, privatization, isolation. But most important, I think, is really that she worried about a kind of identity-based politics. Representative politics required a kind of unity of the represented in order for the representative to be able to do his or her job, and whether rightly or wrongly – I would think that you would say rightly – she worried about that, about the way that representative democracy presupposes a certain level of unification and group identities, to which she was hostile for reasons that I think you sympathize with. So, she may not have offered and she may be wanting an alternative, an institutional alternative for the daily politics to which she was somewhat hostile. But I think the reasons for her hostility are reasons that are important to many people here, and to just say that she was contemptuous of it and to dismiss her is to miss out on some of the best aspects, I think, of her contribution to political theory.

ERNST VOLLRATH: As far as I can remember there is only one singular instance where she speaks about representation, where she connects representation with judging, and I think the most sound moments of her think-ing are connected with her theory of political judgment. One can connect her theory of judgment from her old work, I think, with the renewal of the theory of representation in democratic sense.

Well, the other point I would like to make refers to her own capability of understanding the political in its normal ways. This has something to do with the Germans' drive for authenticity, at least in these intellectual cir-cles, in these Heideggerian circles, coming out from the woods, from the Black Forest, they want to be authentic. Okay, in this context I would like to quote again Helmut Plessner from the *Verspätete Nation* where he iden-tifies this moment of our culture as attributable to something we lack, what our culture, the German culture lacks: the specific Western spirit of mun-dane normalcy, and she shared this view, I think.

ROBERT PIPPIN: I would like to bring the discussion somewhat back to Strauss since there is a kind of similarity here, not only in relation to Hei-degger but on the question that Tim Fuller was talking about. The ques-tion of sovereignty or authority. A couple of people have mentioned that Arendt and Strauss appear in the American context as exotic, and because of that some of their influence, in a way, constituted a strangeness to the American, as well as their attempt to understand America. But on the ques-tion of political life, I think it is fair to say that for both of them the prob-lem of sovereignty, the great British problem was not anywhere near the center of their political thought, in the way it was for the Anglo-American political tradition. Their conception of the origin of democratic principles was quite different. I do not know whether it has anything to do with Hei-degger or not, but the conception, for example, that Arendt has of why po-litical life is important, is in a way too perfectionist to generate a theory of obligation. It just does not follow because a political life is good that one has an obligation to participate in it, that is a non sequitur. In Strauss, the authority of the claim on citizens to be citizens by a public body is in a way not even a problem for him. The question of sovereignty is, it seems to me, not the main issue or in no way resolved by the central solution, namely, no injury can be done to the willing, that sovereignty essentially is self-constituted, there are no obligations that are not self-imposed, and so forth. They pretend a conception of politics as ideal, as an ideal life, that it is some-how flourishing or fulfilling to be political in this sense, or to be citizens in the Straussian sense, for the reasons that Strauss gives. But there is some-thing about that whole position that does not fit into the central problems that developed from the sort of religious conflict and its relationship to the modern state, which many other thinkers have studied in a different way. Thus, part of what this problem, it seems to me, is we just do not have a theory of sovereignty.

ALFONS SÖLLNER: Any theory of representation under modern conditions is closely connected to the idea of the functional representation as process, as the will of the citizen is imputed to the sovereign. One of the reasons why Arendt does not have a worthwhile theory of representation is that her idea of politics is based on identity, as you say, and under modern conditions, such a concept of politics is just not able to understand the differentiation of power, the division of labor, the division of powers, and so on. This is one of the features that unites Strauss and Arendt as well as Voegelin. If you read *The New Science of Politics,* there are the long chapters on representation, and what he develops is an existentialist concept of representation that is nearly premodern. So, your norm of the ability to develop a worked-out theory of functional representation, to develop the legal forms of representation in a constitutional form, hangs together with all these people's premodern sort of orientation and ideas of politics. They are just not able or not willing to step into the conditions of modern politics.

ERNST VOLLRATH: I would like to respond to the comment Söllner just made. Arendt indeed, except for that singular instance to which I have alluded, does not identify always with representative representation. She never was able to see the multifaceted political phenomenon that representation is, and it is very strange to me, since in the chapter on the division of power, much admired by her, Montesquieu speaks also on representation, and representation to him is a kind of division of power. It is very strange. It has something to do with her rejection of politics in the normal sense, in her rejection of normalcy.

TIMOTHY FULLER: I see Voegelin somewhat differently. I think his theory of representation or that theoretical excursion into the problem of representation was designed very carefully. He was very interested in the English legal tradition and he speaks at great length about these things particularly in the footnotes to *The New Science of Politics.* I think that he is trying to develop a concept of representation that has a certain kind of universality but is compatible with constitutional government in the sense that, when he finally comes to concluding it, is fundamental to establishing any kind of constitutional regime, regardless of its specific provisions, that is not to be equated with some cosmic truth, that there is a sense of limitation which has to be built into the self-understanding of the participants in the regime, which makes whatever set of institutions they use work in a satisfactory way. So, I see him to be much closer to working out such problems than Arendt.

With regard to Strauss, I think Strauss's problem is a simpler one. I think he thought the thing to do was to study and understand very well the American Constitution and to use that as the basis for thinking about the daily problems of a constitution in a democratic society. Thus, it was not necessary for him to construct a theory, it was necessary to appreciate the theory already operating quite satisfactorily. So, I see the three as quite different.

HORST MEWES: I will make my remarks short, they are related to Strauss. We have, I think, gotten the overall impression that he is not a genuine democrat. We know that presently the discussion of democracy, at least in the United States, mostly revolves around communitarianism versus individualism, liberal democracy versus strong participatory democracy, and a variety of other kinds of types. I think in this context of the typology of democracy that Strauss represented a type, and that is the type of the Federalist's democratic republic. The type of democracy that is essentially based on a representative republic governed by an elected, natural aristocracy of merit. Now I regard that to be a genuine type of democracy in the self-understanding of the founders. Whether it is or not, he is providing the most profound theory at the moment that is available for that type of democracy. Now, the fact that this is an extremely unpopular type of democratic theory right now is more than obvious. It is quite clearly a perfectionist theory, as it provides a theory of human excellence. I completely agree with Robert Pippin that after building this edifice Strauss does not provide the tools for the most profound answers as to the relation between natural consciousness, modern science, post-Kantianism, etc., and one can hardly blame him for that.

# Select Bibliography of Works by Arendt and by Strauss on Modern Political Science and Philosophy

## ELISABETH GLASER-SCHMIDT

This bibliography contains the first editions of Arendt's and Strauss's books and articles. It also includes some of Arendt's and Strauss's comments on contemporary politics. Thus, it presents the works of Arendt and Strauss on early modern as well as nineteenth- and twentieth-century European and American political philosophy and science as it relates to their influence on American political thought after 1945. This compilation illuminates the common intellectual concerns of Hannah Arendt, the modern political philosopher, and Leo Strauss, the scholarly political theorist. It also highlights the process of their intellectual migration from Germany to the United States and their different explorations of modern politics.[1] Titles are presented chronologically.

### HANNAH ARENDT

*1930*

"Philosophie und Soziologie. Anlässlich Karl Mannheim, 'Ideologie und Utopie.' " *Die Gesellschaft* [Berlin] 7 (1930): 163–76.

*1932*

"Aufklärung und Judenfrage," *Zeitschrift für die Geschichte der Juden in Deutschland* [Berlin] 4, nos. 2–3 (1932).

*1941*

"Moses oder Washington." *Aufbau*, March 27, 1941: 16.

*1942*

"From the Dreyfus Affair to France Today." *Jewish Social Studies* 4 (July 1942): 195–240.
"Die Krise des Zionismus 1–3." *Aufbau*, Oct. 23, 18, Nov. 6, 17, and Nov. 20, 1942, 17.

*1943*

"We Refugees." *Menorah Journal* 31 (Jan. 1943): 69–77.
"Französische Politische Literatur im Exil 1–2." *Aufbau*, Feb. 26, 7–8, March 26, 1943, 8.

---

1 See also the *Chronological Bibliography of the Works of Hannah Arendt,* in Elisabeth Young-Bruehl, *Hannah Arendt: For the Love of the World* (New Haven, Conn.: Yale University Press, 1982): 535–547; and Joseph Cropsey "Leo Strauss: A Bibliography and Memorial," *Interpretation* 5, no. 2 (Winter 1975): 133–47, on which this select bibliography is partly based. Compare also the bibliography "Hannah Arendt," compiled by Joan Northquist, *Social Theory* 14 (1989).

*1944*

"Race-Thinking before Racism." *Review of Politics* 6, no. 1 (Jan. 1944): 36–73.
"The Jew as Pariah: A Hidden Tradition." *Jewish Social Studies* 6, no. 2 (Feb. 1944): 99–122.
"Concerning Minorities." *Contemporary Jewish Record* 7, no. 4 (Aug. 1944): 353–68.
"Frei und Demokratisch." *Aufbau,* Nov. 3, 1944, 15–16.
"Die Entrechteten und Entwürdigten." *Aufbau,* Dec. 15, 1944, 13 and 16.

*1945*

"Christianity and Revolution." *Nation,* Sept. 22, 1945, 288–89.
"Imperialism, Nationalism, Chauvinism." *Review of Politics* 7, no. 4 (Oct. 1945): 441–63.
*German Guilt.* New York: Jewish Frontier Reprint, 1945.
"Approaches to the 'German Problem'." *Partisan Review* 12, no. 1 (Winter 1945): 93–106.
"Organized Guilt and Universal Responsibility." *Jewish Frontier,* Jan. 1945, 19–23.
"The Stateless People." *Contemporary Jewish Record* 8, no. 2 (April 1945), 137–53.
"The Seeds of a Fascist International." *Jewish Frontier,* June 1945, 12–16.
"Zionism Reconsidered." *Menorah Journal* (Aug. 1945): 162–96. German translation in *Die verborgene Tradition: Acht Essays.* Frankfurt: Suhrkamp, 1976.
"Parties, Movements and Classes." *Partisan Review* 12, no 4 (Fall 1945): 504–12.

*1946*

"Imperialism: Road to Suicide." *Commentary* 1 (Feb. 1946): 27–35.
"The Jewish State: 50 Years After, Where Have Herzl's Politics Led?" *Commentary* 1 (May 1946): 1–8.
"Expansion and the Philosophy of Power." *Sewanee Review* 54 (Oct. 1946): 601–16.

*1947*

"Creating a Cultural Atmosphere." *Commentary* 4 (Nov. 1947): 424–26.

*1948*

"To Save the Jewish Homeland: There Is Still Time." *Commentary* 5 (May 1948): 398–406.
"The Concentration Camps." *Partisan Review* 15, no. 7 (July 1948): 743–63.

*1949*

" 'The Rights of Man': What Are They?" *Modern Review* 3, no. 1 (Summer 1949): 24–37.

*1950*

"Religion and the Intellectuals, A Symposium." *Partisan Review* 17 (Feb. 1950): 113–16.
"Social Science Techniques and the Study of Concentration Camps." *Jewish Social Studies* 12, no. 1 (1950): 49–64.
"The Imperialist Character." *Review of Politics* 12, no. 3 (July 1950): 303–20.
"The Aftermath of Nazi Rule, Report from Germany." *Commentary* 10 (Oct. 1950): 342–53.
"Mob and Elite." *Partisan Review* 17 (Nov. 1950): 808–19.

*1951*

*The Origins of Totalitarianism.* New York: Harcourt, Brace, 1951. German ed.: *Elemente und Ursprünge totaler Herrschaft.* Frankfurt: Europäische Verlagsanstalt, 1955.

"Totalitarian Movement." *Twentieth Century* 149 (May 1951): 368–89.
"Bei Hitler zu Tisch." *Der Monat* 4 (Oct. 1951): 85–90.

*1953*
"Rejoinder to Eric Voegelin's Review of *The Origins of Totalitarianism*." *Review of Politics* 15 (Jan. 1953): 76–85.
"The Ex-Communists." *Commonweal* 57, no. 24 (March 20, 1953), 595–99.
"Ideology and Terror: A Novel Form of Government." *Review of Politics* 15, no. 3 (July 1953): 303–27.
"Gestern waren Sie noch Kommunisten . . ." *Aufbau,* July 31, 1953, 19 and Aug. 7, 1953, 13 and 16.
"Understanding and Politics." *Partisan Review* 20, no. 4 (July–Aug. 1953): 377–92.
"Religion and Politics." *Confluence* 2, no. 3 (Sept. 1953): 105–26.

*1954*
"Tradition and the Modern Age." *Partisan Review* 22 (Jan. 1954): 53–75.
"Europe and the Atom Bomb." *Commonweal* 60, no. 23 (Sept. 17, 1954): 607–10.
"Europe and America: Dream and Nightmare." *Commonweal* 60, no. 24 (Sept. 24, 1954): 551–54.

*1956*
"Authority in the Twentieth Century." *Review of Politics* 18, no. 4 (Oct. 1956): 403–17.

*1957*
*Fragwürdige Traditionsbestände im Politischen Denken der Gegenwart.* Frankfurt: Europäische Verlagsanstalt, 1957. [These essays are included in *Between Past and Future* (1961).]
"History and Immortality." *Partisan Review* 24, no. 1 (Winter 1957): 11–53.
"Jaspers as Citizen of the World." In *The Philosophy of Karl Jaspers,* ed. P. A. Schilpp, pp. 539–50. La Salle, Ill.: Open Court Publishing, 1957.

*1958*
*The Human Condition.* Chicago: University of Chicago Press, 1958. German ed.: *Vita Activa oder vom tätigen Leben.* Stuttgart: Kohlhammer, 1960.
*Karl Jaspers: Reden zur Verleihung des Friedenspreises des Deutschen Buchhandels.* Munich: Piper, 1958.
*Die ungarische Revolution und der totalitäre Imperialismus.* Munich: Piper, 1958.
"Totalitarian Imperialism: Reflections of the Hungarian Revolution." *Journal of Politics* 20, no. 1 (Feb. 1958): 5–43.
"The Crisis in Education." *Partisan Review* 25, no. 4 (Fall 1958), 493–513.
"The Modern Concept of History." *Review of Politics* 20, no. 4 (Oct. 1958): 570–90.
"Totalitarianism." *Meridian* 2, no. 2 (Fall 1958), 1.

*1959*
"What Was Authority?" In *Authority,* ed. Friedrich (Cambridge, Mass.: Harvard University Press, 1959).
"Reflections on Little Rock." *Dissent* 6, no. 1 (Winter 1959): 45–56.

*1960*

*Von der Menschlichkeit in Finsteren Zeiten: Gedanken zu Lessing.* Hamburg: Hauswedell, 1960.
"Freedom and Politics: A Lecture." *Chicago Review* 14, no. 1 (Spring 1960): 28–46.
"Society and Culture." *Daedalus* 82, no. 2 (Spring 1960): 278–87.
"Revolution and Public Happiness." *Commentary* 30 (Nov. 1960): 413–22.

*1961*

*Between Past and Future: Six Exercises in Political Thought.* New York: Viking Press, 1961.

*1962*

"Revolution and Freedom: A Lecture." In *Zwei Welten: Siegfried Moses zum Fünfundsiebzig-sten Geburtstag.* Tel Aviv: Biaton, 1962.
"Action and 'The Pursuit of Happiness'." In *Politische Ordnung und Menschliche Existenz: Fest-gabe für Eric Voegelin.* Munich: Beck, 1962.
"The Cold War and the West." *Partisan Review* 29, no. 1 (Winter 1962): 10–20.

*1963*

*Eichmann in Jerusalem: A Report on the Banality of Evil.* New York: Viking Press, 1963. Rev. and enlarged ed., 1965.
*On Revolution.* New York: Viking Press, 1963. Rev. 2nd ed., 1965. German ed.: *Uber die Revolution.* Munich: Piper, 1963.
"Sie haben mich missverstanden." *Aufbau,* Dec. 20, 1963, 17 and 18.
"Kennedy and After." *New York Review of Books* 1, no. 9 (Dec. 26, 1963): 10.

*1964*

"The Deputy: Guilt By Silence." *Encounter,* Jan. 1964, 51–56.
"Personal Responsibility under Dictatorship." *Listener,* Aug. 6, 1964, 185–87 and 205.

*1965*

"Hannah Arendt – Hans Magnus Enzensberger: Politik und Verbrechen: Ein Briefwechsel." *Merkur,* April 1965, 380–85.

*1966*

Introduction to *Auschwitz,* by Bernd Naumann. New York: Frederick A. Praeger, 1966.
Introduction to *The Warriors* by J. Glenn Gray. New York: Harper & Row, 1966.
"On the Human Condition." In *The Evolving Society,* ed. Mary Alice Hinton, 213–19. New York: Institute of Cybernetical Research, 1966.
"The Formidable Dr. Robinson: A Reply to the Jewish Establishment." *New York Review of Books* 5, no. 12 (Jan. 20, 1966): 26–30.
"Remarks on 'The Crisis Character of Modern Society'." *Christianity and Crisis* 26, no. 9 (May 30, 1966): 112–14.

*1967*

Preface to *The Future of Germany* by Karl Jaspers. Chicago: University of Chicago Press, 1967.
"Randall Jarrell: 1914–1965." In *Randall Jarrell, 1914–1965.* New York: Farrar, Strauss and Giroux, 1967.
"Truth and Politics." *New Yorker,* Feb. 25, 1967, 49–88.

*1968*

*Men in Dark Times.* New York: Harcourt, Brace and World, 1968.

"Comment by Hannah Arendt on 'The Uses of Revolution' by Adam Ulam." In *Revolutionary Russia,* ed. Richard Pipes. Cambridge, Mass.: Harvard University Press, 1968.

"Is America by Nature a Violent Society? Lawlessness Is Inherent in the Uprooted." *New York Times Magazine,* April 28, 1968, 24.

*1969*

"Reflections on Violence." *Journal of International Affairs* (Winter 1969): 1–35. Rev. ed.: *On Violence* (1970).

*1970*

*On Violence* (New York: Harcourt, Brace and World, 1970). German ed.: *Macht und Gewalt.* Munich: Piper, 1971.

"Civil Disobedience." *New Yorker,* Sept. 12, 1970, 70–105.

*1971*

"Lying and Politics: Reflections on the Pentagon Papers." *New York Review of Books* 17, no. 8 (Nov. 18, 1971): 30–39.

"Thoughts on Politics and Revolution." *New York Review of Books* 16, no. 7 (April 22, 1971): 8–20.

"Thinking and Moral Considerations: A Lecture." *Social Research* 38, no. 3 (Fall 1971): 417–46.

*1972*

*Crises of the Republic.* New York: Harcourt, Brace Jovanovich, 1972.

*Wahrheit und Lüge in der Politik: Zwei Essays.* Munich: Piper, 1972.

"Washington's 'Problem-Solvers' – Where They Went Wrong." *New York Times,* April 5, 1972, Op-Ed Page.

*1973*

*Karl Jaspers in der Diskussion. Mit Beiträgen von Hannah Arendt.* Munich: Piper, 1973.

*1974*

"Karl Jaspers zum fünfundachtzigsten Geburtstage." In *Erinnerungen an Karl Jaspers,* ed. H. Saner, pp. 311–15. Munich: Piper, 1974.

*1977*

"Public Rights and Private Interests." In *Small Comforts for Hard Times: Humanists on Public Policy,* ed. Mooney and Stuber. New York: Columbia University Press, 1977.

*1978*

*The Jew as Pariah: Jewish Identity and Politics in the Modern Age,* ed. Ron H. Feldman. New York: Grove Press, 1978.

*The Life of the Mind,* ed. Mary McCarthy. New York: Harcourt, Brace Jovanovich, 1978.

"From an Interview." with Roger Errera, *New York Review of Books* 25, no. 16 (Oct. 26, 1978): 18.

*1990*

"Herzl et Lazare." In *Le Fumier de Job* by Bernard Lazare, followed by *Herzl et Lazare* by Hannah Arendt. Strasbourg: Circe, 1990.

*1992*

*Hannah Arendt–Karl Jaspers Correspondence, 1926–1969,* ed. Lotte Kohler and Hans Saner; trans. Robert and Rita Kimber. New York: Harcourt, Brace Jovanovich, 1992.

*1993*

*Was ist Politik? Fragmente aus dem Nachlass,* ed. Ursula Ludz. Munich: Piper, 1993.

LEO STRAUSS

*1923*

"Anmerkungen zur Diskussion über 'Zionismus und Antisemitismus." *Jüdische Rundschau* [Berlin] 27, no. 9 (1923).

*1924*

"Paul de Lagarde." *Der Jude* (Berlin) 7, no. 1 (1924): 8–15.

*1930*

*Die Religionskritik Spinozas als Grundlage seiner Bibelwissenschaft: Untersuchungen zu Spinozas Theologisch-Politischen Traktat.* Berlin: Akademie-Verlag, 1930.

*1932*

"Anmerkungen zu Cal Schmitt, Der Begriff des Politischen." *Archiv für Sozialwissenschaft und Sozialpolitik* 67, no. 6 (Aug.–Sept. 1932): 732–49.
"Das Testament Spinozas." *Bayerische Israelitische Gemeindezeitung* 7, no. 21 (Nov. 1, 1932): 322–26.

*1933*

"Quelques remarques sur la science politique de Hobbes." *Recherches Philosophiques* III (1933): 609–22.

*1935*

*Philosophie und Gesetz. Beiträge zum Verständnis Maimunis und seiner Vorläufer.* Berlin: Schocken, 1935. [The English translation was published as *Philosophy and Law. Essays Toward the Understanding of Maimonides and His Predecessors.* Philadelphia: Jewish Publication Society, 1987.]

*1936*

"Quelques remarques sur la science politique de Maimonide et de Fârâbi." *Revue des Etudes Juives* 100 (1936): 1–37.
*The Political Philosophy of Hobbes: Its Basis and Its Genesis.* Oxford: Clarendon Press, 1936.

*1937*

"On Abravanel's Philosophical Tendency and Political Teaching." In *Isaac Abravanel,* ed. J. B. Trend and H. Lowe, pp. 93–129. Cambridge: The University Press, 1937.

*1943*

"The Law of Reason in the *Kuzari*." *Proceedings of the American Academy for Jewish Research* 12 (1943).

*1945*

"On Classical Political Philosophy." *Social Research* 12, no. 1 (Feb. 1945): 98–117.
"Fârâbi's Plato." In *Louis Ginzberg Jubilee Volume*, pp. 357–93. New York: American Academy for Jewish Research, 1945.

*1948*

*On Tyranny: An Interpretation of Xenophon's "Hiero."* New York: Political Science Classics, 1948. Rev. ed.: *Tyranny and Wisdom*. Glencoe, Ill.: Free Press, 1963.

*1949*

"Political Philosophy and History." *Journal of the History of Ideas* 10, no. 1 (Jan. 1949): 30–50.

*1950*

"On the Spirit of Hobbes' Political Philosophy." *Revue Internationale de Philosophie* 4, no. 14 (1950): 405–31.
"Natural Right and the Historical Approach." *Review of Politics* 12, no. 4 (1950): 422–42.

*1951*

"The Social Science of Max Weber." *Measure* 2, no. 2 (Spring 1951): 204–30.

*1952*

*Persecution and the Art of Writing*. Glencoe, Ill.: Free Press, 1952.
"The Origin of the Idea of Natural Right." *Social Research* 19, no. 1 (March 1952): 23–60.
"On Locke's Doctrine of Natural Right." *Philosophical Review* 61, no. 4 (Oct. 1952): 475–502.

*1953*

*Natural Right and History*. Chicago: University of Chicago Press, 1953.
"Maimonides' Statement on Political Science." *Proceedings of the American Academy for Jewish Research* 22 (1953): 115–30.

*1956*

"Kurt Riezler, 1882–1955." *Social Research* 23, no. 1 (Spring 1956): 3–34.
"Social Science and Humanism." In : *The State of the Social Sciences,* ed. Leonard D. White, pp. 415–25. Chicago: University of Chicago Press, 1956.

*1957*

"Machiavelli's Intention: *The Prince*." *American Political Science Review* 51, no. 1 (March 1957): 13–40.

*1958*

*Thoughts on Machiavelli*. Glencoe, Ill.: Free Press, 1958.
*What Is Political Philosophy?* Glencoe, Ill.: Free Press, 1958.

*1959*

"The Liberalism of Classical Political Philosophy." *The Review of Metaphysics* 12, no. 3 (March 1959): 390–439.

*1960*

"What Is Liberal Education?" Commencement Address at University College, University of Chicago, June 6 1960. Chicago: University of Chicago, 1960.

*1961*

"Relativism." In *Relativism and the Study of Man,* ed. Helmut Schoeck and J. W. Wiggins. Princeton, N.J.: Van Nostrand, 1961.

*1962*

"Liberal Education and Responsibility." *Education: The Challenge Ahead,* ed. C. Scott Fletcher. New York: Norton, 1962.
"An Epilogue." *Essays on the Scientific Study of Politics,* ed. Herbert J. Storing, pp. 302–27. New York: Holt, Rinehart, and Winston, 1962.

*1963*

"Reply to Schaar and Wolin II." *American Political Science Review* 57, no. 1 (March 1963): 152–55.
"Perspectives on the Good Society." *Criterion* 2, no. 3 (Summer 1963): 2–9.

*1964*

*The City and Man.* Chicago: Rand McNally, 1964.
"The Crisis of Our Time" and "The Crisis of Political Philosophy." In *The Predicament of Modern Politics,* ed. Harold J. Spaeth, pp. 41–54 and 91–103. Detroit: University of Detroit Press, 1964.

*1965*

"Preface to Spinoza's Critique of Religion." In *Spinoza's Critique of Religion.* New York: Schocken Books, 1965.
*Hobbes politische Wissenschaft.* Neuwied/Berlin: Hermann Luchterhand Verlag, 1965. The German original of *The Political Philosophy of Hobbes* (1936).
"On the Plan of the *Guide of the Perplexed.*" In *Harry Austryn Wolfson Jubilee Volume,* 775–91. Jerusalem: American Academy for Jewish Research, 1965.

*1966*

*Socrates and Aristophanes.* New York: Basic Books, 1966.

*1967*

"Jerusalem and Athens. Some Preliminary Reflections." *The City College Papers,* no. 6. New York: City University of New York, 1967. Abridged in *Commentary* 43 (1967): 45–57.
"Liberal Education and Mass Democracy." In *Higher Education and Modern Democracy,* ed. Robert A. Goldwin, pp. 73–96. Chicago: Rand McNally, 1967.

205

157; and history, 73.
common sense,
107; and reve-

200

Schmitt aus den Jahren 1932/33
buchhandlung, 1988.

189

An Introduction to Political Ph
versity Press, 1989.
The Rebirth of Classical P
say, and Lectures by
Chicago Press, 198

1991
On Tyranny. Rev
York: Free P

1993
Faith and P
1934–1

A
ve

1971
"Philosophy as a
1971): 1–9.

1972
"Correspondence with Ha
dent Journal of Philosophy / U.
"Machiavelli." In History of Politica
Rand McNally, 1972.
Renaissance Socrates. Ithaca, N.Y.: Corne

1973
"Note on the Plan of Nietzsche's Beyond Good an
1973): 97–113.

1975
The Argument and Action of Plato's Laws. Chicago: University
"The Three Waves of Modernity." In Political Philosophy: Six Es
lail Gildin. Indianapolis and New York: Bobbs-Merrill/Pegasus,

1979
"The Mutual Influence of Theology and Philosophy." Independent Journal o
(1979): 111–18.

1981
"Progress or Return? The Contemporary Crisis in Western Civilization." Modern Judaism
(1981): 17–45.

1983
"Correspondence Concerning Modernity: Karl Löwith and Leo Strauss." Independent Jour-
nal of Philosophy 4 (1983).
Studies in Platonic Political Philosophy, ed. Thomas L. Pangle. Chicago: University of Chicago
Press, 1983.

1988
Carl Schmitt, Leo Strauss und der "Begriff des Politischen" Zu einem Dialog unter Abwesenden: Mit
Leo Strauss' Aufsatz über den "Begriff des Politischen" und drei unveröffentlichten Briefen an Carl

, ed. Heinrich Meier. Stuttgart: J. B. Metzlersche Verlags-

*llosophy. Ten Essays,* ed. Hilail Gildin. Detroit: Wayne State Uni-

*olitical Rationalism: An Introduction to the Thought of Leo Strauss.* Es-
*Leo Strauss.* Selected by Thomas L. Pangle. Chicago: University of
9.

*sed and expanded edition, including the Strauss-Kojève Correspondence.* New
*ess,* 1991.

*olitical Philosophy: The Correspondence between Leo Strauss and Eric Voegelin,*
*64.* University Park: Pennsylvania State University Press, 1993.

# Index

absolute monarch, 14–16; beheading of, 15

abstraction and modernity, 66–7

Adams, John, 56

Adorno, Theodor: American experience of, 173, 174–5, 176; on democracy, 174; *Dialectic of Enlightenment*, 173

*Akademie für die Wissenschaft des Judentums*, 91, 94, 122

*aletheia*, 106

*Alltäglichkeiten*, 170

Almond, Gabriel, 83

American education, *see* liberal education

American experience: Arendt on, 34, 45–58; and European framework, 34

American Political Science Association, 83, 176

American Revolution: intellectual origins of, 56; and public freedom, 23, 55; reassessment of, 170–1; and social contract, 18, 20

*Amerikanische Regierungssystem, Das* (Fränkel), 182

animalist power, 123

anthropology, philosophical, 99

anthropomorphism: and Plato, 113; and skepticism, 119

antiquity, *see* Greek antiquity; Roman antiquity

*apeirokalia*, 77

*aporia*, 150, 157-8

*arche*, 50, 108

Arendt, Hannah: American experience of, 163, 170, 171–82; background of, 45, 47; *Between Past and Future*, 12, 32, 35; continuity of, 172; *Crises of the Republic*, 36; *Eichmann in Jerusalem*, 54; and German philosophy, 163–71; her theory of decline, 3, 11, 24, 26; "Home to Roost," 54; *Human Condition*, 12, 13, 25, 32, 35, 54, 184; on layers of mean-

ing, 13; *Life of the Mind*, 38; *Merkur*, 166; as modern political philosopher, 191; *Origins of Totalitarianism*, 30, 32; as postmetaphysical thinker, 12; "Thoughts on Politics and Revolution," 31; "What Is Authority?," 36n, 50n, 53, 185; writing method of, 12; *see also On Revolution* (Arendt)

Aristophanes, 133

Aristotle: Arabic approach to, 124; and *arche*, 50; on being, 106–7; constitutional doctrine of, 8, 130; on human nature, 107, 110, 113; idealism of, 41; on moral virtue, 110; pragmatic politics of, 133; on reason, 108; scholastic approach to, 126

Athens, *see* Greek antiquity

Athens–Jerusalem theme of Strauss, 125, 137, 146n, 198

Auschwitz and breakup of civilization, 125

authenticity in politics, 48

authority, *see* political authority

Bacon, Francis, 110, 113

Beard, Charles, 170

behavioralism, 134

*Behemoth* (Neumann), 172

being: cause of, 110; dualism of, 119–20; and fate, 118; Heidegger on, 111, 113–20; as highest essence, 106, 107, 120; poetic prophet of, 117; primordial understanding of, 106, 107, 117, 118; and truth, 106–7, 108; as unconcealment/*aletheia*, 106, 110, 113, 114–15, 117

*Being and Time* (Heidegger), 126, 164, 165, 166

Compiled by Eileen Quam and Theresa Wolner.

201